BLACK SATURATION

BLACK
SATURATION

Selected Works of Stephen E. Henderson

Edited by Hazel Arnett Ervin, E. Ethelbert Miller,
Phillip M. Richards, and Emily Ruth Rutter

University Press of Mississippi / Jackson

Margaret Walker Alexander Series in African American Studies

The University Press of Mississippi is the scholarly publishing agency of
the Mississippi Institutions of Higher Learning: Alcorn State University,
Delta State University, Jackson State University, Mississippi State University,
Mississippi University for Women, Mississippi Valley State University,
University of Mississippi, and University of Southern Mississippi.

www.upress.state.ms.us

The University Press of Mississippi is a member
of the Association of University Presses.

Names: Henderson, Stephen, 1925–1997, author. | Ervin, Hazel Arnett, editor. |
Miller, E. Ethelbert, editor. | Richards, Phillip M., 1950–editor. | Rutter, Emily Ruth, editor.
Title: Black saturation : selected works of Stephen E. Henderson /
edited by Hazel Arnett Ervin, E. Ethelbert Miller, Phillip M. Richards, and Emily Ruth Rutter.
Description: Jackson : University Press of Mississippi, 2025. |
Series: Margaret Walker Alexander series in African American studies |
Includes bibliographical references and index.
Identifiers: LCCN 2024048190 (print) | LCCN 2024048191 (ebook) |
ISBN 9781496855084 (hardback) | ISBN 9781496855091 (trade paperback) |
ISBN 9781496855107 (epub) | ISBN 9781496855114 (epub) |
ISBN 9781496855121 (pdf) | ISBN 9781496855138 (pdf)
Subjects: LCSH: American literature—African American authors—History and criticism. |
African American critics. | Criticism—United States—History—20th century. |
African Americans—Intellectual life—20th century. | LCGFT: Literary criticism. | Essays.
Classification: LCC PS153.B53 H46 2025 (print) | LCC PS153.B53 (ebook) |
DDC 811.009/896073—dc23/eng/20241031
LC record available at https://lccn.loc.gov/2024048190
LC ebook record available at https://lccn.loc.gov/2024048191

British Library Cataloging-in-Publication Data available

CONTENTS

BLACK SATURATION

INTRODUCTION

HAZEL ARNETT ERVIN AND EMILY RUTH RUTTER

Stephen E. Henderson (1925–1997), one of the most influential African American literary critics to emerge from the Black Arts era, is probably best known for his anthology *Understanding the New Black Poetry: Black Speech and Black Music as Poetic References* (1973). In this landmark volume, Henderson showcases a continuous African American poetic tradition, focusing in particular on folk sources—the spirituals, work songs, field hollers, blues, sermons, and folktales—in an attempt to define the "organizing principles" by which "to recognize, to interpret, to value" Black poetry.[1] Henderson's prefatory essay in that publication, "Introduction: The Forms of Things Unknown," has been especially significant in building and framing critical knowledge of Black poetry traditions. *Black Saturation: Selected Works of Stephen E. Henderson* is designed to expand and enrich understandings of Henderson's critical corpus beyond this anthology by showcasing many of his most essential essays, presentations, and syllabi. These works were among Henderson's papers when he retired from Howard University in 1992 and, knowing their importance for scholars and students of African American letters, were saved by Hazel Arnett Ervin and E. Ethelbert Miller, two of this volume's editors. With the permission of Henderson's son Philip, our editorial team recently set about transposing and arranging these pieces under one cover. It is our hope that revisiting Henderson's scholarship in the third decade of the twenty-first century will inspire further appreciation of his imprint on Black literary studies while introducing new readers and researchers to his salient theoretical frameworks, not to mention his persuasive critical style.

While they vary in topic, Henderson's essays and presentations emphasize the source (artistic origins), form (artistic modes and structures), and function (art's sociocultural and political work) of Black literature. In an interview with Miller, Henderson described his earliest introductions to the sources of

Black literary art coming from his family and community in Key West, Flor-
ida, where he was reared among relatives from the Gullah Geechee–speaking
coastal areas of South Carolina and Georgia as well as the Bahamas.[2] From
an early age, therefore, Henderson, the prospective academic, heard language
and observed cultural traditions that are comparatively close to West African
roots.[3] Coming of age in this distinct sociocultural environment, Henderson
received an early and influential education in the African diasporic origins
of Black literary art, especially speech and music. These sources became the
focus of his work as a scholar and professor.

In 1946, Henderson graduated from Morehouse College with a major in
English and a minor in sociology; in 1959, he earned his PhD in English and
art history from the University of Wisconsin, completing a dissertation on
form in the work of Alfred Tennyson and the Pre-Raphaelites Dante Gabriel
Rossetti and William Morris (entitled "A Study of Visualized Detail in the
Poetry of Tennyson, Rossetti, and Morris"). With his coeditorship (with
Mercer Cook) of *The Militant Black Writer in Africa and the United States*
(1969) and, certainly, with the aforementioned publication of *Understanding
the New Black Poetry*, Henderson made clear his commitment to showcasing
both the artistic sophistication and political use value of Black poetry and
poetics. As Henderson understood it, the source, form, and function of written Black literature must be understood within the context of—recalling the
influence and residue of West African cultural tropes within his own family
and community—longstanding oral and vernacular traditions. As he noted
in an interview with Jerry W. Ward, scholars of Black literature "have to show
that our poets and writers have not only mastered the current techniques
but have access to other kinds of techniques."[4] This is precisely the task to
which Henderson dedicated his scholarly life.

Henderson also shaped generations of students' understandings of Black
poetry in particular and Black literature more generally. He began his teaching career at Virginia Union University in 1950 while still earning his doctor-
ate at the University of Wisconsin. From 1962 to 1969, he served as the chair
of the Department of English at Morehouse College, leaving this post for a
two-year senior research fellowship at Atlanta's Institute of the Black World,
where he worked closely with the historian and civil rights activist Vincent
Harding. Henderson joined the faculty at Howard in 1971, teaching in the
African American Studies and English Departments until 1992. He was also
responsible for bringing the poet and essayist Sterling A. Brown out of retirement to teach again at Howard. From 1981 to 1984, Henderson edited *Sagala:
A Journal of Arts and Ideas*, the organ for Howard's Institute for the Arts and
Humanities, where he served as director from 1973 to 1985. As the present

volume makes clear in such remarks as Henderson's introduction to the Image of Black Folk in American Literature Conference held at the Institute for the Arts and Humanities in 1979, his director role included facilitating, synthesizing, and documenting dialogues among leading Black writers and critics about trends and directions in the field. In particular, he collaborated with novelist John Oliver Killens and poet Haki Madhubuti (also known as Don L. Lee) to organize and host the National Writers Conference as well as the first National Conference of Black Folklorists.

Following Henderson's retirement from Howard—a retirement prompted by Parkinson's disease—he was honored at several events celebrating his impact and legacy. For instance, at the Smithsonian Institution (i.e., the National Museum of American History) in Washington, DC, former classmates, friends, and colleagues—such as Andrew Billingsley, Vincent Harding, Harold Burke, Roland Freeman, Eleanor Traylor, Marilyn Sanders Mobley, Jennifer Jordan, Niani Kilkenny, Reuben Jackson, David Nicholson, Russell Adams, James Early, blues singer Archie Edwards, and the poets Pinkie Gordon Lane, Madhubuti, Eugene Redmond, Sonia Sanchez, Ahmos Zu-Bolton, E. Ethelbert Miller, and Amiri Baraka (previously known as LeRoi Jones and Imamu Baraka) (with David Murray on the saxophone and Rudy Walker on drums)—paid tribute to him in a two-day symposium titled In Search of Blueprints: The Making of an African American Literary Critic. The present volume extends this much-deserved recognition of Henderson's critical contributions to African American literary and cultural studies.

Throughout his esteemed career, Henderson was cautious about public misunderstanding, appropriation, and commodification of the Black art he held dear. During his tenure at the Institute of the Black World, he presented "Black Art and Culture: The 70s" (1970), a polemical paper about Eurocentric educational models in which he calls on other Black scholars and educators to use their platforms to respond "to the lives and needs of our people and not merely to a privileged minority of specialists." In "Inside the Funk Shop: A Word on Black Words" (1973), he warns against the consequences of allowing white America to proliferate false narratives of Black cultural production. "A word which has special significance for the Black community," Henderson points out, "becomes useful or titillating to the white community. Then a process of justification and sanitizing begins. The media, the critics, and eventually the scholars take their roles. The chief thing, however, is to deny the original Blackness of the new usage out of ignorance or by design." In his own work as a scholar, editor, and professor, Henderson militated against such cultural erasure, tending Black artistic roots and elucidating the source, form, and function of Black speech, music, and literary arts in particular.

Committed to developing frameworks for defining and evaluating Black poetry (oral and written), Henderson tarried at length with the question of what makes a poem *Black*. In the opening essay to *Understanding the New Black Poetry*, "Introduction: The Forms of Things Unknown," Henderson delineates critical criteria to answer this question and repeats them in an essay included here, "The Question of Form and Judgment in Contemporary Black American Poetry: 1962–1977" (1977):

1. Any poetry by any person or group of persons of known Black African ancestry, whether the poetry is designated Black or not
2. Poetry which is somehow *structurally* Black, irrespective of authorship
3. Poetry by any person or group of known Black African ancestry, which is *also identifiably* Black, in terms of structure, theme, or other characteristics
4. Poetry by any identifiably Black person who can be classified as a "poet" by Black people. Judgment may or may not coincide with judgments of whites
5. Poetry by any identifiably Black person whose ideological stance vis-à-vis history and the aspirations of his people since slavery is adjudged by them to be "correct"

As Henderson concedes, these criteria have limitations for critics attempting to adjudicate what is or is not a *Black* poem and also for appreciating the diverse range of verse composed by people of African descent. At the same time, the questions of how and who should judge Black poetry are crucial considerations for him (and indeed are live questions in our own time). As he emphasizes in "The Question of Form and Judgement," "The canons, the categories, the dynamics must be as clear and as reasoned as possible. These must rest on a sound empirical base." As the selected writing ahead makes clear, Henderson himself spent much of his career devising and clarifying these frameworks, providing contemporary scholars with a firm foundation from which to build scholarly knowledge of what constitutes the past, present, and even future of Black art.

In his critical approach, Henderson prioritized form but not at the expense of source and function (or context) and, in so doing, developed convincing theoretical frameworks for examining African American lyric expressions, especially that of Black Arts poets. Beginning with his introduction to *Understanding the New Black Poetry* and continuing through the writings gathered here, Henderson deftly conceptualizes the ways in which aesthetic innovations were interwoven with revolutionary exigencies—a marriage of poetry and politics that became a hallmark of the 1960s and 70s but was not limited to that era. As Henderson avers in "The Literature of Power: Black American Poetry of the Sixties" (1976), "The poetry was electrifying. . . . It spoke of Black pride, of Black beauty and the problems which beset a Black Nation. . . . Many were disturbed by the language but few could deny its power." While other critics often either ignored or fumbled to construct an adequate rubric for evaluating (and celebrating) Black Arts verse penned by Baraka, Carolyn Rodgers, Sanchez, Jayne Cortez, Mari Evans, Sarah Webster Fabio, Madhubuti, and Larry Neal, among many others, Henderson constellated a triad of interdependent characteristics—structure, theme, and saturation—through which he examined Black literature in general and poetry in particular.

While structure and theme may be the concern of critics examining non-Black literature, *saturation* indexes an artwork's "'Blackness' and fidelity to the observed or intuited truth of the Black Experience in the United States."[5] For Henderson, saturation is also a curricular goal and even a metric by which the sociocultural use value of courses or knowledge may be assessed. In his galvanizing talk alluded to in the present book's title "Black Saturation: A View of the Humanities" (1974), Henderson insists, "Let us create a generation of Black people who are not specialists in Blackness but who are *saturated* in Blackness, who understand it and act from it, out of mission, yes, and out of love." For Henderson, an education in saturation will result in collective Black empowerment and ultimately liberation. Moreover, Black music and speech provide felicitous examples of saturated forms and structures. As Henderson observes in an essay included here, "Saturation: Progress Report on a Theory of Black Poetry" (1975), "One may call the blues a *saturated form* and blues imagery, *saturated structures*."

In poetry, saturation may manifest in what Henderson terms "mascons," or images and phrases indexical of a "massive concentration of Black experiential energy." The poet Sterling A. Brown, one of Henderson's frequent critical subjects, deploys such a mascon image in "Ma Rainey," his lyric tribute to Gertrude "Ma" Rainey from his exquisite 1932 collection, *Southern Road*. Brown's image of the iconic blues singer among her adoring fans— "Git way inside us, / Keep us strong,"[6] they implore Rainey—exemplifies the deep blues structure (the "massive concentration") to which Henderson refers. The essay "The Heavy Blues of Sterling Brown: A Study of Craft and Tradition" (1980) further argues that Brown's poetry is profitably examined through the "Afro-American culture in which it is saturated," especially the blues, which Brown immersed (even saturated) himself in as he composed the poignant, blues-inspired verse that comprises much of *Southern Road*.

In the aforementioned "Saturation," Henderson also provides the example of contemporary singers ranging from Aretha Franklin to James Brown whose music is thoroughly saturated, structured according to and perceived as the "embodiment and experienc[e] of Blackness as a valuable artistic (aesthetic) whole."

Nearly a decade later, opining about the epistemological implications of saturation in "One More Time: The Black Agenda Revisited" (1982), Henderson observes, "The truth, then—that's what saturation is about," and this concept "comes out of a great educational need, one that certainly is with us still." For Henderson, these fundamental truths and needs are met most poignantly through the cultural power of Black music and, by extension, poetry. In another essay in this volume, "Black Poetry: The Continuing Challenge" (1979), Henderson writes that "in our poetry, rooted in this music, rooted in the *moral* character of this music we have invented a way of speaking which, when the world one day listens, will fill it with astonishment." In the most chronologically recent of the essays included here, "Worrying the Line: Notes on Black American Poetry" (1988), Henderson highlights the poetic innovations developed by Black Arts poets in repeating with an inflected difference (or worrying the line) the nuances of avant-garde jazz via typographical experimentation on the printed page (and vocally in readings and performances) all the while remaining politically committed to the material needs of the Black masses. In these varied pieces, Henderson conveys an underlying argument that a Black poem—a *saturated* poem—is not simply an aesthetic object; it is also a way of feeling, doing, and being predicated on the beauty and the struggle of the Black world.

Indeed, this insistence on placing written Black literature within a broader cultural context is a hallmark of the Henderson selections included here. In "The Blues as Black Poetry" (1977), which began as a conference presentation and was subsequently published as an essay in a 1982 issue of the journal *Callaloo*, Henderson subverts the supposed binary distinction between folk forms and written forms, redefining the blues, as well as the spirituals, ballads, and work songs, as Black poetry. Put another way, Henderson objects to evaluating the lyrics according to Anglo-European rubrics for poetic merit and instead asserts the importance of understanding the blues as a poetic form distinctly reflective of the African American condition of "being an alien in one's native land." He ends "The Blues as Black Poetry" with a powerful call to account for the circumstances that engendered the painful experiences conveyed in the blues: "Perhaps the American public will have the courage to take the next step—a full responsibility for our collective past and for our future. We have the mechanism for that exploration. Our Black and unknown bards invented it. We call it Black poetry; they called it the blues." In another conference presentation, "Modernity and Other Directions in Afro-American Literature: Reflections on the Past Two Decades" (1984), Henderson similarly enjoins his audience to look to "our music" not only for inspiration but for answers to epistemological and ontological questions. Black musical traditions are "problem-solving—in a technical as well as an emotional sense," Henderson affirms. Moreover, "the music is not afraid of new philosophies or new technologies or old philosophies and technologies, for the music deals with time filtered through the pulses of African sensibility." The music points the way for Henderson, whose critical observations reflect the outsized impact of (and often reciprocal relationship between) Black oral and aural traditions, especially blues, jazz, and hip hop, and their poetic counterparts on the printed page.

The essays and talks that follow also elucidate Henderson's commitment to celebrating sociocultural and artistic achievements that offer fresh ways of seeing and knowing. For example, his perspicacious analysis of Neal's collections of poetry "Take Two—Larry Neal and the Blues God: Aspects of the Poetry" (1985) calls attention to the poet's syncretic fusion of blues tropes and African mythology to create a rejuvenating "ideology and iconography of Afro-American cultural history, an achievement as significant as the Black Aesthetic itself." In "Home to *Nommo*" (1975), a review of June Jordan's *New Days: Poems of Exile and Return* (1975), Henderson reminds readers of the important role that Black women writers "have brought to the flowering of Black consciousness," lauding Jordan for her poetic mobilization and realization of *nommo*, the West African concept referring to the creative power of the word to actualize change or to bring about a new kind of reality. Henderson echoes this emphasis on the agential significance of the lyric word in his eloquent eulogy for the Negritude Movement poet Léon Damas (1912–1978), which is also included in the present volume. "The poet is a danger to oppression," Henderson proclaims. "The poet's function is to speak the truth."

There is still much to be learned from Henderson's published essays, presentations, and syllabi that follow. Here was a scholar, editor, anthologist, professor, and socially conscious citizen dedicated to championing the especial significance of Black poetry (oral and written) through the development of theoretical frameworks that would honor it on its own terms—that would, in other words, do Black lyric traditions critical justice. In his syllabi in this volume's appendix, we observe a pioneering pedagogue who engaged his students in probing questions about the relationship between literature and music, as well as the traditions of Black letters—for example, among activist writers, among Black women, and across continents. The afterword by Phillip M. Richards, one of this volume's coeditors, highlights the importance of Henderson's "enormous authority as a student of Black literature and a builder of Black cultural institutions." As Richards—who was mentored by Henderson at Howard University—points out, his critical methodology has had an often-unacknowledged but profound influence on contemporary Black scholarship.

We can readily observe Henderson's influence on the volumes that have shaped African American literary criticism over the last several decades. A long list of persuasive critical texts—including Houston A. Baker Jr.'s *Blues, Ideology and Afro-American Literature: A Vernacular Theory* (1984), Henry Louis Gates Jr.'s *The Signifying Monkey: A Theory of Afro-American Literary Criticism* (1988), Dolan Hubbard's *The Sermon and the African American Literary Imagination* (1994), Larry Neal's *Visions of a Liberated Future: Black Arts Movement Writings* (1989), Karla F. C. Holloway's *The Character of the Word: The Texts of Zora Neale Hurston* (1987) and *Moorings and Metaphors: Figures of Culture and Gender in Black Women's Literature* (1991), Aldon Lynn Nielsen's *Black Chant: Languages of African-American Postmodernism* (1997), Hazel Arnett Ervin's *African American Literary Criticism, 1773–2000* (1999), Winston Napier's *African American Literary Theory: A Reader* (2000), Tony Bolden's *Afro-blue: Improvisations in African American Poetry and Culture* (2004), Fred Moten's *In the Break: The Aesthetics of the Black Radical Tradition* (2004), Jennifer Ryan's *Post-Jazz Poetics: A Social History* (2010), Meta DuEwa Jones's *The Muse Is Music: Jazz Poetry from the Harlem Renaissance to Spoken Word* (2011), Emily J. Lordi's *Black Resonance: Iconic Women Singers and African American Literature* (2013), Anthony Reed's *Freedom Time: The Poetics and Politics of Black Experimental Writing* (2014), and Howard Rambsy II's *Bad Men: Creative Touchstones of Black Writers* (2020), among others—owe something essential to the critical precedent set by Henderson.

Returning to Henderson now, therefore, allows contemporary scholars (alongside their students) to more fully appreciate the ways in which the seeds he planted have taken root in contemporary African American literary criticism. We also hope this renewed engagement with Henderson's selected works will plant new seeds, ensuring that his critical insights (e.g., his eschewing of a false binary between Black folk and written literature; his emphasis on sources, form, and function as equally significant in theorizing African American literary and cultural traditions; his triadic constellation of form, structure, and saturation used to analyze Black poetry; and his concept of "mascon" images, among other theoretical frameworks and insights) are nurtured and sustained in the pathbreaking literary criticism to come.

The pieces in this book are reproduced as they initially appeared with only minor changes to punctuation, capitalization, and the like. Some lines of poetry were cut as indicated in brackets. The editors have made every effort to honor Henderson's distinctive style.

NOTES

1. Stephen E. Henderson, *Understanding the New Black Poetry: Black Speech and Black Music as Poetic References* (New York: William Morrow, 1973), 3.

2. Stephen E. Henderson, "A Conversation with a Literary Critic," interview by E. Ethelbert Miller, *New Directions* 13, no. 2 (1986): 20–27, https://dh.howard.edu/cgi/viewcontent.cgi?article=1422&context=newdirections.

3. In *Talkin and Testifyin*, Geneva Smitherman explains that "Geechee speech is spoken by rural and urban Blacks who live in the area along the Atlantic coastal region of South Carolina and Georgia. . . . Most of the ancestors of these Blacks were brought direct from Nigeria, Liberia, Gambia, and Sierra Leone, and other places in West Africa where Ibo, Yoruba, Mandingo, Wolof, and other West African languages were and still are spoken. Today, Gullah people form a special Black American community because they have retained considerable African languages and cultural practices." Geneva Smitherman, *Talkin and Testifyin: The Language of Black America* (Detroit: Wayne State University Press, 1986), 14.

4. Stephen E. Henderson, "Saturated Situations: An Interview with Stephen E. Henderson," interview by Jerry W. Ward, *Obsidian* 7, no. 1 (1981): 92.

5. Henderson, *New Black Poetry*, 10.

6. Sterling A. Brown, "Ma Rainey," in *Southern Road* (1932; repr., Boston: Beacon Press, 1974), 63.

BLACK ART AND CULTURE

THE 70s

Paper presented at the Institute of the Black World, Atlanta, GA, July 1970.

The areas of Black art and culture are, of course, vast. They subsume and permeate all of Black life as well as the life of the society that oppresses us. Notwithstanding, it is necessary to begin again the process of assessing our knowledge of ourselves so that we may order our priorities for research, for criticism, and for creation to the end of Black liberation and Black celebration. This paper is thus a brief tentative statement of those concerns and makes no pretense of completeness, if such a thing were indeed possible.

It seems to me that our present knowledge and awareness of Black art and culture leave a great deal to be desired, especially as we move from the relatively few persons with great masses of specific information to the vast majority of Black people, both schooled and unschooled, who still believe that European standards and tastes and contributions to a vague "universal culture" should govern our preferences, our education, our aspirations—should, in short, govern our lives. The problem is thus one of education, and although I said that it is one both for the schooled and unschooled, paradoxically enough, it is chiefly one for the schooled. By this I mean that although the man on the street may admire Euro-American book learning or might be deferential when one of his educated brothers extols the virtues of symphonic music, he still knows what he likes and understands what is meaningful to him in Black Culture. The problem for him then is to become aware of the value of the culture which he knows and, in addition, to become aware of the fact that certain aspects of Black Culture rival or exceed anything comparable in Euro-American culture. For the schooled person, the problem is much more complex because it involves, first of all, a systematic questioning of the assumptions upon which formal education was largely based, particularly in those areas, disciplines, and subjects which involve concepts of beauty, morality, sensibility, taste; which involve value judgments and concepts of reality; and which raise the questions that are usually crystallized by or embodied in the arts, practical and applied, and in that group of studies and techniques which address themselves to an evaluation or interpretation of the arts, or, by extension, of the interior life of a people.

Put another way, the educational problem of Black art and culture may be broken down as follows:

1. Discontinuous knowledge
2. Neglected areas of knowledge
3. Undefined areas of knowledge
4. Apathy and inferior feelings regarding Black Culture
5. Problems of personal vision vs. commitment to collective movement

These topics may be further resolved into specific kinds of research and artistic and political concerns; but for the present let us spell them out, or at least illustrate what they may involve. By discontinuous knowledge, I mean knowledge of segments of a whole without any comprehensive sense of the whole. This is obviously the case of much of human knowledge, for various reasons; so, for example, one might speak of medical knowledge—which has no cure for cancer—as discontinuous. Notwithstanding, the disease is being attacked in systematic fashion, which includes theory as well as laboratory analysis and experimentation. So, an attempt is being made to eliminate the discontinuity, chiefly because dedicated and skilled people can see the problem. Admittedly, questions which involve value judgments, and, hence, questions of art and culture, are less subject to the kind of precise response which science and technology can make. Still there are precise responses which can be made which violate neither intellectual integrity nor the larger human concerns of the people whose art and culture are being discussed. In this case, we are, of course, talking about the art and culture of Black people, chiefly in North America. And many of the gaps in our knowledge are painfully obvious. Still the obvious may be with us for so long that we take it for granted and fail to respect its significance to our larger struggle and ultimate well-being.

A good case in point would be in music, the most obvious aspect of Black Culture anywhere, but especially here in the United States. Where is the Black college or university which has seriously examined the sources of our music? Where are the Black scholars who treat the complexities and modern jazz with the intelligence and compassion which they deserve? Where are the seminars in jazz history which examine the development and the influence of our music? Where is the historian of the blues? Where is the historian of gospel music? Where is the historian of the music of the civil rights movement? Where is the analysis of the music of the World War II generation?

Where is that much-needed analysis of the economics of Black music which would indicate why men of genius have had to starve to death or make humiliating compromises in order to survive in a white-consumer-oriented society? Where is the analysis of the role of the mass media in suppressing and distorting Black music? The questions could go on ad nauseam, but the point is that one of the chief ironies of the education of Black people in the United States is that these questions have largely been ignored by the very people who produced the music, and although one has to respect the sincerity and dedication and basic fairness of scholars like Gunther Schuller and Paul Oliver, they are solitary beacons in a sea of willful distortion and uninformed and, apparently, unconscious racism.

The reprint industry, too, has brought mixed blessings, for although it is useful and necessary to have available the research of men like [Henry] Krehbiel, George Pullen Jackson, Guy Johnson, and others, their works are either left with no modern introductions or the introductions are done by white scholars who, when not overtly racist, lack knowledge of the intimacies of Black life which severely curb the validity of their interpretations of the music; thus stereotypes and false assumptions are reinforced and perpetuated. Sometimes these false assumptions verge on complete falsehood, as, for example, in Robert Bone's preface to the Atheneum reprint of Sterling Brown's *"Negro Poetry and Drama" and "The Negro in American Fiction,"* where he flatly asserts that Brown's basic thrust was integrationist, and that he was not a "Black chauvinist." The fact of the matter is that he was neither "chauvinist" nor "integrationist," but a brilliant scholar and poet, and a great teacher, dedicated to the uplift of his people through scholarship and art. He made no apologies either for his exploration and celebration of Black Soul life or for his knowledge of, and influence by, the literature of the United States mainstream, or, for that matter, of western Europe.

Another example of the duplicity of the reprint industry is the Apollo reprint of Benjamin Brawley's *The Negro Genius*, which is described on the paperback cover as "a new appraisal of the achievement of the American Negro in Literature and the Fine Arts," despite the fact that the text was originally published in 1937, when most of the contemporary writers, artists, and musicians were hardly more than toddlers. Still worse, however, is the advertisement for the volume, which appeared in major literary periodicals, and implies that the late Dr. Brawley is currently serving as professor of English at Howard University.

All this, to be sure, is very serious business, and the most effective way to uproot it is with concerted response by Black scholars and their allies. But the task is indeed formidable and more polemics and rebuttals will not do. Instead of this, the Black intellectual community must build on the work of the Brawleys and the Browns and the Reddings, and they must build with daring, with imagination, with sensitivity, and with impeccable scholarship. But even this is not enough, for in music and literature and art especially, the problem of discontinuous knowledge is not only one of information, but one of organization, interpretation, popularization, and, indeed, of application.

Janheinz Jahn's *Neo-African Writings* has many flaws, but no one can deny this man's serious involvement in the problems to which we must address ourselves, again, *in this generation*, if we mean anything at all by the words Black Culture, Black pride, Black power, and, especially, Black liberation. We must establish texts and canons, we must set the criteria for the evaluation of Black creations, we must bridge the gap between *The Negro Genius* and *Blues People*; we must perform the "enabling" acts of criticism and scholarship which will make it possible for Black art in the 70s to be fully responsive to the lives and needs of our people and not merely to a privileged minority of specialists.

In some respects, the problem of discontinuous knowledge is less serious than the problem of *neglected areas of knowledge*. This is so because the areas involved are so crucial to a proper understanding of the Black Experience, and they have generally not been explored on any large-scale basis. Nor has the knowledge which has been discovered been sufficiently energized and disseminated among the Black population. Of course, this is truer of some areas than others. Notwithstanding, I have listed areas which seem to me to be crucial, and, indeed, areas in which some Black persons have excelled but which have traditionally been either totally neglected on the undergraduate level or have been taught from essentially a European perspective. The list is as follows:

1. Graphic arts, painting, and sculpture
2. Photography
3. Folklore
4. Architecture
5. Philosophy
6. Aesthetics
7. Anthropology
8. Archaeology

Our artists have made significant efforts to interpret the lives of our people in this country and abroad, and to some extent our schools have assisted in this task. Yet there is great work to be done. The treasures of local collections at Atlanta, Hampton, Tuskegee, Nashville, Washington, DC, Chicago, and Detroit, for example, need to be made available in inexpensive form for courses in general education both in college and in the public schools.

Our artists need to be supported by the community, especially the business and the intellectual community. Murals ought to be commissioned not only for academic buildings, but also for public buildings—for any buildings which the community uses, to remind it of its past and to inspire its future. Textbook illustration needs serious attention, especially for the very young. Art history texts need to be written so as to show the full contribution of Black men and women to world art. In the cities, the spread of the Chicago *Wall of Respect* idea is encouraging, suggesting as it does art for people's sake, a living, outdoor, museum. Other encouraging ventures are the private museums and the Black artists organization in Los Angeles—Contemporary Crafts, Inc.—which prints art books, films, and slides especially for use in courses on the Black Experience.

Allied with the graphic arts and sculpture is architecture. Here is, indeed, a great challenge for the Black artist to synthesize the old and the new, to build livable habitations which are at once reasonably priced, attractive, and true to the soul force, the design, the movement of Afro-American life. Where is the Black business, the Black college which will lend its support to the vision of, say, Black architect Max Bond? When Black people inherit the inner cores of our Great American cities, will they continue to live in degradation and ugliness; or will the new Black political leadership realize the necessity for transforming the urban environment into forms which enhance the lives of its citizens? Will they encourage our architects to build 21st-century Zimbabwes, or will they settle for functional cubes and African echoes by Picasso?

Some interesting developments are taking place in photography which need to be encouraged in a formal way by our educational institutions and the Black business community. Classes in photography are being offered on a number of educational levels and in various kinds of settings, both formal and informal. Black professionals are getting involved in filmmaking and in the teaching of their skills to others. Among the kinds of projects which need to be further encouraged are photographic essays in Black Culture history, drawing upon the archives of places like Hampton Institute [now Hampton University] and the resources of Black newspapers and magazines. These could be used to document trends in fashion, dance, and other forms of cultural expression. Other kinds of essays would document the specific history of institutions and cities, for example, a documentary history of all of our major educational institutions, a documentary history of Harlem, of Black Atlanta, Chicago, and New Orleans, to name just a few.

In another context, the use of movies to capture the fluid lifestyle of Black people is in an embryonic state. It needs to be systematically encouraged, both as sheer documentation and as artistic creation. Educationally, it seems to me, the problem lies in giving to photography the place which it deserves in the high school and college curriculum, and in having courses taught by professionals who have demonstrated their imagination and their skill but who may not have formal college training, which they may not need.

Philosophy, aesthetics, and folklore are intimately linked in any serious examination of the Black Experience. Perhaps, though, one should begin with the folklore, since it forms the substratum of any consideration of the culture of Black people in the United States. Indeed, it forms the substratum of any consideration of so-called American culture, since so much of that culture is Black derived, whether it be music, dance, language style, or dress. Notwithstanding all of this, the study of folklore has been ironically and seriously neglected at Black schools in the United States. Perhaps the reason is not hard to come by. There are certainly enough indications in our history that we have associated our folklore with the stereotyped images of the American minstrel tradition and with all of those ethnic aberrations which we hoped would be melted away in the American melting pot. It is high time now to reassess our position vis-à-vis our folklife and to realize just how valuable that heritage is. Unfortunately, a great deal of the material that we need to study folklife has been collected and interpreted by non-Black people, and distortions abound, to say the least. Still we have the records, and we have access to living sources of information which will aid us in understanding those records. What we need, then, is a systematic examination of the field of folklore as it now exists in the United States; and a critique of that field so as to derive the maximum benefit from the work which has already been done; at the same time seeking to eliminate methods, techniques, and interpretations which do not actually contribute to a sound understanding of the lives of our people. In short, the study of Black folklore must be freed from 19th-century bias and from Eurocentrism. The major works must be critiqued, the major theories must be critiqued, the major collections must be reevaluated. But above all, the study of Black folklore must be humanized and popularized. One could start, perhaps, by eliminating the notion of folklore itself and substituting for it the concept of Black Humanism, out of which and upon which will develop the kinds of specific knowledge and strategies which will help us to build upon the lifestyle of our parents. This task is so enormous that it must be the exclusive work of a group of dedicated workers, perhaps of an entire institute, for what we are fundamentally talking about is refining and controlling the source of the spiritual energy of American life, which is to say, the basic forms of the Black Experience.

Black aesthetics and philosophy are simply refined and self-conscious forms of this basic energy source, abstracted ways of viewing and handling the Black Experience in its various permutations. Thus Aretha Franklin doesn't have to speak very precisely about Soul, or the Black Aesthetic—her singing embodies these qualities; but if future generations are to avoid the prodigality of the past and the present—if we are to avoid being merely the suppliers of Energy and not the Users and the Controllers—then Black people have to define themselves and their contributions, not only to keep the record straight, but also to ensure the proper transformation of Black Humanistic Energy into Black-Liberating Economic Potential.

What we are talking about, of course, is Black books, Black records, Black audio-visual materials for public school and college and other educational uses; but we are also talking about Black publishing houses, record companies, and multimedia companies. We are also talking about a systematic thrust for important positions on editorial and other policymaking boards in the publishing industry and in government agencies which deal with public education.

But to move back to the theoretical and the programmatic, the concept of Black Humanism over Black Folklore takes us to what I designated earlier as *Undefined Areas of Knowledge* of Black Art and Black Culture. It means that we need to know how to talk precisely about our distinctiveness, whether we call it Soul or Negritude or something else. It means that we have to talk about our experience in such a way that statements about the blues in 1970 will be valid for discussing the blues in 1995. It means that a critique of Negritude, instead of a simple condemnation or exultation of it, has to be made by Black people. It means that we have to study the processes by which the larger society co-opts the language and the style of Black Culture. It means that we have to seek systematically to discover and to describe and to utilize the processes of Black Creativity. We have to seek to understand the psychological bases of that creativity, especially looking toward that day when we react no longer to our oppressors but still realize the historic importance of the blues and the spirituals and our survival—in short, toward the day when we no longer protest but celebrate.

Further, it means that we must systematically seek to extend the boundaries of our knowledge, especially of our recent past, through the acquisition of manuscripts, documents, and other artifacts which we need. The recent discovery in Harlem of over 10,000 papers of Marcus Garvey's Universal Negro Improvement Association is a good case in point. They perhaps should have been searched for a generation ago. At any rate, the cultural growth and movement of our people, especially in urban areas, should be systematically and scientifically documented through the introduction of the methods and techniques of the anthropologist and the archaeologist into the urban environment, the creation, so to speak, of an urban archaeology, an urban anthropology, scientific, yes, but suffused with Black Humanism, with that Black verve which we call Soul.

The *empathy and the inferior feelings* which obstruct our present drive, the *personal ambitions* which distort our collective commitment, will not be easily dispelled. We have no monopoly on these human failings, yet of all the world's people, because of our unique past and the strategic importance of our present consciousness in this country, we can at least afford to indulge them. There is work for all. There is work for a generation. Let us, then, at the risk of the displeasure of those who called themselves our friends, boldly strike out wherever we are to define, refine, and to control the sources and the directions of our culture.

The dangers in all of this are obvious. Private collectors control important segments of information, important artifacts, and important living resources. Private foundations and governmental agencies still think that Black people are fundamentally incapable of interpreting their lives and goals in this country and around the world. Some Black people share that distrust, and unfortunately some of these people are highly influential in the Black community. Moreover, the problems of Black people tend to be viewed strictly in economic and political terms, and anything which sounds "artsy-craftsy," which smacks of "culture," is suspect. This is perhaps as it should be. Our basic problems *are* economic and political. However, behind any realistic drive to reach permanent solutions there must be a regeneration of the spirit. And this regeneration has been the historical role of art. It has always been the role of Black art, especially here in America. In our drive for economic and political liberation, then, we can avoid the mistakes of other people and other generations by drawing consciously from those deep wellsprings of Being which we call by so many names, especially now by the beautiful term Soul.

INSIDE THE FUNK SHOP
A WORD ON BLACK WORDS

Published in *Black Books Bulletin* 1 (Summer–Fall 1973): 9–12.

"Ain't it funky now!" James Brown screamed for days at the top of the Soul Brothers' chart. "Ain't it funky!" The obnoxious word had been given a new Black meaning and public respectability. It wasn't a new word certainly, and it retained the original meanings which Black people had given it in the days of the funky butt dance. But there were other meanings too, which jazz critics especially liked. In fact, they used the word so much that a decade ago Imamu Baraka (LeRoi Jones [Amiri Baraka]) declared it "almost useless." Now while the word "funky" is being revived, another Black word, "Soul," that surfaced during the time Imamu wrote, is apparently on its way out—done in by overexposure and the Man.

Though both of these words have special Black meanings and are, in effect, Black words, they also have "standard" English meanings that both whites and Blacks know. The whites have, however, responded to the vital Black meanings in a way which epitomizes their historical response to Black Culture: for although one may dismiss the emergence and popularity of words like these as linguistic fads, and the white imitations as merely innocuous, commercial, racist, or sick, that would be a grievous error, for this concern with Black language is part of a subtle system of co-optation and control which involves all major aspects of Black Culture. If examined even with cursory attention, in fact, it epitomizes this system. It thus embodies (a) the virtual compulsion (personal and national) of whites to control Black distinctiveness, (b) the mythic and unconscious aspects of that control, (c) the commercial aspects of it, and especially, (d) the educational and political aspects of it.

First there is the level of fad—with the popularity and abuse of the words in question. The media plays an important role, chiefly in the dilution and distortion of Black meaning. The net effect is political control. For example, a few years ago, *Time* magazine did a feature story on the word "Soul," in which *Time* decided what that quality was and even determined the people and *literary characters* who possessed it. Among them were Jackie Kennedy, Caliban (but not Ariel), and other personages, white and Black. *Time* provided a kind of do-it-yourself kit and made the whole business a kind of game. *Newsweek*, not to be outdone, also sought for the mysterious essence of Black life encompassed in the word "Soul." They were a bit less presumptuous and more pragmatic. They interviewed Black people themselves and published some, at least, of what they had to say. What the people said, in effect, was that "Soul" was the Black lifestyle, the Black wisdom of the race, born in suffering, but proud, flexible, hip, shrewd, loving, tough, lyrical, patient, tender, and full of virtuoso elegance.

All of this, to be sure, wasn't obvious in the *Newsweek* story, and I flushed it out with a study which I conducted in Atlanta, Georgia, in 1967–1968. I pointedly asked people whether they thought that white folks had "Soul." The responses were canny sometimes, at other times naïve or hopeful, or just plain Christian democratic. That is to say, people regarded "Soul" as a special something that Blacks possessed, but were often reluctant to press the point. Others defined "Soul" in a quasi-religious sense, though again centering on the Black Experience. "Soul," for most, became a deep-down feeling that Black people had which sometimes whites imitated. And if they wanted to call what they were doing and feeling "Soul," why not let them. That's their business! Which, of course, was a most soulful way of dealing with the situation.

The response to "funk" can be seen in an article which appeared in the January 11 issue of the *Washington Post* entitled "Funk Is in the Eye of the Beholder," by Henry Allen. Funk in the eye! Wow! But the author is certainly not uninformed. He knows something about the various meanings. He states: "Funk once meant a shameful condition shunned by millions, a quality lent to aging bedclothes, depression, various low rent-odors and incapacitating fear." "This," he declares, "is no longer true, and 'funk' may become the hottest cultural property since organic food." He knows the usage of the jazz critics. He cites the music of Les McCann. Next, he examines current usage. "Funk is," he writes, "a way of life that only yesterday you no doubt considered tacky, old-fashioned, obnoxious or irrelevant. Funky is what things are before they become camp." Funk is not a "nostalgia for the mud, or a sentimental attraction for the lower classes," although these things are found in Thomas Wolfe, who uses the word "funk." Funk is doing the unexpected, but that which your "peer group" will also loathe. Getting high on a dollar-a-bottle wine, drinking beer out of the can, while sitting around in your undershirt listening to a ball game—all of this is very funky, especially if you also eat a peanut-butter-and-jelly sandwich, which, in fact, "comes about as close as anything to epitomizing the new funk." And, finally, "funk turns life into a costume party which you attend dressed just like everyone else."

The pattern is important. A word which has special significance for the Black community becomes useful or titillating to the white community. Then a process of justification and sanitizing begins. The media, the critics, and eventually the scholars take their roles. The chief thing, however, is to deny the original Blackness of the new usage out of ignorance or by design.

Here, as in the *Time* article on "Soul," the point is to capitalize on the excitement aroused by Black usage and turn it into white ends. Just as *Time* reduced "Soul" to a kind of do-your-own-thing game, the *Post* article reduces "funk" to a sentimental free-associational kitsch, and further links it to the stylized sensibility which produced the notion of camp. All of which has nothing to do basically with the Black Experience, and the proof is easy. Listen to James Brown. Or listen to the DJ who says, "Oooooooo-Weeeeeeee! I'm fonky as I wanna be! Fonky as a can of Magic Shave! Can you dig it!" That kind of funk doesn't have anything to do with costume parties and campy old clothes. Sometimes Black folks wear old clothes because they want to be comfortable, but usually because they can't do any better. And Magic Shave is a thing unto itself.

The Black response to white imitation has been to ignore it, to tolerate it, to show whites what the real thing is by appearing to share it with them, to go back to the original basic meanings involved, to invent new meanings which defy white acceptance, or to discard the expression altogether and take up another. Thus, many Blacks didn't care whether white people said that they had "Soul" or not, and Black DJs even invented the term "blue-eyed soul." And James Brown diplomatically allowed that Merv Griffin just might have "Soul." And Dionne Warwick said that Dick Cavett had it. Aretha said Frank Sinatra had it too. And Jesse Jackson taught Mayor Daley the handshake. Finally, *Liberator* magazine got mad and said to hell with it, and declared that Soul was useless—officially dead—and printed a picture of the gravesite to prove it. And so we became "funky"—like calling ourselves "n[*****]s" in public. There are, of course, whites who try to call themselves "student n[*****]s" and "new n[*****]s" and "gay n[*****] s" and "women's lib n[*****]s," but Dick Cavett hasn't called Bill Russell "my main n[*****]" on TV yet. And Johnny Cash hasn't called Flip Wilson that either. And Johnny Carson hasn't called himself "funky" yet, and one doubts that any of the presidential candidates would address Black voters as "my fellow funky Americans."

Thus, there is a temporary detente, so to speak, while the deodorizing machinery goes into action. The *Post* article shows how it works. Reduce the whole thing to a game played with "class" values—not racial ones—then retreat from the real world of the present to the nostalgic world of "O Mein Papa," in which everyone returns to the mythical melting pot of musical comedy and television commercials.

This would all be quite harmless and funny if we were merely talking about acculturation and if the pattern of white response merely indicated national emptiness, or neurosis, or greed. It would be hilarious if the only thing involved were the "soulful strut" and the "funky butt" finding their way to the White House, for a fascination with the exotic African ranges through American—indeed, Western life and history—culminating in an all-pervasive lust-hate-envy syndrome which is everywhere apparent. But it is part of a larger picture: the imperialistic intrusion of Europe into the continent of Africa. The story is familiar by now: the initial peaceful contacts before the Industrial Revolution, the wondrous tales of wealth and exotic civilizations, the cancer of the slave trade, the coming of the missionaries and the settlers, the wholesale dismembering of the continent and its people, and the bitter years of colonial subjugation. And on this side of the water, the need to justify the action—the system of exploitation and oppression—in a country supposedly democratic, founded on the assumption of universal human worth and the inalienable right to the pursuit of happiness.

What was needed was a mythology to justify slavery, and after that, segregation, and, as the truth becomes generally known, the expansion and perpetuation of political and economic power through whatever means those in control have at their disposal. One of the chief means is education, both formal and informal—through the schools, through the churches, through the publishing industry, and through the communications media.

It is at this point that the question of language and of distinctive Black language and culture in the United States becomes crucial. It is here that we see in the apparently faddish concern with Black "slang" and lifestyle the powerful and subtle workings of a massive system of economic and political control. To view such questions as merely the concern of poets and academicians is dangerous, for as I noted earlier, the movement of unofficial and official response toward Black Culture in this country has been toward the denial of Black distinctiveness. The point is to convince all people, white and Black, that everything of value which Black people possess they owe ultimately to the white man. In this manner it is possible to thwart any serious large-scale organization of Blacks on a nationalistic basis.

This strategy has been employed whenever a distinctive feature of Black life seemed to resist the "melting pot." It has been used to discredit the originality of the blues, the spirituals, jazz, Black literature, and even large segments of Black folklore by pointing to European similarities or analogues. And the enormous energy spent in these attempts, sometimes by seemingly unwitting and "objective" scholars, has confused many of our people who not only fail to see our own strength but the devious weakness of our oppressors. Thus, words like "funky" and "Soul" are important indicators of our awareness as a unique people. They are important also because they signal that knowledge to the larger society, which must control our identity images if it is ultimately to control us.

Historically, this has been done by raising certain kinds of "academic" and "scientific" questions with regard to our distinctiveness. The problem for the "scientists," then, becomes one of measuring and defining and limiting and predicting that something which makes us distinctive. Quite understandably they have had problems with funk and Soul. But they have also questioned the capacity of Blacks to master the "complex" European language which they were forced to adopt. They have questioned our capacity for "abstract" thought. In the process, they have conveniently forgotten about Juan Latino, Phillis Wheatley, Aesop, Terence, St. Augustine, Rameses II, Akhenaton, Paul Cuffey, [W. E. B.] Du Bois, and others. They have forgotten the pyramids and the Spirit World to the South.

The president of the United States himself—Thomas Jefferson—had his doubts about whether a Black man could master the Greek verb. And so we knocked ourselves out and learned Greek verbs and made Greek a requirement in our colleges for generations. But underlying all that formal linguistic demonstration was the sheer poetic genius of the people which burst into the grandeur of the spirituals and the bitter precision of the blues. Funk and Soul are part of this too. And the white response was predictable. They invented the minstrel tradition, both as a staged performance and as "literature," and they wrote in a language which, however entertaining they thought it to be, was certainly not Black. Imagine the popularity, for instance, of Hamlet's "to be or not to be" speech done up in "plantation English"! Yet such was the case. On the other hand, the response toward the "noble savage" was one of appreciation for his simple, broken, picturesque language which he mercifully dissolved in ineffable sweet, though "monotonous" song. Even "educated" Black people still accept that judgment of "an empty jingle in a broken tongue."

But the crucial response has been on the level of formal education with the myth of "Standard English" which all Americans had to learn if they were to get on in the world. In a somewhat disguised form it is still with us.

It appears in conservative and liberal packages. The one believes in holding all noses to the same grindstone; the other saying, a fat nose is just as good as a long nose, as long as I'm selling the Kleenex, or doing the nose jobs. Accordingly, there has grown up in this country over the past decade a dangerous collusion of forces in industry, government, private foundations, and professional language researchers and teachers. To date, their most seductive appeal has been the notion that the "culturally deprived" or "disadvantaged," i.e., a Black child can be moved into the mainstream of American life—to use the cliché—if he is taught to be "bidialectal," that is, if he learns to use "standard" English in those situations which would guarantee success for him in the white world. He is to be taught that his own dialect, his social approach, is to be reserved only for private and intimate occasions. For his attempts at this kind of self-mutilation the child is rewarded with transistor radios and other products of the "Great Society."

Industry has moved into the picture with the blandishments of contract teaching. Fortunately, its corruption has already been exposed and its premises and results brought under fire. But there is a more sophisticated operation afoot which involves professional linguistics of national reputation. Although they are confronted with evidence that they are unprepared to produce real "double-speakers," they have a vested interest in the money and prestige and power involved. And if the Black child fails to become "bidialectal," the fault will be found in him, not in the system. And the final question is whether those who control the system and those who fund it are concerned with learning anyway, or with the circulation of money and the pacification of the Black community.

So Black English worries these people. They know the political significance of language. They knew the power of "Ain't Gon' Let Nobody Turn Me Round." They somehow co-opted it, but they have never been able to define "jazz," to say nothing of "Soul." And it's not dead. We're just letting it rest a while, gathering up that ancestral energy, for as long as we have vital contact with that, we can get it together. Well, it may be a costume party to Henry Allen, but it's real to us, and everything we do from now on gonna be FONKY!

BLACK SATURATION

A VIEW OF THE HUMANITIES

Paper presented at Howard University, Washington, DC, 1974.

If the Black Studies / Black University debates of recent years have taught us anything, they have taught us that if we are to serve the needs of our people today, mere skill is not enough, more professionalism is not enough, and token integration into the so-called mainstream is not enough because that stream is obviously polluted. These debates have taught us that our older, deeper, historic sense of pride and movement and service must be recaptured and renewed. They have taught us that we must face the contradictions in American life head-on, with our own definitions and sense of direction. They have taught us that unless our schools and colleges and universities have a special function to perform, then, indeed, they should be abolished, and other people continue to control and direct our lives. However, we have also learned in our pursuit of new modes of organization and thought, new instruments and mechanisms, that we cannot afford to lose *any* of the Black institutions which have been dedicated in principle to the acquisition and dissemination of what can still be called humanistic knowledge, for that knowledge serves a very vital function.

The function of humanistic knowledge (with the qualifications implicit in this discussion) is to provide individual and group answers, albeit tentative ones, to the ultimate questions of human existence. These are usually phrased as follows: Who are we? Where do we come from? Where are we going? And as abstract as they may seem, these questions and their logical derivatives are deeply rooted in the gritty facts of everyday existence.

Moreover, these questions and problems are the special formal concern of that group of studies which we call the humanities. They are the alleged concern of everyone in American education—student or teacher—whether he is associated with the school of engineering or a so-called liberal arts college, the Free University, or the Independent Black Institution. In a way, they represent the distilled life of the people, the unexpressed assumptions behind their thoughts and actions, their values, their judgments, their aspirations. The term "humanities" comes from Latin and originally described an education based on Greek and Roman civilization; its history provides a kind of capsule of Western life and thought, which has, indeed, circumscribed Black people on the continent as well as in this hemisphere. But Black students are saying now, "We are an African people." Thus, they are calling for a view of the world which is radically different from the ones which their schools are prepared to give them. If the recent history of Black student thought is any indication, this trend will doubtlessly continue, for the "Black Curriculum" debates quickly escalated to "Black Studies." While the term was being dissected and analyzed by whites and Blacks alike, the theoreticians abandoned it because it was too limiting and, moreover, had been co-opted by white administrators and book publishers for their own interests. Meantime, student and faculty theoreticians were moving to the new and challenging concept of the Black University and the noble ideal of education for the liberation of all Black people, of all Africans, wherever they may be.

The colleges on the whole have moved very cautiously, sometimes to their disadvantage, but that struggle is well documented, and fairly well known. What needs to be better known is the amount of faith that Black students still have in the ability of their colleges to reconstruct themselves in order to meet the challenges of life in the 70s. Despite the recent highly publicized meeting of Black college presidents with President Nixon, our schools still remain in a crisis, which results not only from budgetary problems, but chiefly, I feel, from a failure of nerve, a loss of vision and a sense of mission.

This loss shows itself especially in those courses which embody the philosophy of the college, its objectives, and its sense of direction. These courses chiefly include the humanities and the social sciences, as well as mathematics and elementary science, and are generally required of all students. A typical list of courses would include the following: Freshman English Composition, an Introduction to Literature, a Survey of Western History or Western Civilization, an Introduction to Economics, Introductory Sociology, and Political Science. In addition, there may be a semester each of music and art, and, for good measure, a year of Western Philosophy, sometimes, a semester or year of Religion. Sometimes, a group of these subjects are organized thematically or chronologically into a one- or two-year sequence called General Humanities.

Finally, many schools still require two years of a modern foreign language. What is immediately striking about this list is that it contains so much that is required. What is even more striking is the fact that a student taking all these courses over a two-year period or so could write dozens of papers, engage in virtually endless debate, without once realizing that Black people not only helped shape this culture of the West, but have an important and viable one of their own which is rarely acknowledged in the classroom.

The other reason I say *rarely* is that the men and women who not only acknowledged but interpreted, shaped, and helped to define this culture are rare persons themselves—Black National Treasures—who should be better known today: Sterling Brown and the galaxy of brilliant professors at Howard University—to name a few—[William Leo] Hansberry, Miller, Davis, Locke, Dodson, Cook, Logan, Butcher, and Lee; Chivers, Tillman, and Brawley at Morehouse; Willis James at Spelman; Horace Mann Bond at Atlanta University; Margaret Walker Alexander at Tougaloo and Jackson State; and others who lived and taught the Black Experience, even, as in Tillman's case, if the ostensible subject matter were Shakespeare. Because of their style, their Blackness, some of these people suffered the essential neglect of their colleagues and peers. These men and women, along with [Frantz] Fanon and [W. E. B.] Du Bois and Malcolm [X], [Martin Luther] King [Jr.], and [Marcus] Garvey, are the heroes and quiet prophets of the present Black Awakening.

To return to these courses—the general requirements of the Black college—they provided the nucleus of a student's education, so that even if he dropped out, or transferred after the first two years, he would still be "educated"—"well-rounded," able to "cope" with the fundamental problems of the world. During these years the institutional stamp was placed on its product—a Howard or Fisk man or woman, a Spelmanite, a Morehouse man. These courses served their function—to spread the attractive but essentially false philosophy of universal man, molded, of course, in the European form.

Memphis, really, was the symbolic end of all that. And that is why these courses are presently failing, why they have been particularly singled out for demolition. Generation after generation of Black youths have been taught not only that western European civilization epitomizes the highest reaches of the human mind and spirit but that they should be grateful for being allowed to experience, although vicariously, that noble leap of inexpressible sensibility. All of which, to be sure, is not to deny Dante, or Shakespeare, or Beethoven. And the question is not the opposition of the civilizations of the East, or even of Africa, but the intellectual imperialism of the European which followed so swiftly in the wake of his economic and political conquest and enslavement of the nonwhite world.

But particularly Africa. For we are, indeed, an African people, and in that realization lies our salvation. Even if we were reluctant to give up certain notions of universalism, we could still make the case, based on the Europeans' own scientific discoveries, that Africa is the cradle of mankind, of human civilization. That kind of speculation, however, is too easy for us. We cannot afford the luxury of it—of living, as it were, under the aspect of eternity. Our problems exist in time, in history, and historically the Europeans are our oppressors. They must be judged, as we must be ourselves, by human actions, in time.

And on what grounds can we make judgments? On the basis of our own experience or that of others, the family, the clan, the nation, and the people and how is that experience preserved and transmitted? [Experience is] transmitted through history, through culture—through religion and art, law, science, and the forms of belief. And who . . . is listening? Our artists? Our great men of science? We ask ourselves these questions, and our answers are vague, blurred, superficial, for we want to pronounce those European names, and we realize that, really, they are not ours. No matter how hard we try—at a certain fundamental level, Dante's Europeanness, his Italianness, resists us; Beethoven's Germanness overwhelms us. For all of its Latinate language, for all of its "universality," *Paradise Lost* is an English poem. Chartres Cathedral appeals to our sensibility, not to our soul.

Our ancestral names and actions, our moral philosophy, our music, our religions, our languages, our inventions were shut out from our minds even in our own Black schools, and we became ourselves and made of our students Victorian ladies and gentlemen, suffering from the delusion of universality, the European version, which the English poet [Percy] Shelley expressed in his dictum "We are all Greeks," apparently unaware of the Greek expression "Always something new out of Africa."

The "newest" something is the oldest perception of all—identity. And our students say, "We are an African people." If our people are to survive, therefore, our schools must address not "Black Curriculum" or "Black Studies," but the monumental problem of transforming "Greeks" into Africans.

Now, although the recent curricular changes in Black colleges to accommodate the Black Experience may have their own parochial logic, seen as a large national picture, they reflect all the confusion, the acrimony, the fear, and the endless debate which characterize the national pattern. Briefly, the changes may be ranked in order of the degree of involvement in the totality of the Black Experience—a condition which we shall call *saturation*, and which shall be elaborated later as it particularly relates to the humanities.

First, there is the notion of "Blackening," or "Blackenizing," courses, which may mean as little as using "Black" examples to illustrate concepts which are irrelevant or inimical to Black life using a traditional course as a vehicle for Black liberation, however one defines that oft-used expression.

Next is the concept of balance in courses, which often seems to mean that in a course, or text, say in American literature, a couple of Black representatives need to be brought in to demonstrate presumably the democratic nature of American life, notwithstanding the fact that in a given text Phillis Wheatley may be a better poet than Anne Bradstreet; and Amiri Baraka, better than a host of white poetasters, may be represented by a few of his earlier poems and those oftentimes not his best; and other Black writers, like A. B. Spellman or Bob Kaufman or Larry Neal or Margaret Danner, may not be mentioned at all. And this is even true of a text which was copyrighted in 1968 and entitled *American Literature: A World View*.

The next pattern is, I take it, part of a more serious attempt to deal *structurally* with the Black Experience in the curriculum. It is called a "concentration" in a particular major, and means, for example, that a student, again majoring in literature, would take a sizable number of his courses in "Black areas," but would still be required to take, in effect, the basic requirements for a traditional English major. This is at least an intelligent compromise, but it suffers from a lack of daring, a lack of commitment, and a lack of imagination.

The last important pattern is the so-called "Black Studies major," which is modeled on the traditional concept of *the major* field of study, with its general courses on the lower level and the more specialized ones offered during the junior and senior years. Aside from the conceptual weakness implicit in the idea of fitting this experience into a traditional major is the fact that only a few students (as also in the *concentration*) would be affected by it, and the problem of transformation from "Greek" to African involves everybody.

This brings us back to the general requirements, especially to the social sciences and the humanities. They deal with basic problems affecting the Black community, and they should, ideally, not be in conflict with one another, for, in effect, the social scientists provide the means for realizing the visions of the poets and for embodying the concepts of the philosophers. The model of Amiri Baraka, the significance of his work in the elections recently held in Newark, should also serve to remind the artists and the students of the humanities how practical, in action, art can be. On the national level, how important and far-reaching would such an influence be! And of our social scientists, to name just one, Andrew Billingsley, of Berkeley, how different would our lot be if his views, rather than Daniel Moynihan's, helped to determine federal policy toward the Black families of this land!

This kind of awareness cannot be left to chance, if we are to survive. The experience of Blackness, in all of its dimensions, cannot be left to a handful of students who specialize in literature, or art, or history. It must be an integral part of any serious attempt to prepare our children and our youth to live and to flourish and to prevail in this country. On the level of formal education it means a total involvement—to the point of illumination, commitment, and action—in the life of the Black community, by whatever means the structures and mechanisms from the school can provide us. I am not speaking about indoctrination. I am speaking of *saturation*, which means, again, simply absorbing as much of the Black Experience as one can, as much as one needs to find out who he is and what he must do to go where he must, with his people, for without them there *is* no identity except the one which the West has foisted upon us and which we know all too well. Again, *saturation* is reached when the Black man in America understands, accepts, utilizes, and celebrates his Blackness, then becomes as unselfconscious about it as his brothers are on the ancestral continent. He and his community are one and move together, for as we discover who we are, we realize what we have to do, and we exert our energies toward the acquisition of the proper skills and techniques.

Thus, *saturation* can be spoken of as (a) a condition or goal, specifically, a kind of total health or well-being; (b) a mechanism or process in attaining that condition or goal; (c) a strategy for attaining that condition or goal. With specific reference to education, *saturation* can be viewed as the end product of the Black University, replacing the outworn concept of the "well-rounded man," the Victorian gentleman of John Henry Newman, who seems to be the model in theory for so many of our colleges and schools.

As a mechanism, *saturation* is the device by which "value" courses, especially the "humanities," are tested for relevance and effectiveness—the end result being, as stated above, not only self-illumination but creative integration of one's total self into the family and the larger community through study and action. Thus, information is changed into energy; energy into action—intellectual, social, political, and spiritual—and the ultimate end of this action is Black liberation.

As strategy, saturation provides the individual student, teacher, or administrator with a means for the radical transformation of value courses—hence, the rationale and ultimate direction of the most conservative institution—into pockets of Black energy, into the cells of the Black University. The strategy can be as simple as asking questions—the teacher of the class, or the class of the teacher—or demanding specific answers, factual answers or value judgments, which energize even apparently irrelevant information. (Strategy thus sets the process in motion.)

For example, courses in the humanities are either offered in a kind of package which comprises art, history, philosophy, literature, and music; or they are offered as separate courses. They are usually organized either chronologically or thematically; in both cases the frame of reference is Western civilization. Any teacher or student worth his salt could raise fundamental and disturbing and liberating questions in even a World Literature, i.e., Western Literature, type of course, simply by finding out what people in India were doing at the same time that Sappho was writing. If one is turned off as being irrelevant, then the point needs to be made that Sappho was not only the greatest Greek lyric poet but also a Black woman, and the Greeks said so. One could raise the further question of Homer's conception of the Ethiopian, and still further of the Greek gods and their relationship to the Egyptians. And behind all of this, one could raise the question of the origin of Egyptian civilization with its very considerable Black substratum. When this is done—and one doesn't have to be a specialist—the notion that we are all "Greeks" will be seen for what it really is. This is but a single, simple example. Any hardworking and imaginative student or instructor could raise dozens of others.

In the area of music, for example, for a course organized that way, a serious student armed with the research of Alan Lomax or with a good ear and a collection of African records could challenge fusty notions about who invented counterpoint, and about simple rhythm. The average Black student, I would venture to say, is more knowledgeable about Black music in America than most professors. Let this average student insist upon [John] Coltrane and [Thelonious] Monk and Cecil Taylor in his humanities classes. Or let him read Spellman's *Four Lives in the Bebop Business* and see what Taylor has to say about the Black Experience. Let him make it possible for Taylor to leave Wisconsin and create in dignity at Howard or the Atlanta University Center, where gifted young Marion Brown was not appreciated.

Or in literature, let our students raise the serious questions, the profound questions about the current writing; and let them ask why Ebon Dooley has to struggle with his Timbuktu Bookstore and is not lecturer or writer in residence at the AU Center. Starving our poets and artists is also a form of "Black genocide"! Let our students tell our presidents that! Perhaps, they don't really know.

Let them raise the question of qualifications again—in a nonracial, nonideological manner, in a "scientific" manner—and let them find out why in many of our colleges whites constitute so large a percentage of our humanities teachers. Are the whites being exploited? What are the criteria? Why are the blues not included in our textbooks? The poetry is as moving, to say the least, as that of the English and Scottish ballads. Let them raise the questions! Let them raise the questions! Let them question the qualifications of those whose textbooks we use. Let them do this on the freshman level. Who decides who or what a *major American* poet is? Who decides whether no Black poetry should be printed in an anthology? Who determines that there is no such thing as Black art? Hilton Kramer? What are his qualifications? Let us raise the questions. Let us create a generation of Black people who are not specialists in Blackness but who are *saturated* in Blackness, who understand it and act from it, out of mission, yes, and out of love.

HOME TO *NOMMO*

Review of *New Days: Poems of Exile and Return,*
by June Jordan. *Black World / Negro Digest,* September 1975.

One of the most significant aspects of Black American poetry is the prominent role which Black women have always assumed. Accordingly, women
bring and have brought to the flowering of Black consciousness of the present
and the recent past an extraordinary range of insight and sensitivity textured
and shaped by the special fact of being both Black and female. At best they
illuminate and help to define the elusive interior dimensions of our history
by exploring areas of feeling and thought which have seemed inaccessible to
men. A case in point is Gwendolyn Brooks's poem on Malcolm X, appearing
in Margaret Burroughs's and Dudley Randall's commemorative volume *For
Malcolm X* (Broadside Press, 1969):

> [lines 1–10 from "Malcolm X: For Dudley Randall"]
> He opened us—
> Who was a key.
>
> Who was a man.

It is difficult to imagine that poem being written by a man, and it gives us a
perspective which is startling in its primitive archetypal power. It is not only
a Black love poem but also a poem about history, history as love.

This is also the unifying theme of June Jordan's latest book, *New Days:
Poems of Exile and Return.* It is a book about love and about identification
and identity, about family and time, about art and death and struggle. It is
a book about lovemaking. It is a book about courage, about keeping on,
about Eternal Return. One is immediately struck by the poet's remarkable
gift for language, for the flashes of highly compressed, memorable imagery,

the subtle intellectual connections, the rhythmic versatility, the courage to tackle difficult and complex subjects, to risk failure with intractable material, as in some of the "Roman" poems in "Poems of Exile" and some of the topical poems in "Poems of Return." Jordan doesn't apologize for her virtuosity, so when the poem works completely, as in the opening poem "May 1, 1970," she is at home with sly scatology: "Here am I / a dark spot on / the underwear of ivory snow." She can run changes on lovemaking, and give lines like these: "no love will hurt / me lover lift me lying down." Or like these: "When he comes on top of me / I am high as I can be." Or the following: "In your love I am sometimes redeemed / a stranger / to myself." In a tantalizing and evocative work, "Fragments from a Parable," she explores family relationships, the creative process, the nature of the artist, and identity. Metaphysical concerns suffused with imagination are stated with passionate precision: "The immovable of your awareness is The Wall. You and what you do are optional. That is the secret, he said, that is the secret of your tragic spontaneity. Be glad you are optional, he told me. His voice was deep. His eyes were shut. . . . / My father said: There shall be shadow. / I am shining shadows on The Wall. / / And my father was only a shadow. His shadow of flesh divulged / me: I was an apology of bone." There is thus a wide range of tone and technique in these poems, moving from simple lyrical statement through the nuances of Black idiom to complex combinations of slang and history, myth and politics. But underlying the individual poems, there is a strong sense of design, of pacing, of structure, so that the book makes a complete statement, the parts of which are sensibly ordered.

The book is divided into five sections and four thematic groupings. "Conditions for Leaving" consists of three short poems, one lyrical and elegiac, "On the Twenty-Fifth Anniversary of the United Nations: 1970," preceded and followed by two tartly satirical poems on America, "May 1, 1970" and "Memo to Daniel Patrick Moynihan." The tone and the arrangement are calculated for maximum effect. "Poems of Exile" consists of seventeen "Roman" poems, a series of lyrics in which the poet comments on or dramatizes a variety of topics and moods. Two memorable ones are number fourteen, an ecstatic love poem, and number five, the longest in the series, which meditates on the human condition as symbolized by the destruction of Pompeii. It is a difficult, ambitious work, flawed perhaps, but intellectually daring and notable for what it reveals of an extraordinary talent.

"Poems of Return" embraces sections three and four. It is a somewhat uneven performance. Some poems seem merely topical and don't come off, like the rhetorical "May 27, 1971: No Poem," or [are] too flip, like "Poem: On Divine Adaptation to an Age of Disbelief." Others, though slight, vibrate with the poet's sincerity, as in "Poem: On the Spirit of Mildred Jordan," or "Poem: On Your Love." In addition, two of her finest love lyrics, "It's about You," and "After All Is Said and Done," appear in this section. But the strongest works in the entire book, "Fragments from a Fable," a splendid prose poem, and "Getting Down to Get Over," appear in section four of this group. "Poem against a Conclusion" is the final unit. Its philosophical stance suggests a pun on the word "against," meaning simultaneously being opposed to a conclusion, in anticipation of, or in payment for a conclusion.

The most moving poem in the book and, I think, one of the most important to come out of the recent Black Arts Movement is "Getting Down to Get Over," from "Poems of Return." Containing most of the themes of the book, it first appeared in *Essence Magazine*, and is dedicated to the poet's mother. Here the poet makes a wonderful synthesis of the many levels of language at her command. Here she exerts a fine control over a verbal virtuosity which in other places—in this volume, and in *Some Changes*, her first—threatens to dominate our impressions, somewhat as the poetry of [Melvin] Tolson does, or early LeRoi Jones [Amiri Baraka], or early Gwendolyn Brooks. It is a long poem, so the control is even more admirable. It deals with the Black woman / Earth Mother theme in a way which raises it above all the tired litanies to Black women which were unfortunately too common in the sixties. Here is a successful attempt to gather the many-faceted image of the Black woman into a statement which is at once both mythic and personal.

She begins with a simple, passionate, primal call: "MOMMA MOMMA MOMMA." The subsequent changes which she runs on the name delineate a wide variety of man-woman relationships. She continues: "hey daddy! hey / bro! / we walked together (an') / talk together (an') / dance and *do* / (together) / dance and do/hey! / daddy! / bro! / hey! / nina nikki nonni nommo nommo / momma Black / Momma." At this point something magical happens as the poem is energized by the poet's intelligence. First, the mention of two strong Black women, Nina [Simone] and Nikki [Giovanni], whose impact has a directness that goes beyond art, whose names have become the concrete symbols of Black creativity. Next, a momentary playful flirtation with childhood and with English song. Then the quick illumination of *nommo nommo*—the creative force of the word and the realization that *Momma* is the creative force of the universe—and here is the achievement of June Jordan's imagination. The force is expressed in African terminology, but this is the first time since it became current with [Janheinz] Jahn's book *Muntu* that the term *nommo* has become domesticated. And that is, I feel, a historical achievement, a watermark of Black consciousness in the United States.

In the passage immediately following, we find the poet mastering a great deal of sociological information without becoming either abstract or prosy. Her wit dominates and vitalizes the abstractions before they crystallize. There is a volume of analysis compressed in the bitter brilliance of these lines: "to be Low-down / Black Statistical / Low Factor / Factotum / Factitious Fictitious / Figment Figuring in Lowdown Lyin / Annual Reports." That was a comment on the white male exploitation of the Black woman. The comment on the Black male is equally precise and much more elaborate. No summary can do justice to it. She demands: "What does Mothafuckin mean? / WHO'S THE MOTHAFUCKA / FUCKED MY MOMMA . . . / a macktruck / mothafuck / the first primordial / the paradig/digmatic / dogmatistic mothafucka who / is he? / hey! / momma momma." Beyond the mythic, historical, and sociological associations rapped in those lines, there are the personal relations of man and woman, suggested with deeply felt rhythm and image: "dry eyes on the / shy/dark/hidden/cryin Black / face . . . / and no poem / take you through the whole night / and no big / Black / burly / hand / be holdin yours / to have to hold onto / no / big Black burly hand / no nommo / no Black Prince / come riding from the darkness / on a beautiful Black horse / no bro / no daddy." And the encounter with the father takes place through a complex series of cinematographic images which compress multitudes of family relationships, at the center of which is momma momma as the girl becomes a woman.

Section II of the poem is a moving series of fundamental images of the many roles of the Black woman—as field hand, as wife, as mother, as urban worker, as lover. It concludes: "Consider the Queen / a full/Black/glorious/a purple rose / aroused by the tiger breathin / beside her / a shell with the moanin / of ages inside her / a hungry one / feedin the folk / what they need // Consider the Queen." After that multidimensional passage, there is a remarkable change of pace as section III states with staccato directness: "Blackman / let that white girl go / She know what you ought to know. / (By now.)" The final section harkens back to the opening, but moving more quickly this time to social commentary, which includes the "national gross product," "the trickbag university," the "infest/incestuous investigators." These are all things to avoid, to turn away from, and the word "turn" itself becomes the driving motive of a powerful rhythm that doesn't subside until the final line of the poem: "teach me to survive my / momma / teach me how to hold a new life / momma / help me / turn the face of history / *to your face.*" This poem is the emotional and spiritual climax of the book—the homecoming— but it is not the end of the book, or of the quest. The book, in fact, though it stops, does not end, and the last section, section five, is appropriately entitled "Poem against a Conclusion." It contains these lines:

These words
they are stones in the water
running away

They are also wise words—touchstones that lead to that knowledge which is the first step toward home.

SATURATION

PROGRESS REPORT ON A THEORY OF
BLACK POETRY

Published in *Black World* 24, no. 8 (June 1975): 4–17.

In *Understanding the New Black Poetry* (William Morrow & Co., 1973), I attempted to sketch a critical framework which would help make the poetry accessible to a larger number of people. I tried to do this in a serious, nonpolemical fashion, because although some of the attacks on the poetry deserved to be simply blasted away by the polemic, other attacks and misunderstandings were more challenging. And much of this misunderstanding was—to be frank—in the minds of the Black people to whom the poetry was addressed. Not all of them were over thirty, or reactionary, or brainwashed. Many of them were young, bright men and women who wanted to know more fully what was going on. Some of them were even poets themselves. I conceived of the book with them in mind, and their teachers, and, frankly, in order to clarify some things for myself. All in all, the book has been well received, but like most attempts to explain or explicate or verbalize art, it also raised some questions which need some systematic response.

These questions revolve mainly around one of the three categories that were basic to my discussion—*saturation*. The other two categories are *theme* and *structure*. Before I address those questions, however, I shall summarize briefly the entire argument. It says that there are two traditions or levels of Black poetry—the folk and the formal—which must be seen as a totality, since they often intersect and overlap one another, and since the people who create them are one people. It says further that the overriding theme of Black poetry is the idea of *freedom* and/or *liberation*, expressed in various ways and on various levels. This, of course, is not to deny the existence and the importance of other themes—both public and personal; but the poetry reflects the concerns, the consciousness of the people—and freedom/liberation has been and still is obviously the main objective of Black American life, and as a theme it virtually leaps from the pages of our poetry.

Structure is a crucial category because it is the one so loosely discussed and so open to damaging attack from enemies of the literature and enemies of the people, but sometimes even from well-meaning and "objective" friends of the literature and teachers of the people. Here are two examples. In a review of *Black Fire*, ed. LeRoi Jones [Amiri Baraka] and Larry Neal, William Morrow & Co., 1968, Peter Berek makes the following observation:

> A few of the assembled works have a scatological energy that succeeds in impressing one with the violence and passion of the author's emotions, but the expression never achieves the precision and control which are the hallmarks of successful art (including the "black" arts of jazz and rhythm and blues). Characteristically (and sometimes ludicrously) the poet substitutes the announcement of an intention for its fulfillment. Thus, Yusuf Rahman glorifies Black womanhood by saying
>
> > naturally Black & beautiful
> > LOVE ME EBONY LADY
> > Yes! I see blue-crystal teardrops
> > burning scars on your soul's cheeks
>
> A burning heart is not the same as acid indigestion. (*Saturday Review*, Nov. 30, 1968, 36)

What makes the review damaging is the fact that the editors had compared the lines of this poem to a Charlie Parker solo. In another review, this one in the *New York Review of Books*, the same poem and the same statement are taken to task.

Despite the implicit chauvinism in these reviews, polemic is certainly not sufficient answer to them. The question which they raise is structural and should be answered, if possible, in structural terms. If it cannot be, then the writer/critic/editor should be more careful with his similes. With these kinds of responses in mind, then, I tried to set down the structural patterns that I saw, and that I felt were identifiably Black. In the process, I assumed that anyone in the Western world who took the time to read a critical essay on poetry in the first place would already have some specific ideas in mind about what European, specifically English, and Euro-American, specifically Anglo-American, poetic structures were.

This leaves, of course, the concept of *saturation*, which is the subject proper of this discussion. This category, while the most briefly discussed in my "Introduction: The Forms of Things Unknown," is actually the most important, in my thinking, of the categories, simply because it poses the most difficult questions on the one hand, and presents a logical category in which they can be profitably discussed.

In the essay I observed that by saturation I mean "several things, but chiefly (a) the communication of Blackness in a given situation, and (b) a sense of fidelity to the observed and intuited truth of the Black Experience. I postulate this concept as a third category for describing and evaluating Black poetry. As in the other two, theme and structure, this category exists only in relationship to the entire work and is employed merely to deal with an aspect of the poetry that warrants discussion and appreciation. In other words, just as it is misleading to speak of them to the exclusion of structure and vice versa, it is difficult, if not impossible, to speak honestly about saturation without considering these other two. In addition, one must not consider the poem in isolation but in relationship to the reader/audience, and the reader to the wider context of the phenomenon which we call, for the sake of convenience, the Black Experience" (*Understanding the New Black Poetry*, 62).

Saturation may thus be seen as (1) a perception, (2) a quality, and (3) a condition of theme and structure. The *perception* occurs in the reader/audience in a situation of communication involving the poem/poet/reader/performer. If the poem "works," then the reader perceives something in it which he identifies as Black and meaningful. He perceives this as being true to his knowledge of the experience recorded in the poem, according to his *observation* or according to his *intuition*. The important thing, at any rate, is that he considers the communication of this "Blackness" to be significant and his reception of it to be significant, whether he agrees with it or not. This communication of Blackness may be related to theme, or what is commonly called the subject or meaning of the poem; or it may be related to the structure of the poem—the way it is put together. With regard to theme, saturation may occur when the theme is simply, obviously, and naturally Black—as in a tiny poem by Sterling Plumpp, entitled "Heaven Here": "on asphalt / dance floors / in sure control / o i see / little alcindors be" (*Half Black Half Blacker*, Third World Press, 1970, 12). On the other hand, as I pointed out in *Understanding the New Black Poetry* (63), it may occur in poems which do not ostensibly deal with Black themes at all, which yet impress us somehow as Black, as having a Black "quality." The analogue in real life is the very fair-skinned person who may or may not be "Black" whom we somehow take to be Black on the basis of some subliminal gesture, or tone, or "quality." I cite again two examples from Mari Evans's *I Am a Black Woman* (William Morrow & Co., 1970): "I am not / lazy . . . just / . . . battered." Evans continues: "where have you gone / with your confident / walk your / crooked smile the / rent money / in one pocket and / my heart / in another." I noted that, "In cases like these, the awareness is largely unverbalized and comes across as a 'typical' situation, which we identify as true-to-life or part of the Black Experience" (63). And there are poems which we simply draw into the dynamics of our Blackness because they do not contradict it but flow into it freely, stamped with our own personal and group impress. Many poems on love, for example, are of this variety, as are innumerable popular songs on the same theme.

But to return to my argument, poets have made Blackness—in a thematic and structural sense—the subject of their poems. And when they do so with the skill of Sterling Brown in "Ma Rainey," then the least the critic can do is to try to meet the work on its own terms. As far as I know, there are no traditional categories, or practices, or attitudes in American or English literature which make this possible. On the contrary, they try to make it impossible, to erase it, to pretend that it doesn't exist—as in Louis Simpson's cavalier dismissal of Gwendolyn Brooks, or in the general liberal platitudes about "the human tradition" or "universals."

If the critic is worth his salt, then he would attempt to *describe* what occurs in the poem and to *explain*—to the extent that it is possible—how the "action" takes place, i.e., how the elements of the work interact with one another to produce its effect. And if one of those elements is Blackness—as value, as theme, or as structure, especially the latter—then he is remiss in his duty if he does not attempt to deal with it in some logical, orderly manner. Finally, he must place some value judgment on the work, on the totality of the work—not just its theme, its sociology, or its ideology, but also its structure. And if the theme involves Blackness as value, and if the structures are Black, whether in a traditional sense or not, then the judgment must involve that Blackness as well.

Surely some structures are more distinctly Black, more recognizably Black than others. Thus, the three-line blues form is more distinctly Black than a sonnet by Claude McKay, for example. The ballad because it is a form (in the Anglo-American tradition) which was early appropriated by Blacks—on both folk and formal levels—is also more definitely "Black" than the sonnet. But the blues, an invention of the Black people, is "Blacker" than both. In fact, one may call the blues a saturated form and blues imagery, saturated structures.

This perception of a Black quality can take place on various levels of significance, thus making some poems "Blacker" than others or more significantly "Black" than others. Thus Plumpp's "Heaven Here," though saturated by its fidelity to observed events and evoking the towering model of "alcindor" weighs less in terms of meaning than, for example, Langston Hughes's "I wish the rent / Was Heaven sent." Or, "I got the blues but I'm too damn mean to cry." Both of these "poems" represent different conditions of Blackness, of saturation. This perception of Blackness, then, means that Blackness is, or can be, or should be a value in the *creation*, in the *description*, and in the *criticism* of Black poetry. This is so, of course, not because I say so, but because poets say so, musicians say so, and audiences say so, either directly, or by implication. Now, I know that this is an unpopular view, especially with those artists and those critics, like [J.] Saunders Redding, who think that they live in a colorblind homogeneous United States of America. I can in all honesty merely give them my respect as writers and my pity as Black people.

At this point we begin discussing *saturation* as a function or condition of structure. And we may say briefly that certain characteristics of Black speech and music may so imbue the poetry as to warrant our calling certain poems or features of poems "structurally saturated." The musical referents themselves are quite clear: boogie-woogie style, blues tonality and changes, the pulse of jazz. So also are those of speech. Moreover, if we look at the broad structural categories of literature—prose fiction, drama, and poetry—and if we further divide these, we will produce a kind of spectrum of concreteness which will parallel the forms of saturation which I have described as "a sense of fidelity to the observed and intuited truth of the Black Experience." One may arrange the categories in this way:

Science → OBSERVATION		INTUITION → Music	
Factual Writing	*Fiction*	*Drama*	*Poetry*
History	Novel	Tragedy	Epic
Anthropology	Novella	Comedy	Ballad
Sociology	Short story	Tragicomedy	Ode
Geography	Parable		Personal lyric
Economics	Fable		
Journalism, etc.			

In Black writing, the form which would depend most on the sustained *observed* factual truth of the Black Experience would be the novel; the form which would depend least on factual truth and most on the intuited truth would be the lyric. Yet both of these forms can be "saturated," the novel because it approaches the quality, the nature, the character of history; the lyric because it approaches the *condition* of music, with all of the special advantages and disadvantages of that medium. However diverse the spectrum, we are speaking of literature, which I define as the verbal organization of experience into beautiful forms.

The forms of Black poetry—to the extent that they are definable—can themselves be arranged into a spectrum of sorts.

History→			*Music*→	
Formal: Literary ballads	Odes	Short formal lyrics		Free verse
				Experimental
				Spirituals
Folk: Work songs	Blues	Seculars		Blues
Ballads				Work songs
				Ballads

It is interesting to note that the folk forms are all basically involved with music, i.e., they are also songs, or primarily songs. The formal poetry based on these types can be measured against them, in a conscious act of criticism. If one knows them, then, of course, this measurement takes place automatically—as saturation, or degree of saturation.

Degree of saturation is a concept of meteorology which is useful for us. For example, just as the atmosphere may be 70 percent saturated with moisture, so theoretically may a poem be 70 percent or more, or less, saturated with *Blackness*, with the referent being on one hand fidelity to the "observed," i.e., personal and historical truth of the Black Experience; and on the other, to the intuited truth as embodied in the cultural forms, especially the music, of the folk life. This is not to say that saturation or fidelity is perceived as imitation of folk forms. To the contrary, it is perceived of as logical and spiritual extensions of those forms. The following comment by James Weldon Johnson on the poetry of Sterling Brown is an elaboration and a particularization of what I mean:

> He infused his poetry with genuine characteristic flavor by adopting as his medium the common, racy, living speech of the Negro in certain

phases of *real* life. For his raw material he dug down into the deep mine of Negro folk poetry. He found the unfailing sources from which sprang the Negro folk epics and ballads such as "Stagolee," "John Henry," "Casey Jones," "Long Gone John" and others. But, as I said in commenting on his work in *The Book of American Negro Poetry*: he has made more than mere transcriptions of folk poetry, and he has done more than bring to it mere artistry; he has deepened its meaning and multiplied its implications. He has actually absorbed the spirit of his material, made it his own; and without diluting its primitive frankness and raciness, truly re-expressed it with artistry and magnified power. In a word, he has taken this raw material and worked it into original and authentic poetry. (Preface, *Southern Road*, xiv–xv)

Sometimes those extensions embody parts of larger forms—quotes from a song or allusions. The most powerful of these I have called "mascons," a term which I borrowed from NASA, which I signify as "the massive concentration of Black experiential energy." These mascons, oddly enough, though they can be used, and are used almost in the manner of chords, almost as abstract structures, are deeply rooted in the spiritual history of the people.

But to pursue the idea of degree of saturation leads us to the idea of incomplete saturation. This is also useful as a critical tool, for if "saturation" is incomplete in a given work, and the poem is presumably complete (i.e., if it makes sense), then it is somehow complete outside of the tradition, or the framework, of Blackness. What, then, do we call such a work? Hybrid? Incomplete? A failure? A new creation? Whatever we call it, it is usually completed by extensions into and reliance upon the Euro-American poetic tradition. And it must, to the extent which it is apparent, be judged by the standards of that tradition. And, it should be emphasized that this applies not only to the poems of Phillis Wheatley and Albery Whitman, who consciously accepted those standards, but also to the popular songs, the gospel songs, and the formal Black poetry, new and old, which either consciously or unconsciously accepted these standards.

With this in mind, it becomes apparent that much of what is bad technically in Black poetry and in popular song is the imperfect assimilation and mastery of vocabulary and other stylistic features of the Euro-American tradition. This often shows itself in "purple passages," as occasionally in [Askia] Touré or [Keorapetse William] Kgositsile, to name two of the newer writers, or in the unconscious use of any arty clichés and, at times, just plain literary detritus.

It should also be apparent that when the writer consciously or unconsciously employs material from the folk tradition he may also fail technically to transform the material into art. On certain, obvious technical levels, this, of course, can be easily demonstrated. One example from a white novelist is [William] Styron's *The Confessions of Nat Turner*; one example from a white poet is [Yevgeny] Yevtushenko's poem on the death of Dr. Martin Luther King Jr., which appeared in *Black World*. For poetry, I take two examples from two fine poets, since their reputations are secure. First, my good friend Keorapetse Kgositsile and his poem "Origins":

> [lines 1–9 from "Origins"]
> the very soul aspires to songs
> of origins songs of constant beginnings
> what is this thing called
> love

Here the poet's usually precise rendering of experience degenerates, in the last line, into bathos. "What is this thing called / love." The referent here is probably not the pop song but a jazz version. At any rate, the poem verbalizes it in a manner indistinct from the original pop.

The second example is from Imamu Baraka [Amiri Baraka]. Here we go to the rough aspect of the tradition, but even here we can make value judgments based on technique and structure. Here is Baraka's takeoff on the dozens in "T. T. Jackson Sings": "I fucked your mother / On top of a house / When I got through / She thought she was / Mickey Mouse." The version recorded by Robert Abrahams is less halting, smooth yet tough. The couplet form is appropriate for the punch ending: "I fucked your mother from house to house / Out came a baby named Minnie Mouse." These, of course, are brief examples, but the poetry of the sixties, and earlier as well, is replete with others, both clean and dirty.

The question must now be raised precisely. What constitutes effective or successful rendering of Black poetic structure? Are there any models, or guidelines? I say yes. There is the example of established writers like [Robert] Hayden, [Gwendolyn] Brooks, [Sterling] Brown, and [Langston] Hughes. There is the standard of observation—of fidelity to the observed truth of the Black Experience. There is also the standard of intuition—of fidelity to the intuited truth of the Black Experience.

Some people—critics, white and Black—have difficulty with this last standard. They call it mysterious, mystical, chauvinistic, and even (in a slightly different context) a "curious metaphysical argument" (Redding). I call it *saturation*. I authenticate it from personal experience. To those critics I say: Remember [John] Keats did the same, proving poetic experience by his pulse and "the holiness of the imagination." Remember Norbert Weiner, the father of cybernetics, who habitually went to bed with a notebook nearby so that he could jot down the solutions to problems which intuitively came to him in sleep. Remember Stephen Spender's description of the proverbial singing of the poetic line, the nagging at his mind before the words came. Remember A. E. Housman whose poetry came to him when he was in a state of depression similar to that produced by illness. Remember T. S. Eliot's "objective correlative," despite current skepticism of its usefulness. Remember Matthew Arnold's "touchstone" theory of criticism. At any rate, what these various and famous people did was to admit that on the deepest levels of experience there is something about the nature of art—about the nature of creativity (and that includes scientific thought as well)—that there is something which eludes analysis, something which is experienced as a whole, as complete, and as valuable. Thus the mathematician J. W. N. Sullivan, in his brilliant study, *Beethoven: His Spiritual Development*, speaks of the capacity of the music to organize experience into meaningful "wholes." Thus, Matthew Arnold's famous "touchstone" theory, which says that passages of great literature should be carried about in the mind to measure other literature against. And thus in other areas of experience we find William James speaking of the "oceanic sense" in religious experience, and [William] Wordsworth's transcendental "spots of time." And thus, too, the Christian confronted by unbelief in the risen Christ: "I know that my Redeemer liveth."

But these are all analogues to the *condition* of saturation and the *perception* of saturation, to the embodiment and experiencing of Blackness as a valuable artistic (aesthetic) whole. For the real thing, we must go to the experience itself. I cite two examples, one of which explains itself and is from Sterling Brown's "Ma Rainey": "O Ma Rainey, / Sing yo' song; / Now you's back / Whah you belong, / Git way inside us, / Keep us strong . . ." The other example is a review of Aretha Franklin's gospel album *Amazing Grace*, by Carman Moore, the Black composer and music critic. He calls it "all perfect musical experience." And he continues:

You can hear Aretha as she hits upon an idea and turns it into triumph—as in "Amazing Grace" where she turns the line "and grace will lead me home" into "and grace will lead me right on" (echoed by the choir of course), "right on home." And in the early part of the same hymn we go with her as she vainly tries to call the spirit into her singing, first by moaning, then by singing a verse, and we exult with her as finally over the next two verses she goes out after that spirit and seizes it or is seized by it on a thrilling high A. A special moment, too, for me is all of "Precious Memories," a great big firm three-four tune that is more than a waltz, with James Cleveland joining Aretha to serve up what could only be called a succulent Baptist meal of soul. But the most memorable and telling passage on the album occurs on the tag end of one of the hymns when Aretha breaks out and does what a gospel singer is supposed to do in the first place—testify out loud and inspire the congregation to do likewise. She suddenly begins fervently, and over and over, to sing "I'm so glad I got religion . . . my soul is satisfied." And contained in that one outburst are the reasons why AM radio soul music can never be the real thing, why those Blacks who insist on breaking the back of the church before starting the revolution will never see any revolution in their lifetimes, and why any government or mystic klan that expects someday to crush the spirit of Black America can forget it. Aretha, James Cleveland, and yes Wilson Pickett, and Patti LaBelle, and the rest are not keepers of that spirit: they only show where it comes from, like swaying trees show the presence of wind. The mysteries may not be grace, but they sure are amazing. (*The Village Voice*, July 6, 1972, 31)

What Brother Moore has described is saturation—as experience. He has also employed it as a criterion of Black art. The link with the New Black Poetry has been eloquently made by many poets, but none more succinctly than Larry Neal, in his description of James Brown as "the best poet we got, baby." A link with the old can be seen in the hymn from the Georgia Sea Islands, "I Heard the Angels Singin." It goes in part as follows:

> Lawd, it wuz all 'roun' me shine
> All 'roun' me shine
> All 'roun' me shine
> Ah heard the angels singin'.

That, of course, is the ultimate experience of Blackness—saturation, as value, as perception of Black structures, Black themes. That can stand, too, for Black Transcendence. Below that height, however, there are many significant gradations. It is the task of the present generation of critics to make these explicit and to use them, so that our creative Brothers and Sisters can "move on up a little higher."

THE LITERATURE OF POWER
BLACK AMERICAN POETRY OF THE SIXTIES

Paper presented at the Colloquium on Culture and Development, Dakar, Senegal, Oct. 1976.

On first glance the thought of literature in the context of development seems frivolous, and the idea of Black American literature having a bearing on development (especially in an African context) seems either presumptuous or absurd. Nonetheless, if we accept the definitions of culture and development as offered by President [Leopold S.] Senghor and expressed with variations by others, then perhaps a reflection on the Black American literature of the 1960s will serve some useful purpose.

Briefly, the literature was an expression of the Black Consciousness Movement, a manifestation of the Black Power Movement, and a convergence of forces, ideas, and events which involve our common history. I speak, of course, of our African origin, of the slave trade, and the experience of slavery. I speak of the Black Experience of colonization. But I speak also of the African diaspora, or the African continuum. Continuum is a better word, for although we have been scattered and have taken root in other lands, our origin and our lifestyle are African.

The great discovery of Black Americans in the 1960s was just that. Not only that Black is beautiful, but more meaningfully the idea, the realization— "We are an African people." This discovery energized the writers and artists of the decade. It is still doing so. It didn't matter really whether we knew an African language or, like Alex Haley, could trace our ancestry back to particular persons or groups on the continent. What *was* and *is* important was that we dared to say this, that we believed it, that we dared to grapple seriously with its implications; and, finally, that others have found the conviction disquieting and are seeking to neutralize it.

49

Time does not allow me to discuss these strategies, but I shall refer to them in my brief characterization of the movement. At any rate, they center on the expression of power through definition. The period under discussion begins really in 1954, with the outlawing of segregation in the public schools. Until 1963 the main ideological and strategic thrust of the movement was integration into the so-called mainstream of American society. This activity culminated in major legislation which benefited Blacks and other American minorities. Nevertheless, fundamental problems remained unsolved, among them the economic, the political, and the cultural. "Integration" so-called had its price. Many were not willing to pay for it, and Black nationalism reasserted itself dramatically in the Black Power movement and in the Nation of Islam. Both the integrationist and the Nationalist aspects of the struggle had their martyrs—Medgar Evers, 1963; Malcolm X, 1965; Martin Luther King Jr., 1968; and the countless unnamed thousands who suffered physical or mental death.

The death of Malcolm X galvanized the consciousness of the writers. It made them search for meanings along the path he had chosen—through tough spirituality and dedication to the people. The death of Martin Luther King Jr. was America sending back its check from the bank of justice marked "insufficient funds." The rioting. The violence. The revolutionary fervor. The espionage. The decimation of the Black Panthers. The political exiles. All of this is history now and quite familiar. But we lived it. It was real. It informed the literature.

The literature took two chief avenues, in Thomas De Quincey's words from the past century—the literature of knowledge and the literature of power. The "function of the first," he states, "is to *teach*; the function of the second is to—*move*: the first is a rudder; the second, an oar or a sale." De Quincey continues:

> The first speaks to the *mere* discursive understanding; the second speaks ultimately, it may happen, to the higher understanding or reason, but always *through* affections of pleasure and sympathy. Remotely, it may travel towards an object seated in what Lord Bacon calls dry light; but proximately, it does and must operate—else it ceases to be a literature of *power*—on and through that *humid* light which clothes itself in the mists and glittering *iris* of human passions, desires, and genial emotions.

Specifically, the Black literature of knowledge of the 1960s eventuated in the Black University concept, which called for a rethinking of the role of the universities which serve Blacks in order to make them more relevant to the people. Among other things, proponents called for greater knowledge of Africa—African languages especially and African institutions. They called for greater community involvement. They cited institutional examples on the continent, especially in Tanzania. They called further for a restructuring of all institutions which serve Black people, from the family to the school and the church. Essentially, they called for revolutionary change, and the impact of this thinking has been significant. For example, one of the best-known poets of the generation was a crucial voice in the Black University Movement. I speak of Sonia Sanchez.

The literature of power manifested itself chiefly in poetry and drama and, to a lesser extent, in fiction and critical essays. The poetry was electrifying. It was crude at times, but seldom dull. At best, in the hands of Amiri Baraka or Larry Neal, or Haki R. Madhubuti, or Sonia Sanchez, Mari Evans, or Jayne Cortez, it was brilliant by anyone's standards. It spoke of Black pride, of Black beauty and the problems which beset a Black nation. It preached open hatred for the enemy and for those who collaborated with him. Many were disturbed by the language but few could deny its power. Baraka, writing in "Black Art," described his poetic creed:

> [lines 1–19 from "Black Art"]
> Let the world be a Black Poem
> And Let All Black People Speak This Poem
> Silently
> or LOUD

Ted Joans, who lives in Timbuktu for a part of the year, brought a grigri to activist Stokely Carmichael in the United States. Stokely, in a symbolic gesture, throws away his Saint Christopher medal. He no longer needs the false Christian protection. Joans writes:

> The medal no longer hangs from his Black neck
> He has a gri-gri of his own made of spiritual materials
>   living elements
> [lines 4–13 from "Gri-Gri Poem"]

And in a poem entitled "People of Gleaming Cities, and of the Lion's and the Leopard's Brood," New York poet Sharon Bourke calmly states the new/old wisdom.

[lines 1–8 from "People of Gleaming Cities"]
We have never stopped wearing the life masks of ancestors
[lines 11–12 from "People of Gleaming Cities"]
We have never stopped being what we have preserved.
And now we flourish.

The poets wrote endless variations on this theme, fascinated by their discovery. Chief among these was Amiri Baraka.

The critical name and drama were the same, first LeRoi Jones, then Amiri Baraka. With others in New York, Philadelphia, Chicago, and Watts, Los Angeles, he sought to bring drama to the people. He sought, as in his poetry, to employ his art as a weapon. However, neither the poetry nor the drama became a real issue until the writers constructed a theoretical and ideological framework for their work. This framework, despite inconsistencies, was the Black Aesthetic.

The Black Aesthetic in the most specific sense was formulated by Ron Karenga, who had been making a serious study of African philosophical and social thought. He borrows specifically from President Leopold S. Senghor. In an article in the January 1968 issue of *Negro Digest*, he wrote, "Tradition teaches us, Leopold Senghor tells us, that all African art has at least three characteristics: that is, it is functional, collective and committing or committed. Since this is traditionally valid, it stands to reason that we should attempt to use it as the foundation for a rational construction to meet our needs."

Karenga's concept of the Black Aesthetic has been highly influential, being adopted by Baraka, Haki Madhubuti, and others. Notwithstanding it raised questions for many artists and writers. It is significant to note that the problems which arose are similar to those in Africa and the Caribbean, the problems of form, structure, language, theme, and the question of modernity vs. tradition. At any rate, what is important here, it seems to me, are the following:

(a) The influence of President Leopold Senghor and other African thinkers, including two who have rejected negritude—President Sékou Touré and Dr. Frantz Fanon
(b) The reawakened interest in Africa in specific historical, cultural, and political terms
(c) The identification with the culture of Africa, both the western and the eastern countries
(d) A deepening of the dialogue with African intellectuals and artists, some of whom were living in the United States, among them Chinua Achebe, Es'kia Mphahlele, Keorapetse Kgositsile, and others

What is also important is:

(a) The rediscovery by the writers of the 1960s of Langston Hughes, Sterling Brown, Frank Marshall Davis, and others who had themselves inspired and influenced the pioneers of the Negritude Movement
(b) The rediscovery of the political and social dimensions of the Harlem Renaissance, or New Negro Movement, which also inspired the Negritude Movement
(c) The discovery of the revolutionary potential of Black American culture, and, by extension, of African culture in a Western context

The writers, of course, made mistakes. There was ignorance, envy, misunderstanding, distrust, and disillusionment, so that today some are plagued with a "sense of responsibility without power," in the words of June Jordan. Nonetheless the writing and the movement itself have had positive effects. They have:

(a) Stung the reactionary elements of American society and have encouraged and influenced the progressive
(b) The movement has encouraged the political struggles in South Africa and the Caribbean (Black Power)
(c) It has increased a general sense of pride and dignity among American Blacks
(d) It has contributed to an emergent international African consciousness
(e) It has put the cultural forces of the common oppressor on the defensive
("The Arts in Black America," *Saturday Review*, Nov. 15, 1975; "Point of View," *The Chronicle of Higher Education*, Nov. 17, 1975)

Finally, what is the relevance to this conference? Essentially, the Black American Experience may provide a laboratory of sorts for testing theses about the direction of African cultural development in the next several decades. We need not despair. We have survived in the Americas, in the United States, where all of the stresses and strains and seductions of Western society are magnified; and we have done so because of our difference—the part which could not be assimilated, the part which is reflected in the literature not of knowledge, but of power. You have called it negritude and African personality. We call it Soul. Its roots are in the Black church, and our music, and in our dance. The blood of many African peoples courses through our veins. We have maintained the essential Africanness—the philosophical.

That part we do not learn in books, or even in spoken language. We have never forgotten it.

I invite you, therefore, to follow the examples of Es'kia Mphahlele, "Bra Willie" Kgositsile, and Leopold Senghor. You need not repeat our mistakes. You may in fact discover how very well you already know us.

THE QUESTION OF FORM AND JUDGMENT IN CONTEMPORARY BLACK AMERICAN POETRY

1962–1977

Published in *A Dark and Sudden Beauty: Two Essays in Black American Poetry*,
edited by Houston Baker Jr., 19–36. Chicago: University of Chicago Press, 1977.

For one reason or another, the question of how to judge a Black poem has been fudged, blurred, evaded, or ignored. Now that the spectacular Black Arts Movement seems to have run its course, the question of evaluation takes on crucial importance. Among the signs that the movement is over, or is entering a new phase, are the demise of *Black World* magazine, the most important cultural periodical of the Black Consciousness Movement; the intensified sniping by scholars, Black and white, who disagreed with the idea of a Black Aesthetic; the systematic efforts by white scholars either to blunt, appropriate, or discredit the artistic achievements of the sixties, and their attendant critical justifications; and the defection of important writers to other camps, both aesthetic and political.

Although sniping at the Black Aesthetic is not new, its critics have not relented. In some instances, the concern is largely scholarly, as in the case of Arthur P. Davis, for example. In others, it is essentially polemical. Whether scholarly or not, reactions to the Black Aesthetic rest overtly or implicitly on a political base. At any rate, no one can accuse Prof. Davis for inconsistency, for throughout his long and distinguished career he has made plain his views on integration, on American literature, and the role which Black writers have played in shaping that literature. Yet the achievement of *From the Dark Tower*, his recent admirable history, is marred by his failure to grapple with the hard issues raised by Black Aesthetic. He lumps all the critics together, calls them honorable men, but asserts that to date they have failed either to destroy the white aesthetic or to erect another in its place. So, then, the question remains a matter of ranking authors according to their craftsmanship, their thematic concerns, in historical and social context, or the size of their output. Prof. Davis solves the problem of judgment by avoidance or oversimplification.

Another example of scholarly fudging is found in Roger Rosenblatt's recent book *Black Fiction*. He disposes of the problem of judgment by a retreat into formalism. The social issues are not important—technique is technique and pattern is pattern. Although he discusses fiction, not poetry, many of the issues are the same. Professor Rosenblatt solves the problem of judgment by ignoring it.

In Helen Vendler's review of a series of Broadside books for the *New York Times Book Review*, September 29, 1974, liberal sympathy is tempered by unconscious liberal condescension which reveals an essential ignorance of the issues involved in the Black Aesthetic in general and the evaluation of Black poetry in particular. After praising the range and variety of Black "verse" and the pioneering rule of Dudley Randall, she expresses the fond hope that in the future some single giant Black poet will unite all of those varied threads and themes in one single giant voice—as [Walt] Whitman did, for example, for the American nation. What she fails to realize is that the Black epic voice is collective and communal, and it has already achieved what she speaks of, though in forms, perhaps, which she doesn't understand or recognize—in the tales and the spirituals especially, but also in the work songs and the blues. Prof. Vendler also solves the problem of judgment by oversimplification.

Not so the editors of the *Saturday Review*. They solve it by overkill. In their infamous issues of November 15, 1975, devoted to "The Arts in Black America," the intent is clearly political, clearly designed to give a *coup de grâce* to the Black Arts Movement. The article, written by Robert F. Moss, describes the state of the arts in Black America in pathological and racist terms. It linked the political problems of FESTAC [World Festival of Black Arts] and the Nigerian government with the author's views on Black art in general. Of the Black Aesthetic, he predicts that it seems "destined to produce more heat than light." But one important byproduct, he asserts, has been the building of Black audiences, presumably for legitimate art, by whites or based on white models. Matters of "form and style" in Black art, he states, "have not really been ignored so much as they have been translated into ethnic terms, and in some cases thoroughly politicized. Black verse is perhaps the most obvious example" (15). He continues:

The elder statesman among Black poets—notably Robert Hayden, Melvin B. Tolson, and Gwendolyn Brooks—achieved recognition from the literary establishment by adjusting their timbre and rhythms, their style and vocabulary, to the requirements of mainstream verse, although their subject matter was sometimes racial. Perhaps the last important 'accommodationist' was [Amiri] Baraka, a competent Beat poet who was beached by the receding currents of that short-lived movement in the early sixties. Taking the techniques of Ginsburg & Company—a declamatory voice, deliberate formlessness, street language—and fusing them to virulent outbursts of racial protest, Baraka was able to found a new school of Black poetry. (15–16)

It should be apparent that Moss would not think very highly of that poetry. Speaking of technical matters, Moss states:

Baraka-ites such as Don L. Lee, Nikki Giovanni, Sonia Sanchez, and David Henderson profess to have tossed every scrap of whitey's *ars poetica*—along with his "diseased civilization"—onto the cultural bonfire. In its place they have introduced Black consciousness, carefully equipped with a Black literary technique to articulate it correctly. In practice this usually means a free use of obscenities (especially the omnipresent m-f), ghetto slang, phonetic spellings, typographical hijinks a la Cummings, a striving after oral effects, and a tone of voice pitched at megaphone level. (16)

After examining examples of "verse" that he disagrees with from Carolyn Rodgers, Don Lee [Haki R. Madhubuti], and Baraka, Moss concludes his observations on Black literary technique with the following:

Beyond this, there is a taste for Black word games like "Playing the Dozens" and "Signifying." Such is the route favored by Ishmael Reed, though he is better known as a novelist than as a poet. A devout follower of William Burroughs' comic surrealism with generous helpings of Black folklore, pop culture, and ghetto sociology. Despite its imitativeness, his writing has a creative energy and a stylistic reach that is beyond most Black writers today. (17)

An analysis of these views and others will be made later in this essay. Suffice it to say at present that Prof. Moss repeats most of the clichés which critics of Black art, especially of the poetry, have made for some time. He adds a special virulence couched in the self-satisfaction of one who feels that he has done his homework and who knows, in addition, that his views have the editorial support of a powerful and influential periodical. That does not, of course, make them either accurate or important.

A further sign of reaction to the Black Consciousness Movement can be seen in two other recent books by white scholars, *Folklore in Nigerian Literature*, by Bernth Lindfors, and *Invisible Poets*, by Joan Sherman. Lindfors's book is relevant to our discussion for several reasons: (a) the aggressive, defensive tone of the introduction; (b) the rejection of white critics of their literature by both African and Afro-American critics; and (c) the theoretical implications of some of the chapters, especially the two listed under "Critical Perspectives" (6, 23) and the one under "Rhetoric," entitled "Characteristics of Yoruba and Ibo Prose Styles in English" (153).

Like numerous other white critics of "Black" literature, Lindfors is concerned about the "territorial imperative" which Black critics asserted during the sixties. Lindfors quotes a statement which I made in *The Militant Black Writer* (1969) that "despite the proliferation of 'experts,' whites are unable to evaluate the Black Experience, and, consequently, any work of art derived from it or addressed to those who live it." He adds: "Whites should therefore abandon the field to Blacks, who are innately better qualified to understand and appreciate their own literature" (1). Lindfors calls attention to a similar rejection of white critics by African writers. Then he proceeds to some tacky logic and linguistic sleight of hand: "While these statements condemning the incompetence of white critics are not as extreme as those heard in America today, they do point in the same racial direction: Black critics are acclaimed as the best possible interpreters of their own literature" (1). And Prof. Lindfors gives what he calls the "standard reply" to these views.

> A favorite tactic is to reverse the argument by asking, "Should all the Black critics—and this includes Africans as well as Afro-Americans and teachers and professors of literature throughout the world—be given a similar 'hands off' ultimatum on non-Black writing?"

"An affirmative answer to this question," Lindfors concludes, "would be very hard to justify." And, one might add, hardly worth the time.

The reactions cited above have one important common factor: they substitute for the question, "How does one judge a Black poem?" the related question, "Who is to judge a Black poem?" While the substitution reveals a great deal about those who make it, it nonetheless leaves the prior question unanswered. To repeat, then, How does one judge a Black poem?

Curiously, very few answers were given to that question during the sixties. The responses among Blacks tended to be mystical, ideological, defensive, or hostile. Among whites, they tended and still tend to be condescending, defensive, or preemptive, when not narrowly or naïvely academic. At any rate, there has been poor and uninformed criticism written by Blacks and whites alike. And, conversely, there has been on occasion, some useful criticism by Blacks, less frequently by whites. (A major exception is the forthcoming study of Baraka, *The Renegade and the Mask*, by Kimberly Benston.) Older Black poets and poets who are not Nationalist have stated that they would rather be reviewed by a good white critic than a poor Black one. And writers as diverse as Frank Marshall Davis, Robert Hayden, and Clarence Major have said that they were not especially writing for a Black audience.

To begin with, the question of judgment is tied up with the question of definition. What is a Black poem? What is Black poetry? In *Understanding the New Black Poetry*, I made an approach to that question in a series of statements, which I repeat below. These statements may be approached in a historical or empirical manner. In either case, one could say with varying degrees of validity that Black poetry is chiefly:

1. Any poetry by any person or group of persons of known Black African ancestry, whether the poetry is designated Black or not
2. Poetry which is somehow *structurally* Black, irrespective of authorship
3. Poetry by any person or group of known Black African ancestry, which is *also identifiably* Black, in terms of structure, theme, or other characteristics
4. Poetry by any identifiably Black person who can be classified as a "poet" by Black people; judgment may or may not coincide with judgments of whites
5. Poetry by any identifiably Black person whose ideological stance vis-à-vis history and the aspirations of his people since slavery is adjudged by them to be "correct" (7)

Since an empirical approach has the advantage of historical anchorage and verifiability, let us place that perspective on the foregoing statements. Again, since I have discussed the complications of these statements in *Understanding the New Black Poetry*, I shall not pursue them here. Nevertheless, when the statements are examined from the perspective one must consider the following items: (a) *what the record or canon says*, (b) *what the poets say*, (c) *what the reader/audience/critic says*, and (d) *the notion of standards and evaluation*. In the following pages, I shall address each of these items in some detail.

a. *What the record reveals* is a rich tradition of both oral and written poetry which is usefully designated the folk and the formal. In the United States the oral traditions go back to the emergence of distinctive Afro-American verbal expression—the field cries and hollers, work songs, ballads, spirituals, sermons, and blues. The size of this literature, though not so complex as that of the West Indies or Africa, is enormous. John Lovell Jr. estimates the number of spirituals alone at over 10,000, with no way of knowing how many were not recorded. The tradition continues today in children's songs, in rapping, the dozens and its contemporary descendants, in the sermon, and in gospel and pop songs at their best. But gospel and pop songs are individually composed and written down, so here the oral tradition merges with that of the formal literary tradition. The literary tradition itself dates back to Lucy Terry's "Bars Fight" (1746), a long ballad of historical rather than literary merit, and to Jupiter Hammon and Phillis Wheatley.

The nineteenth century produced dozens of published poets, some of significant talent. Notable among them were George Moses Horton, Charles L. Reason, Francis E. W. Harper, and Albery A. Whitman. An introduction to these writers can be obtained from Benjamin Brawley's *Early American Negro Writers*; H. Robinson's *Early Black Poets*; Sterling A. Brown's *Negro Poetry and Drama*, and *The Negro Caravan* edited with Arthur P. Davis and Ulysses Lee. An important work in this area is Joan Sherman's recent book *The Invisible Poets*. In addition, there are individual volumes which are listed in Sherman's bibliographies and in checklists by Arthur Schomburg and Dorothy L. Porter.

Paul Laurence Dunbar, W. E. B. Du Bois, and James Weldon Johnson open the twentieth century. Their work was followed by Langston Hughes, Claude McKay, Jean Toomer, Sterling Brown, Countee Cullen, and the various poets of the New Negro Movement. The next generation produced Margaret Walker, Owen Dodson, Gwendolyn Brooks, Robert Hayden, and others. Some of these poets were active in the fifties and the sixties. And, of course, the 1960s produced a veritable explosion of Black poetry, with such notable names as Amiri Baraka, Larry Neal, Sonia Sanchez, Nikki Giovanni, Don L. Lee (Haki Madhubuti), and others. Much of the work of this period has probably never been published so no one has a complete picture of the phenomenon. Notwithstanding, one can easily acquaint himself with this poetry by reading the individual volumes published by Broadside Press, Paul Bremen Press, and by major publications such as the *Journal of Black Poetry*; *Liberator*; *Negro Digest / Black World*; *Soul Book*; *Black Creations*; and *Umbra*. Some journals had limited, regional circulation, such as college publications like *Ex Umbra*.

Some poets printed their works themselves. Many of these are listed in *Negro Digest / Black World*. Other sources include useful anthologies such as *Soul Script*, June Jordan; *Dices or Black Bones*, Adam David Miller; *Natural Process*, Tom Weatherly and Ted Willenz; *Understanding the New Black Poetry*, S. E. Henderson; *The Black Poets*, Dudley Randall; *The New Black Poetry*, Clarence Major. Current publishers of Black poetry include *Essence, Black Arts South, Yardbird Reader, Black Books Bulletin*, etc. In addition, Black poetry is being published at workshops, on campuses, etc., as well as by white publishers. At any rate, this brief account merely hints at the corpus of poetry produced by Black Americans. To this (if one were talking about the entire range of modern Black poetry) could be added the poetry published in English by Caribbean and African poets living in the United States. Less tenable, but logical would be the addition of all poetry in English by Africans on the continent and in the Dispersion. While that could be done and, eventually, must be done, the problem of focus would thereby be greatly increased. Thus for the purpose of this study, Black poetry must be studied in historical context— with Black people in the United States as the focus. The justification for this is simple. Modern Black formal poetry has existed longer in the United States than it has in Africa or the West Indies (cf. Jahn, *Neo-African Literature*, 50, table 1). In addition, the poetry of the Harlem Renaissance helped stimulate the flowering of modern Black poetry in Africa, Europe, and the West Indies during the Negritude Movement. With that in mind, one could still benefit from studying work produced in Africa and the West Indies, not only in English, but in Portuguese, French, Dutch, Spanish, as well as the various African languages. Conversely any serious and extended study of the oral tradition of Afro-American poetry must recognize the vast resources of that tradition in Africa and the West Indies. This includes not only traditional materials but popular contemporary expression as well.

b. *What the poets say.* Historically, the question of what constitutes a Black poem or how to judge one does not really come to a head until the 1960s and the promulgation of the Black Aesthetic in literature and the other arts. In a special sense, then, "Black" poetry was invented in the 1960s along with the radicalization of the word "Black" and the emergence of the Black Power philosophy. From the beginning, however, there were problems of definition, contradiction, ideology, and taste, resulting from differences in personal background and in political and cultural orientation. In the January 1968 issue of *Negro Digest*, Hoyt Fuller, the executive editor, conducted a survey of the opinions of 38 Black writers on some 25 questions which included the following:

19. Do you see any future at all for the school of Black writers which seeks to establish "a Black aesthetic"?

20. Do you believe that the Black writer's journey toward "art" should lead consciously and deliberately through exploitation of "the Black experience"?

25. Should Black writers direct their work toward Black audiences?

Some older writers, like Robert Hayden, felt that a writer's chief concern should be with the truth of all people everywhere. Others stressed craftsmanship and felt that writers should write to be read. Others felt enthusiastically that they should write about what they knew best, themselves and their people. There was, in effect, no simple consensus as to what Black writing was, could be, or should be, though there was a fairly general agreement that Black writers should write about Black people, for Black people, and sometimes for sympathetic whites. Some younger writers were immersed in the self-consciousness of other "modern" writers; others still were rigidly nationalistic. The split among the younger writers was best exemplified in an exchange between Ron [Maulana] Karenga, of US [Organization], and James Cunningham, of OBAC [Organization of Black American Culture]. Their views were polar. Karenga set forth his famous and influential dicta that literature must be functional, collective, and committing, and must support the revolution. Cunningham felt that the writer should be free to express himself.

Perhaps the most insightful statement in the 1968 *Negro Digest* survey was made by Larry Neal. On the question of the Black Aesthetic, he said:

> There is no need to establish a "Black aesthetic." Rather, it is important to understand that one already exists. The question is: where does it exist? And what do we do with it. Further, there is something distasteful about a formalized aesthetic. This is what the so-called New Critics never understood. Essentially, art is relevant when it makes you stronger (35).

In that opening statement, Neal not only demonstrated an understanding of the aesthetic questions under discussion but also an extensive grasp of the roots of Afro-American art, thereby linking up with a tradition of "criticism" which includes James Weldon Johnson, W. E. B. Du Bois, Alain Locke, and Sterling Brown. That was an important linkage, for it not only insured historical continuity but kept the field of discussion open to a wide range of approaches. At the same time that it claimed for the poet much of the personal freedom which Cunningham advocated, it insisted on the wider dedication advocated by Ron Karenga. But this was done with a greater degree of subtlety, as, for example, in his sensitive understanding of the blues and the central importance of the Black Church.

c. *The reader/critic/audience.* Specifically, the question of the poet's audience was crucial to the sixties. It was encapsulated in the *Negro Digest* survey. The response ranged from Karenga's paraphrase of [Leopold S.] Senghor that art is "functional, collective and committing or committed," to Gwendolyn Brooks's shrewd comment that Black writers "should concern themselves with TRUTH. Truth should be put on paper." That phrase, "direct their work," she said in reference to the questionnaire, "suggests a secret contempt for the intelligence of the Black audience" (29). Some other writers hedged their bets, writing for ideal audiences, or for anyone who would buy their books. But the question was not altogether new, nor the consciousness, for Langston Hughes had said to a similar question posed in 1927 by *Crisis* magazine,

> We younger Negro artists who create now intend to express our individual dark-skinned selves without fear or shame. If white people are pleased we are glad. If they are not, it doesn't matter. We know we are beautiful. And ugly too. The tom-tom cries and the tom-tom laughs. If colored people are pleased we are glad. If they are not, their displeasure doesn't matter either. We build our temples for tomorrow, strong as we know how, and on top of the mountain, free within ourselves. ("The Negro Artist and the Racial Mountain")

What is often overlooked in this passage is an individualism that borders on "art for art's sake."

But Langston Hughes also pioneered some of the techniques of direct audience communication which were to become very popular in the sixties. His readings with jazz accompaniment, his strong sense of the aural tradition, of the preacher and the musician, of the oral tradition of the raconteur and the rapper, provided a strong model. So that Larry Neal was to say in 1968:

> To explore the Black experience means that we do not deny the reality and the power of the slave culture; the culture that produced the blues, spirituals, folk songs, work songs, and "jazz." It means that Afro-American life and its myriad of styles are expressed and examined in the fullest, most truthful manner possible. The models for what Black literature should be are found primarily in our

folk culture, especially in the blues and jazz. Further models exist in the word-magic of James Brown, Wilson Pickett, Stevie Wonder, Sam Cooke, and Aretha Franklin. Have you ever heard a Black poet scream like James Brown? I mean, we should want to have that kind of energy in our work. The kind of energy that informs the music of John Coltrane, Cecil Taylor, Albert Ayler, and Sun Ra—the modern equivalent of the ancient ritual energy. An energy that demands to be heard, and which no one can ignore. Energy to shake us out of our lethargy and free our bodies and minds, opening us to unrealized possibilities. (*Negro Digest*, 81)

Again, at this point one sees Neal's understanding of and linkage to the tradition of W. E. B. Du Bois, James Weldon Johnson, Langston Hughes, Sterling Brown, and Richard Wright. He adds two dimensions: popular music and African ritual. The crucial insight is the realization of Black oral expression as a continuum—in fact, oral expression as part of the larger global continuum of Black expressive culture.

Central to that continuum are music and dance. Small wonder then that when Black poets described what they were trying to do they used the language of these arts. Similar wonder still that readers who conceived of poetry and Euro-American terms were unable to come to grips with the New Black Poetry. This was true of some older Blacks as well as many white professional critics. Again, that should have surprised no one, for the history of the criticism of Black music and dance is a systematic attempt to deny the originality, the power, and the ultimate worth of those forms also. This Robert Moss and the others have their tradition too, of denial, presumption, subversion, and neglect.

The beauty and power of Black American poetry, notwithstanding these negative views, have long been recognized. Along the first to bring the oral tradition to national attention was Colonel Thomas Ventworth Higginson, in an article which appeared in the *Atlantic Monthly*, June 1867, entitled "Negro Spirituals." He points out the verbal as well as the musical beauty of the songs. His reaction to one of the songs has been quoted by W. E. B. Du Bois, James Weldon Johnson, Sterling Brown, and John Lovell Jr. It is worth quoting again. He stated:

But of all the "spirituals" that which surprised me the most, I think—perhaps because it was that in which external nature furnished the images most directly—was this. With all my experience of their ideal ways of speech, I was startled when first I came on such a flower of poetry in that dark soil:

XVII. I Know Moon-Rise
I know moon-rise, I know star-rise,
Lay dis body down
I walk in de moonlight, I walk in de starlight,
To lay dis body down.
I'll walk in de graveyard, I'll walk through the graveyard,
To lay dis body down.
I'll lie in de grave and stretch out my arms;
Lay dis body down.
I go to de judgment in de evenin' of de day,
When I lay dis body down:
And my soul and your soul will meet in de day
When I lay dis body down.

"I'll lie in de grave and stretch out my arms." Never, it seems to me, since man first lived and suffered, was his infinite longing for peace uttered more plaintively than in that line. ([quoted in] Jackson, [*The Negro and His Folklore,*] 91)

Note Higginson's expression—"their ideal ways of speech." It not only furnishes a corrective to the stereotypes created by the minstrel tradition, but provides an important literary insight. For speech is a chief element of anybody's poetry. And here the manner of the speech is noted in a useful way. We shall return later to this point.

Frequently the words of these songs are referred to as poems, as they are in this study. Their composers are also referred to as poets, by Blacks and whites alike. This practice is found not only in Higginson and others who appreciated the slaves' "ideal ways of speech," but by those who satirized the songs on the minstrel stage, and even as John Lovell brings to our attention, on the concert stage. At any rate, the language posed a challenge to the serious collector and the casual listener alike. There were problems of intelligibility and of transcription. Regarding the latter, Y. S. Nathanson recounts his difficulty in transcribing a refrain which imitates a wild turkey's gobble. He concludes that "I am aware that no words can express the rich, unctuous, guttural flow of the line, when uttered in perfect time by a full gang at their corn-shucking task" (Jackson, 49).

In "Songs of the Slaves," John Mason Brown observes:

To convey a correct idea of negro pronunciation by ordinary rules of orthography is almost impossible. Combinations that would satisfy the ear would be grotesquely absurd to the eye. The habits of the negro in his pronunciation of English words are not such as minstrelsy would indicate. Just as the French and German characters in our comedies have passed into a conventional form of mispronunciation which the bulk of playgoers firmly believe to be lifelike and true, so have min-strels given permanency to very great mistakes in reproducing negro pronunciation. (*Lippincott's Magazine* 11, Dec. 1868, 617–23)

The problem confronted Black scholars and poets also, just as it was to con-front poets of the 1960s and the present decade [of the 1970s]. Paul Laurence Dunbar, for example, wrote in a dialect tradition popularized by whites, although his orthography was more idealized than satirical or fanciful.

James Weldon Johnson wrote "coon songs" in the white manner of his time, but later turned to a serious confrontation of the problem of render-ing the sounds of Black speech and song. In his two collections of Negro spirituals, *The Book of American Negro Spirituals* (1925) and *The Second Book of Negro Spirituals* (1926), he indicated the importance of preserving the original pronunciation of the words, and in the preface to the first volume, he discussed serious questions of dialect, voiced timbre, and poetry, with informed sensitivity. Like John Mason Brown before him, he attacks visual grotesqueries masquerading as speech:

Negro dialect is for many people made unintelligible on the printed page by the absurd practice of devising a clumsy, outlandish, so-called phonetic spelling for words in a dialect story or poem with the regu-lar English spelling represents the very same sound. Paul Laurence Dunbar did a great deal to reform the writing down of dialect, but since it is more a matter of ear than of rules those who are not inti-mately familiar with the sounds continue to make the same blun-ders. (James Weldon Johnson and J. Rosamond Johnson, *The Book of American Negro Spirituals*, 38)

Later, Johnson spoke thus of his intent and method in his volume *God's Trombones* (1927). These poems were sermons in the folk manner. He wanted to go beyond the limitations of dialect with its twin stops of pathos and humor. What he wanted was "a form that will express the racial spirit by symbols from within rather than by symbols from without, such as "the mere mutilation of English spelling and pronunciation." The form would be "freer and larger than dialect, but which will still hold the racial flavor; a form expressing the imagery, the idioms, the peculiar turns of thought, and the distinctive humor and pathos, too, of the Negro, but which will also be capable of voicing the deepest and highest emotions and aspirations, and allow of the widest range of subjects and the widest scope of treatment" (*The Book of American Negro Poetry*, 41–42).

But Johnson, like others, was acutely aware of the difficulties involved in developing this form. Earlier, he had said of the spirituals:

> What can be said about the poetry of the texts of the Spirituals? Naturally, not so much as can be said about the music. In the use of the English language both the bards and the group worked under limitations that might appear to be hopeless. Many of the lines are less than trite, and irrelevant repetition often becomes tiresome. They are often saved alone by their naivete. And yet there is poetry, and a surprising deal of it in the Spirituals. There is more than ought to be reasonably expected from a forcedly ignorant people working in an absolutely alien language. (*The Book of American Negro Spirituals*, 38)

And Thomas W. Talley makes the point with a Black anecdote. Speaking of the secular rhymes, he observes: "When critically measured by the laws and usages governing the best English poetry, Negro Folk Rhymes will probably remind readers of the story of the good brother, who arose solemnly in a Christian praise meeting, and thanked God that he had broken all of the Commandments, but had kept his religion" (*Negro Folk Rhymes*, 228). Note Johnson's use of the terms "racial spirit" and "racial flavor" as well as the more explicit reference to "imagery," "idioms," and "peculiar turns of thought." Note, too, the humorous but meaningful use of the term "religion" by Talley. To this one might add a remark by an experienced preacher from the folk tradition. When his language was questioned by his self-consciously academic brothers in the seminary, he stated: "A verb is like a nut. You got to crack it to get the goodie out of it." And Sterling Brown reports an encounter with a young minister at Virginia Seminary, in 1923, when he took his first job teaching English. He was so exacting in his grading that the students called him a "red ink man." The exasperated seminarian said to him one day, "Prof., you run them verbs, and I'll drive the thought." And Brown concedes, "He could drive the thought."

And a few years later James Weldon Johnson wrote the preface to Sterling Brown's masterly first volume of poems, *Southern Road*. He said:

> He infused his poetry with genuine characteristic flavor by adopting as his medium the common, racy, living speech of the Negro in

certain phases of *real* life. For his raw material he dug down into the deep mine of Negro folk poetry. He found the unfailing sources from which sprang the Negro folk epics and ballads such as "Stagolee," "John Henry," "Casey Jones," "Long Gone John," and others. But, as I said in commenting on his work in *The Book of American Negro Poetry*: he has made more than mere transcriptions of folk poetry, and he has done more than bring to it mere artistry; he has deepened its meaning and multiplied its implications. He has actually absorbed the spirit of his material, made it his own; and without diluting its primitive frankness and raciness, truly re-expressed it with artistry and magnified power. In a word, he has taken this raw material and worked it into original and authentic poetry. (Preface, *Southern Road*, xiv–xv)

In other words, Sterling Brown had achieved the kind of form that Johnson himself had spoken of and had experimented with in *God's Trombones*. Johnson had singled out other young poets for special mention. Among them were Claude McKay, Jean Toomer, Countee Cullen, and Langston Hughes. Even a cursory examination of their work would reveal a wide range of styles, technique, subject matter, and tone, from the Romantic sonorities of Cullen to the jazzy rhythms of Hughes. Yet they had something in common, their concern with "race" and their response to it. Johnson states, "In their approach to 'race' they are less direct and obvious, less didactic or imploratory; and, too, they are less regardful of the approval or disapprobation of their white environment" (Preface, *Southern Road*, xxxvi).

These statements of Johnson's, taken together with other observations of his, pose most of the larger critical questions of Black poetry, questions of *range, theme, form*, and *structure*, and *judgment*. As far as the theme is concerned, that which makes it Black is "race," in his words, "the principal motive of poetry written by Negroes" (xxxvi). As for form and structure, they are found in "the deep mine of Negro folk poetry" (xxxvi). Yet he includes the sonnets of Claude McKay and Countee Cullen and the free verse odes of Jean Toomer, all written in "Standard English." And we may recall some of the difficulty which Johnson experienced with the language of the spirituals, a difficulty not really unlike that encountered by the white collector John Mason Brown. Not merely the problem of orthography, but of poetic expression. Notwithstanding the beauty of the music, the difficulty of working in an unfamiliar language caused the slaves to produce many lines which "are less than trite, and irrelevant repetition often becomes tiresome. They are often saved alone by their naivete" (Preface, *Southern Road*, 14). Yet Johnson makes judgments, both of the spirituals and, as we have seen, of the formal poets, of whom the "Younger Group" received his special blessings.

On what basis was Johnson able to distinguish the excellent from the trite in this vastly varied body of material? Obviously, he had some means, some measure, some touchstone that would allow him to accept both the Keatsean lushness of Cullen, the sonorous language of the sermons, and the transcendent simplicity of the spirituals. Johnson himself suggests something of his mechanism, his method, and his considerations in several places, among them the two works previously cited in his *The Autobiography of an Ex-Colored Man* (see R. Carroll). The mechanism included a reliance upon the ear rather than the eye, for example, and he states (Preface, *Southern Road*, 13): "Paul Laurence Dunbar did a great deal to reform the writing down of dialect, but since it is more a matter of ear than of rules those who are not intimately familiar with the sounds continue to make the same blunders." This reliance upon the ear includes a deep and sympathetic and sensitive knowledge and love of music, not only that of his own people but of other cultures as well. He could thus say with complete assurance of the motif of the spiritual "Go Down Moses" (Preface, *The Book of American Negro Spirituals*, 13):

> I have termed this music noble, and I do so without qualifications. Take, for example *Go Down Moses*; there is not a nobler theme in the whole musical literature of the world. If the Negro had voice himself in only that one song, it would have been evidence of his nobility of soul. And his knowledge of Black music ran the gamut, from the work songs and the spirituals to ragtime and the newly emergent jazz.

Black music, he says in effect, is the touchstone of Black art. And the touchstone can be applied also to the creative work of other cultures. This is implicit in the statement above. It is more explicit in Johnson's poetic statement in "O Black and Unknown Bards." But Johnson certainly did not slight the verbal component of the songs. He recognized the poetry in their very titles. Although later scholarship has demonstrated that he overstated his case for the originality of the spirituals, it is still essentially correct. Johnson continues:

> The white people among whom the slaves lived did not originate anything comparable even to the mere titles of the Spirituals. In truth, the power to frame the poetic phrases that make the titles of so many of the Spirituals betokens the power to create the songs. Consider the sheer magic of "Swing Low, Sweet Chariot" and confess that none but an artistically endowed people could have evoked it:

Swing Low, Sweet Chariot
I've Got to Walk My Lonesome Valley
Steal Away to Jesus
Singing with a Sword in My Hand
Rule Death in His Arms
Ride on King Jesus
We Shall Walk Through the Valley in Peace
The Blood Came Twinklin' Down
Deep River
Death's Goin' to Lay His Cold, Icy Hand on Me

No one has even expressed a doubt that the poetry of the titles and texts of the spirituals is Negro in character and origin, no one else has dared to lay claim to it; why then doubt the music? (Preface, *Southern Road*, 15–16).

Of course, even the texts were later disputed by George Pullen Jackson. And Johnson's protégé, the young Sterling Brown, was to make the final point with his characteristic wit:

In bringing forth proof that in words and melody many Negro spirituals are traceable to white songs, southern white scholars have succeeded in disproving the romantic theory of completely African origin for the spirituals. All of those who assiduously collect evidence grant, however, that now the Negro song is definitely the Negro's regardless of ultimate origin, and one of them writes as follows: "the words of the best White Spirituals cannot compare as poetry with the words of the best Negro spirituals." It remains to be said that for the best Negro spirituals, camp-meeting models remain to be discovered. (*Negro Poetry and Drama*, 17)

d. *The notion of standards and evaluation.* I have taken this long to suggest the outlines of this argument on the originality and the power of Black folk poetry for two reasons: (1) the poets of the sixties claim a kinship with this poetry and music; and (2) the questions raised cast some light on the latter body of poetry, some of the disputes, some of the achievements, and some of the promise.

Some of the dispute over recent Black poetry is traceable to the experimental nature of much of it, and it follows that this dispute is not necessarily racial in character. For example, Robert F. Moss's reference to the "typographical hijinks" of E. E. Cummings, or W. E. Farrison's peevish dismissal of similar experimentation in his review of Beatrice Murphy's anthology of young Negro poets. White critics, of course, have dismissed white writers in much the same manner. And, of course, one remembers the furor raised over Allen Ginsberg's *Howl* and, earlier, over Walt Whitman's *Leaves of Grass*, to name two works at random.

But the reaction goes deeper than mere resistance to change and experimentation. It seems rooted in white America's perception of the lives and culture of Black Americans, which has been marked by distortion, and by a continuing and systematic attempt to ridicule, to deny, to absorb, or to appropriate that culture. Specifically, both traditions of Afro-American poetry have long been under siege, and just to mention Black poetry is to evoke a history of white critical condescension and snobbery, and more recently, outright pathological ignorance and fear. The roots of this reaction are deep and pervasive. They are entwined in nineteenth-century attempts to justify slavery by proving the innate inferiority of the African slave. They are entwined in the African's supposed inability to master the "difficult" European languages. They are entwined in the questioning of the African's very humanity. They are likewise entwined in European conceptions of the poet and poetry—the poet as maker, or prophet, or divine madman; the poetry as sacred text or as edifying verbal diversion, producing pleasure.

Since a poem is made of words and since the slave was incapable of mastering the "difficult" English tongue, how could one take seriously the idea of a Black American poet? Most did not. A few did, as the history of the early poets, Jupiter Hammon, Phillis Wheatley, and George Moses Horton attests. But essentially, they were curiosities. Phillis Wheatley was a successful experiment to test the strength of nurture vs. nature; and Hammon and Horton were sports of nature (which was, indeed, one eighteenth-century definition of genius).

Other early poets took as their central aim the vindication of their race from calumny and, indeed, the largest task of liberation through appealing to the conscience of the ruling whites. This appeal ranged from direct protest to demonstrations of worthiness as evinced by learning and by mastery of the craft of poetry. Thus, Albery A. Whitman justifies his use of the difficult Spenserian stanza, the "'stately verse,' *mastered only* by [Edmund] Spenser, [Lord] Byron, and a very few other great poets," because "some negro is sure to do everything that anyone else has ever done, and as none of that race have ever executed a poem in the 'stately verse,' I simply venture in" (quoted by J. Sherman, 12).

This emphasis on craftsmanship is historically quite important. It shows the Black poet reflecting the same kind of concerns as other gifted Black individuals. It also shows a continuing need to test oneself according to white standards, and sometimes to receive white praise. Whitman treasured the praise he received from [William Cullen] Bryant, just as Phillis Wheatley had treasured the praise of the literati of her day. And decades later, W. D. Howells was to praise Paul Laurence Dunbar in the same liberal manner. Later still, Gwendolyn Brooks was awarded a Pulitzer Prize for her technical mastery of the forms of Modernist poetry, and Karl Shapiro and Allen Tate were to praise Melvin B. Tolson for having assimilated the language of the Anglo-Saxon poetic tradition and for writing in "Negro" at the same time.

All of this was the recognition of individuals, not of a tradition. Indeed, the attempt has been from the outset to ignore, absorb, or to destroy the tradition in both its folk and formal dimensions. Despite this, however, the beauty and power of the tradition has been recognized by many, even though grudgingly at times.

As I have suggested, a good deal of the confusion comes from the variety of the poetry itself. Some comes from the desire of certain poets to be free of racial identification, which implied inferiority of achievement or judgment by less rigorous standards. Some, too, comes from an unwillingness to be limited to writing on racial themes. One certainly thinks of Cullen, Hayden, [Gloria] Oden, [Clarence] Major, and others.

The central concern seems to be the assumption that poetry which can be identified as Black is "racist" or inferior or un-American, so that one pretends that race is unimportant or that Black poetry is merely a fad or a bad imitation of experimental white poetry (as the Robert Moss analysis states). All of this, of course, is nonsense. Black poetry can and should be judged by the same standards that any other poetry is judged by—by those standards which validly arise out of the culture. Some of it is good, some excellent, and some downright bad. Much of this awareness has been expressed by the poets themselves, some of whom are excellent critics, like Lance Jeffers, E. Ethelbert Miller, Sarah Fabio, June Jordan, Margaret Walker, and Carolyn Rodgers, to name but a few.

At any rate, scattered through their interviews, their essays, and their conversations, there are many critical pronouncements by Black poets themselves. Similarly, there are the pronouncements and preferences of their readers and their audiences, including professional scholars and critics, white, Black, and other. Whether the poets approve or not is now certainly irrelevant since their work has become part of the general consciousness. And that consciousness has been formed by the media, by the national institutions and myths, and by the educational system, both public and private. That, of course, is obvious. What is less obvious is the extent to which the

Black reader/audience/poet has been shaped by these forces and, further still, and more important, how they have created and synthesized the special consciousness out of their special history and experience.

Thus, we have the phenomenon of Tolson outpounding Pound and critics and scholars employing constructs derived from English, European, or American literature to evaluate Black literature. There is nothing necessarily wrong with this. Intellectually, we are to a large extent what we read. And we certainly need not ignore non-Black writing and criticism. Indeed, we do so at our own risk.

Nevertheless, the question, in a practical sense is whether Black poetry can most effectively be understood, experienced, explicated, and encouraged by complete or even major reliance upon methodologies and standards that have evolved out of the larger Euro-American society. To the extent that we share those values and concerns, then perhaps it should be, for the sake of efficiency and simplicity, especially for those readers who are university trained. Yet we all know that even those of us who are so trained and are accustomed to think in certain academic patterns also react in complex ways to the cultural referents and forms which arise from our Black Experience. Since the poetry often consciously or unconsciously draws upon this dual heritage one would expect a useful critical method to do likewise. Accordingly, if one were to approach the work of the past fifteen years, one could begin at whatever intellectual locus he may inhabit and push toward the central experience of the poem. Easily a good deal of the work is approachable in this way, much of early Baraka, for example.

Notwithstanding, we are soon confronted with the ambiguities and densities which make up a wide range of the poems, which make up, in effect, the *Blackness* of the poems. Some of these elements can be explicated through historical and cultural study. Others have to be experienced because they are "saturated" in Black Experience and these may include some which are written in so-called "Standard English."

Let us recall that there are two large categories of Black poetry of this period: (a) the political poetry of Black Power, and (b) the cultural poetry of the Black Experience. Although these categories overlap, they are by no means congruent, and writers shift from one to the other, sometimes without much clarity.

At any rate, purpose is important. The object of a Black Power poem is to raise Black people's consciousness. The classic statement is given by Ron Karenga in his paraphrase of Leopold Senghor and in Baraka's "Black Art." These poems were often frankly propagandistic and, technically speaking, quite often not very interesting. They were meant to be "throwaway" poems.

Perhaps, then, they should be examined in this light—they were raps for the occasion, and the occasion was the revolution.

But all of these were not raps, and certainly not deficient either in execution or in delivery. Excellent examples can be found in Baraka, Neal, Lee, Sanchez, The Last Poets, Ahmed A. Alhamisi, and elsewhere. And one needs to observe that many great poems of the West were highly political in their time, among them the *Divine Comedy* and *Paradise Lost*. So it does not follow that Black Power poems had to be shoddy or trite. In fact, there is a "revolutionary obligation" to make the poem as good as one can. (Cf. Mao.) Too, many of these poems were written by nonpoets, by ordinary people in a state of excitement and fervor which they felt compelled to express. This was not a function of education or class necessarily, though many were obviously written by college students. In a word, then, one would judge these poems in historical context, even that of specific readings and performances where records are available. Did the poet "get over"? That was the criterion. That was all that he was trying to do.

The other category of poems was generally more sophisticated and ambitious. They not only wanted to raise consciousness, they also wanted to do it with style, to celebrate Black life and culture, to seek a larger cosmic consciousness, which, at any rate, was Black, the Original Blackness.

And they wanted to do this with the energy and subtlety and precision of a John Coltrane or with the people-reaching power of a James Brown. In this regard they were certainly following in a long tradition extending formally back to Dunbar and James Weldon Johnson on one hand and to the spirituals and blues on the other. And behind that to Mother Africa.

The more astute among those poets realized that they were seeking interior models, not archaeological revivals of older musical/poetic forms. But what were those forms to be like? How were they to be transmitted, created? They spoke by necessity in metaphoric terms, as Neal's mention of "the modern equivalent of the ancient ritual energy" or "word-magic" or Stanley Crouch's "The Big Feeling." And the object of all of this is, again in Neal's words, "to shake us out of our lethargy and free our bodies and minds, opening us to unrealized possibilities." These "unrealized possibilities," as suggested by the work of Amiri Baraka, Henry Dumas, June Jordan, Ahmed Akinwole Ahlamisi, and many others, go far beyond the narrow political concerns of Black Power to a concern (no less rooted in history) with ultimate philosophical and spiritual questions.

How did the poets approach these problems in terms of craft? How successful have they been? As I have stated in this essay, and at considerable length in others, they employed a wide variety of language, at times drawn from Black speech patterns, at times not. They also through a variety of means—some clever, some clumsy—sought to tap the resources latent in Black music. These are structural considerations, and when they are successful, they form the most striking features of the recent Black poetry.

But again, how successful have these works been? And how do we judge? Essentially on the terms posed by the individual poem. If a love poem is written in blues style, it can be judged against thousands of such poems—from the urban and folk traditions, as well as from the literary versions of Hughes and Sterling Brown. There are individual blues poems which stand up under any critical examination—such as Son House's "Death Letter." For drama, for lyrical intensity, and sensual precision it competes favorably with many literary poems. Blues lovers, Black, white, and Japanese, know the traditionally great blues songs—the masterpieces, the legendary sessions, the mind-melting lines. Any love poem written in the blues manner has to be measured against the bitter humor of "I asked her for water, and she gave me gasoline." Or the pathos of "I folded my arms, I slowly walked away / She's a good old girl—gotta lay there till judgment day." And the self-destructive despair of Tommy Johnson's lines "Canned heat, canned heat, sure, Lord, killin' me." And the poet's angst has to be measured against "the blues ain't nothin' but a low-down shaky chill." Henry Dumas measured against this standard is successful.

But just as jazz musicians have explored and extended the blues experience through technical means, one must ask whether in an analogous way the poets of the sixties were able to extend the achievement of Langston Hughes and Sterling Brown; or better still, whether they have been able to build on the stylistic dynamics of Black language styles (in speech and song) to create the "word-magic" that they aspired to. Intuitively, I know that some like June Jordan, like Baraka, like Larry, like Jayne Cortez, like Carolyn Rodgers—intuitively, I know that they have. However, in criticism, intuition, though vital, is not enough. The canons, the categories, the dynamics must be as clear and as reasoned as possible. These must rest on a sound empirical base. Beneath Larry Neal's "word-magic" lies many subtle and useful linguistic patterns which merit some critical description and organization, not to restrict the poet's freedom to invent and to discover, but to serve as a guide, a framework against which these discoveries may be understood and appreciated. And in the final analysis, the issue is still the problem of definition and the problem of control, not only in literature, but in the life which it refracts and reflects.

THE BLUES AS BLACK POETRY

Address delivered at "Evolution 1976–1977: 200 Years of Progression" lecture series,
Southern University, Baton Rouge, LA, 1977; published in *Callaloo* 16, no. 5 (1982): 22–30.

The theme of your lecture series is "Evolution 1976–1977: 200 Years of Progression."[1] During the sixties, instead of "evolution," you probably would have used the word "survival," as I am tempted to do now. But your theme is apt as it stands, for we have more than survived. And, it may even be said that we have progressed. But perhaps even more than that we have in a subtle sense affected the entire quality of American society. This has been done by our very presence here—by the political, the social, the economic, and the cultural impact of our lives. But greater still than all of this has been the moral impact of the Black presence. It has its greatest manifestation in our struggle for freedom and dignity. We have recently—in the sixties, in the civil rights movement and in the Black Arts Movement borne witness to the drama of our unfolding history. It continues, and the message has begun to seep into the general American consciousness. The television series on *Roots*, by Alex Haley, is thus no isolated phenomenon. It is simply a contemporary adaptation, a commercial, but still a brave strategy to jolt the American public into a confrontation with the central contradiction in our history—the fact of slavery, segregation, and racism in the land of the free. Two centuries ago the "Black and Unknown Bards" that James Weldon Johnson wrote about performed this very task. Their legacy—the spirituals, the ballads, and the blues are a constant reminder of where we have been, how we got over, and where we must go. I would like to speak to you briefly about a segment of this legacy which deals with the contradiction of being an alien in one's native land. I would like to speak to you, then about the texts, the lyrics, the poetry of the blues—of the blues, if you please, as Black poetry.

I have deliberately focused on the notion of "blues as Black poetry" as distinct from the notion of "the poetry of the blues." Because some of the

assumptions behind the latter approach have led to various misinterpretations and have left fundamental problems unsolved.

To begin with, "poetry-of-the-Blues" approach assumes a "universal"
something which one calls "poetry." This "something" is discernible best to
people with considerable formal education, although uneducated people may
sometimes possess natural gifts for the expression of this "something." Thus,
while one may admit to the existence of "folk" poetry or of a "folk poet," the
category of folk critic is unthinkable. And not on the ground of class function
or need, but on the assumption that unlettered people lack sufficient capacity
for judgment, even of works which they create themselves. It is, in fact, this
line of reasoning which further states that a balance of the critical and the
inventive faculties is necessary for the production of great poetry, or even
of "poetry." Folk poetry is thus a lower form of expression which must be
subjected to the informed discursive intelligence before it can become "great
literature" or "real poetry." It follows, of course, that blues being "folk poetry"
must be transformed by the educated intellect before it can merit serious
attention. It follows further that, in this view, since the blues is a variant of or
derivation from the Anglo-American musical and poetic traditions, it must
be judged by the standards and categories of that tradition.

To an extent, this has been done, and the results have not been altogether
damaging. The question is whether this is the only—whether this is the best
way of considering these poems. One must give credit to various pioneers, at
any rate—to Guy B. Johnson, for example, for his discussion of the imagery
and themes of the blues in *The Negro and His Songs*. One must do the same
for Samuel B. Charters, despite the obvious limitations of his *The Poetry of
the Blues*, for someone had to say, in a school-teacherish way, "Look, here
is the use of personification. Here is the use of metaphor," and so on. And
surely, we are all indebted to Sterling Brown, Alain Locke, James Weldon
Johnson, Harry Oster, all of the other students of this poetry.

But in our gratitude, we should not forget those misinterpretations
which I mentioned earlier or those fundamental unsolved problems. Some
of the misinterpretations come from deficient knowledge, of vocabulary,
for instance, or of various kinds of allusions. No one apparently knows precisely, to cite an example, what the word "faro" means as a term applied to
a woman. Most blues commentators say that it is pejorative, but the texts
themselves suggest otherwise. Some speculate that it is a corruption of the
English expression "fair roebuck," but that clearly contradicts Black speech
rhythms, and, in fact, the general drift of the English language. One would
expect, in effect, that the unaccented part of the word "roebuck" would be
lost, but in this explanation, this is precisely the part which is retained.

Two more specific examples may be observed in the interpretations by Paul Oliver in *Screening the Blues* and in Harry Oster's essay "The Blues as a Genre" (*Genre*, 1969). In the chapter entitled "The Santy Claws Crave," Oliver very solemnly sympathizes and empathizes with the Negroes who are learning to celebrate Christmas. What he doesn't realize, however, is that the word Santa Claus and its variants, Santy/Sandy/Claws, means, in the Black speech of pre–World War II days, the female pudendum. There is evidence in folk rhyme and certain gestures, as well as in other blues songs.

And in his essay, Harry Oster makes a questionable reading of "mountain jack" as "mountain jackass." The lines in question are these: "If I could holler just like a mountain jack, I'd get up on the mountain, God knows I'd call my baby (back)." He states that the singer uses a "powerful though conventional" image, in reference to his woman, that "if he had the wild scream of a mountain jackass to express his anguish, he would climb high above the world and summon her." Maybe the term did originally have this meaning. I find few people who seem to remember it, but I do know that in the 1940s it was applied by Black people to the locomotives which, sometimes pulling in tandem, struggled and fought their way up the mountainsides. Their sheer force and their powerful horns must have affected the imaginations of many folks, both Black and white. And how different would it be to holler for your baby like a "mountain jack" in this sense then to bray like a mountain jackass? And linguistically, of course, there are logical parallels with "steeplejack" and "lumberjack," both terms of which refer to one who climbs to get his work done.

But this kind of ambiguity and/or misinterpretation takes place even if one is dealing with so-called "formal literature," with the so-called mainstream literature. This one has to footnote Shakespeare's vocabulary, one has to *learn* [Geoffrey] Chaucer's entire language, even though it is English. This is linguistic decay, historical drag, which Chaucer himself was aware of. What I am speaking about, however, is something different. I am speaking about *cultural displacement*, about the degree of misunderstanding or confusion which results from applying to another person's culture those criteria and values which properly belong to one's own. The displacement is the distortion, the rearrangement of another culture's structures and values so as to make them make sense to an outsider. Some instances of this displacement can be rather precisely described. Others are more arcane, and are detectable chiefly through analysis, because they embody certain aspects of that culture, certain features of its inner workings which are taken for granted by the members of the culture but are unknown to and hidden from others. And to this, to speak about poetry, different meanings of the "same" word and different functions which language assumes as one moves, say, from the larger American culture to Afro-American culture. I am saying, then, that not only must one study the history and the sociology of the blues, one must consider the blues as part of a "universe" of Black poetry/art/culture, which has its own characteristic expression, its own function, its own dynamics, its own centers of gravity. Unless this is done, any study of the poetry is likely to be essentially superficial and condescending.

Let me be more specific about this "universe," or this "spectrum," of Black poetry. It consists basically of two traditions—two strata or streams—the "literary" and the "folk," which Richard Wright labeled the "Narcissistic Complex" and the "Forms of Things Unknown." The first is traceable to Lucy Terry's "Bars Fight" (1746), and continues through Jupiter Hammon, Phillis Wheatley, Paul Laurence Dunbar, James Weldon Johnson, Claude McKay, Countee Cullen, Langston Hughes, Sterling Brown, Owen Dodson, Gwendolyn Brooks, Robert Hayden, Imamu Baraka [Amiri Baraka], Don L. Lee [Haki R. Madhubuti], and Nikki Giovanni. The second, created by those "Black and unknown bards," seems always to have been with us, in one form or another, despite the fact that the first significant collection of these song/poems was not made until 1867. There is of course, abundant evidence of their prior existence, although clouded by disputes over their "originality." The important thing is that both traditions are as old as this country itself and, certain crucial aspects of the folk tradition are much older. It is this older tradition which we are interested in because it embodies a great deal of the distinctiveness of Black poetry, just as folk traditions and culture form the substratum of other literatures.

Both traditions of Black poetry can be profitably discussed in terms of these three categories: (1) theme, (2) structure, and (3) saturation. The first is the most accessible, in both traditions, for the overreaching theme of our literature is liberation or freedom, even when statements are personal. This is not to say that the theme is "protest," but that the specific concerns of Black poetry reflect and embody the general thrust or drift of Black history.

Structure, the second category, is more difficult to handle. Generally speaking, the "literary" tradition is derivative of the Anglo-American tradition until the New Negro Movement, and that which is distinctive comes from the "folk" level—the sermons of James Weldon Johnson and the blues of Langston Hughes, for example. As for earlier writers, Phillis Wheatley uses the heroic couplet, and George Moses Horton, the English hymn stanza. But one must note that imitation of "white" forms persists even in Claude McKay's sonnets and the formal verse of Countee Cullen. Even the succeeding generations are not exempt from this imitation. And there is the absorption of "white" techniques by Gwendolyn Brooks, Sterling Brown himself,

Melvin Tolson, and others. The influence of E. E. Cummings, Ezra Pound, and T. S. Eliot—all of this is well known by now. In short, Black poetry, like Black magic, sometimes uses "white" forms. When it does, however, it runs the risk of compromising its Blackness.

In structural terms, then, Blackness in poetry appears as a tendency to explore Black speech forms and a movement toward Black song forms. We shall return to this point later in the paper.

By saturation, the third category, I mean (a) the communication of "Blackness" in a given situation and (b) a sense of fidelity to the observed and intuited truths of the Black Experience. This category accounts for those situations which one recognizes as "Black" even though such recognition eludes formal analysis, as in the following observation on the spirituals by W. E. B. Du Bois in the introduction to *The Souls of Black Folk*. He states: "Ever since I was a child these songs have stirred me strangely. They came out of the South unknown to me, one by one, and yet at once I knew them as of me and of mine."

Let us now speak more formally of the distinctiveness of Black poetry and the relationship of the blues to this distinctiveness. What does this distinctiveness consist of? Is it to be found in both strata or traditions which we have pointed out?

These questions can be approached by raising a prior question, one which I have deliberately "begged" up to this point. What is Black poetry? In the broadest sense employed in this paper, Black poetry is the verbal organization of the experience of Black people, by Black people, into beautiful forms, as defined or recognized and accepted by Black people. It is immediately apparent that many of the usual distinctions made between poetry and prose and poetry and song are often meaningless in this context. Thus, one notes the "poetic" quality of many sermons and tales. One notes the "poetry" of the spirituals and the blues, which are songs. And beneath all of this, there is the "poetic" character of Black speech and its well-known musicality. For examples one could go, of course, to John Jasper, the famous Richmond preacher, or to the anonymous preachers recorded by Zora Neale Hurston. Here one of them describes Jesus calming the stormy Sea of Galilee:

> And placed His foot upon de neck of the storm
> And spoke to the howlin' winds
> And de sea fell at His feet like a marble floor
> And de thunders went back in their vault.[2] (*Negro Caravan*, 491)

In our own day, we hear Rev. C. L. Franklin, of Detroit, say: "I want God's Word to be shaped like a vessel, and I want my soul to step on board." And who has to be reminded of the golden voice of Martin Luther King Jr. or of his moral imagination?

In the spirituals, the evidence is all but overwhelming. Yet it is there and it survives in many forms, suffused through our entire lives. They ask, they demand: "Were you there when they crucified my Lord?" They shout with ecstasy:

> King Jesus is risen from the dead!
> And they still proclaim to the Wretched of the Earth:
> Go down, Moses, way down in Egypt Land,
> Tell Ol' Pharaoh—Let my people go!

But it is with the "seculars" that we are dealing—the blues, with their roots in the work songs, the ballads, the hollers, and the songs of the church itself. On one level, there is an antagonism toward the religious life and Christian piety. Sometimes this appears as parody. For example, Sterling Brown records the following:

> I seen King Pharaoh's daughter
> Seeking Moses on de water . . .
> Seen ole Jonah sawollin' de whale
> And I pulled de lion's tail (*Negro Poetry and Drama*, 21)

In a blues by Jim Jackson, there is a parody of the hymn "I Heard the Voice of Jesus Say Come unto Me and Rest." It goes, "I heard the voice of a po'k chop say, Come unto me and rest." There is the flavor of the minstrel tradition here, but that simply suggests the complex nature of the forces affecting the blues.

Other secular songs reflect blues-like subjects and situations and suggest how rhymes, aphorisms, song titles, and the like are involved in the process of composition. Some of the rhymes collected in [Thomas W.] Talley's *Negro Folk Rhymes*, for example, still appear in the lyrics of popular songs, or in various guises, such as "raps." At any rate, the point is that this fluid body of folksong and folk speech, although modified by changing social, economic, and political conditions, still exists and forms, indeed, an important embodiment and repository of the Black Experience in America. It is this aspect of the tradition which is most distinctly Black, and which seems capable of supporting literary production which could rival that of our instrumental music.

That, indeed, was the special awareness of James Weldon Johnson as realized in his famous sermons after the folk manner in *God's Trombones*. That was the special achievement of Langston Hughes and later of Sterling Brown. The first historical culmination of that awareness was the movement variously known as the Negro Renaissance, the Harlem Renaissance, and the New Negro Movement. The second culmination occurred in the poetry of the sixties, the "new" Black poetry, an aspect of the Black Arts Movement. Throughout both movements the constant factor is the secular, realistic quality—the blues mood—the entirety of it. As one moves from James Weldon Johnson to Langston Hughes and Sterling Brown to Imamu Baraka and Don L. Lee, there is in effect, a greater appropriation of blues and related forms and materials, as Blacks take an increasingly analytical and hardnosed look at their lives in the United States.

While writers like Langston Hughes and Sterling Brown actually employed the blues as a literary form, and Waring Cuney even wrote a blues which was recorded by Josh White, by contrast, few of the poets of the sixties actually used the three-line blues form as such. Among them are A. B. Spellman, David Henderson, Imamu Baraka, and especially the late Henry Dumas, whose work was heavily influenced by his immersion in blues and gospel music.

Despite this apparent neglect of the blues form, however, there is a good deal of talk about the importance of blues to the contemporary Black poet, and I cite just for a few examples: Larry Neal, "Black Art and Black Liberation"; Gylan Kain and his spoken introductions to "Coagulated Trinity"; Stanley Crouch, "The Big Feeling" (*Negro Digest*) and "Toward a Purer Black Aesthetic" (*Journal of Black Poetry*); Percy Johnson, of the Dasein group; and Imamu Baraka, "The Myth of a Negro Literature." To these, of course, we must add older writers like Richard Wright and Ralph Ellison, both of whom have had major impact on the present generation, and the recent work of Albert Murray, *The Hero and the Blues* and *Stompin' the Blues*.

In short, there has been rich convergence of the two streams of Black poetry ever since the Harlem Renaissance. First the spirituals, then the blues were discovered and explored. Earlier writers explored blues forms as well as blues themes. Poets of the sixties and the seventies go beneath blues forms and overt blues themes to what can be called the blues spirit. Although this was anticipated by earlier writers, Larry Neal, I think, has been the most articulate and explicit in calling attention to this blues spirit. In an essay, entitled "Black Art and Black Liberation," he discusses the spiritual power of the blues and its relevance to Black liberation: "The Black Church . . . represents and embodies the transplanted African memory. The Black Church is the Keeper of that Memory, the spiritual bank of our almost forgotten visions of the Homeland. . . . And when she ceased to be relevant, for some of us, we sang the blues"

(36). Neal continues and makes a crucial point which can be documented in the songs themselves as well as in the conversation of some of the singers:

> At the pulsating core of their emotional center, the blues are the spiritual and ritual energy of the church thrust into the eye of life's raw realities. Even though they appear to concern themselves primarily with the secular experience, the relationships between males and females, between boss and worker, between nature and Man, they are, in fact, extensions of the deepest, most pragmatic spiritual and moral realities. Even though they primarily deal with the world as flesh, they are essentially religious. Because they finally celebrate life and the ability of man to control and shape his destiny. The blues don't jive. (36)

This is a profound insight into the dynamics of the Black Experience in America. That experience has been a struggle against oppression, a struggle for survival and for liberation. That has been the main pattern. But out of this struggle there have emerged great spiritual strengths, and at times, a transcendence. So those who write most truly out of the Black Experience know this essential unity of the sacred and the secular—know the ritualistic importance of the blues as the obverse of the spirituals.

This knowledge is fairly common to us as Black people, although we have not fully explored it as artists or as students. It is becoming increasingly known to other Americans—through popular music and dance. What is needed—what is being realized—is that real people produced this art—out of a direct confrontation with the daily reality of their lives, and the history of degradation, a painful history. Alex Haley made a breakthrough to this level of general consciousness. Perhaps the American public will have the courage to take the next step—a full responsibility for our collective past, and for our future. We have the mechanism for that exploration. Our Black and unknown bards invented it. We call it Black poetry; they called it the blues. "Survival motion set to music."

NOTES

1. Given the discrepancy in date ranges, Henderson may have misprinted the lecture series title as "1976–1977" instead of "1776–1977."

2. [See this "poetic" quality of Black music and speech on] James Cleveland's album and Aretha Franklin and Ray Charles's "Spirit Moving in the Dark." [See also] Lil Green's "In the Dark—And he begs me please be Still—" and the prose poem J. W. J.—"Go Down, Death."

EULOGY FOR LÉON DAMAS

Speech given at Léon Damas's funeral, Washington, DC, Jan. 27, 1978.

Madame [Marietta] Damas, I am honored to have the honor to speak on behalf of my coworkers of the Institute for the Arts and the Humanities at Howard University. Much has been said about Dr. [Léon] Damas. I can't and I shouldn't try to repeat those things. We are privileged, I think, to have the vantage point of various speakers—the very moving message from President [Leopold S.] Senghor; the very moving reminiscences of Dr. Mercer Cook. I haven't known Dr. Damas as long as many of you. I met him in 1970. I am overwhelmed by the fact that his presence links me to so many people; links me to this historic place; links me to Howard University; links me to ideas; links me to a culture; links me to a tradition which at the present time is still under attack. The South African poet [Keorapetse] Willie Kgositsile has written a book of poems which is entitled *The Present Is a Dangerous Place to Live*, and I think that if there is anything that Dr. Damas leaves to us as a legacy it is the fact that the poet represents one means of combating that danger, one means of dealing with it. I think we all know that when oppression overwhelms a land quite often the first persons, the first personalities to be eliminated, are the poets. This, of course, gives the lie to Plato's conception of the role of the poet in a society. He eliminated the poet because he felt that the poet was irrational. We know that the real reason is that the poet is a danger to lies. The poet is a danger to obstruction. The poet is a danger to oppression. The poet's function is to speak the truth.

We have just heard a presentation from Dr. Damas's biographer and I think that if you remember the qualities of Damas's poetry, which he pointed out, you will see the cutting edge of that poetry. Now I represent the Institute for the Arts and the Humanities, a special unit of Howard University which originated as a result of the social and political struggles which students activated here in the 1960s. Those struggles were part of a larger struggle. They did not exist in a vacuum. Thus, the Institute for the Arts and the Humanities was quite pleased and honored to have as one of its chief advisors Dr. Léon Damas. Of all of our advisors, he was the most consistent in his understanding of what we were attempting to do. He was particularly interested in our documentation program which involved the use of videotape and various other media. He was, in fact, instrumental in developing our programs. He taught us. The chief thing he taught us was to be aware—as he used to call it—of the "plantation mentality," whether you are a plantation owner, plantation master, or plantation slave. He told us to beware of tribalism, which speaks for itself. We knew from his work of his international importance. He told us to become aware of our connections with other people in other places. Subsequently, he was instrumental in having the Institute invited to participate in the colloquium in honor of the 70th birthday anniversary of President Senghor in October 1976.

In February of this year, the Institute will be celebrating its fifth year of existence. Last May while we were projecting our national writers' conference and our fifth anniversary, we decided to pay a tribute to Dr. Damas. We felt a sense of urgency because of his illness. We wanted him to know that he had helped us to endure.

We saw him last—I saw him last in October of last year in a typical kind of situation, although it was the last public appearance that I know of. The thing that strikes us most is his encouragement of the young. It was a revelation to me, and it's a beautiful revelation in Dr. Cook's presentation and the others, to realize the consistency of this man's character and the clarity of his vision. Because no matter who the person was he found time. He found time for the youngest of students; he found time to encourage young poets. It's almost symbolic—and I find it difficult to organize my thoughts although I have an outline in front of me—because I see here many people whom I know—especially Dr. Cook, Ambassador Coulbury—and I have beautiful associations with them both. And I think again of the presentation at the Watha T. Daniel Library in October in which many of us attempted to pay tribute to this great man. The presentations were organized by two young teachers who organized an institute—just two young women—an institute for the study and preservation of African and African American literature. It's an enormous undertaking for a *university*! He took that seriously because they took him seriously. They did an exhibit on the Negritude Movement, and they dedicated it to him. What strikes me personally is the fact that he was there, because about a week or so earlier I was visiting him at his house with Harold Burke, my friend, and one of the representatives from the group came, and Damas said that he didn't think that he would be able to make it. I talked to him on the telephone and his voice was gone. And he said—and, of course, when you translate things directly from French to English sometimes the effect is even more startling—and he said, "My voice is broken," and that was a terrible thing to hear a poet say—that his voice was broken. Notwithstanding, that night in a driving rain outside we were there, the African Studies Department was there. Many of his friends were there—Ambassador Coulbury was there with his wife, and Madame Damas, of course. And Damas spoke, and you know that he spoke at length and he was a sick man and his voice was strong—enormous courage, enormous clarity of vision. He knew the importance of the event. Again, another aspect of his character manifested itself that night—his enormous generosity, his enormous generosity with himself. He was talking about the importance of Mercer Cook to the Negritude Movement, and he almost forgot that the tribute was to him; and he was talking about Dr. Cook. And Dr. Cook had trouble getting there because of the rain and lo! And behold! As he was speaking of Dr. Cook, Dr. Cook walked in—and they embraced.

Dr. Damas lived an ordered life, and I think this is the way a poet should live his life. We realize that there are poets and poets and poets. Some poets go merely by inspiration, other poets are informed by a vision, other poets are informed by a political vision as well as a social vision, as well as a mystical vision. And particular in Damas's case is the political vision, the fact that he was a real man in the real world. I think this is what attracted the young people to him. Because you must remember that he was not only a participant in the Harlem Renaissance by indirection, he was not only a sort of product of that, he was also part and parcel of this present social and cultural struggle which continues in this country—indeed, in the world. And you must remember that he influenced and inspired many people. One of his protégés (Jayne Cortez) is here and she will read. Damas has recently—and as I said I met him only in 1970—he has read on the same program with younger poets: Jayne Cortez, June Jordan, E. Ethelbert Miller.

He spoke at the Library of Congress. He honored his friend Sterling Brown. He recorded a tape and the symbolism, as I said, is overwhelming. He recorded three of his poems for *Black Box*. On the tape there are the translations. Sterling Brown reads. Sterling Brown now is 77. E. Ethelbert Miller reads some of the other translations. Ethelbert is also a good friend of Dr. Damas. Ethelbert is 27. And it's a fantastic thing. So his life was a poem. That's one of the important things. One of the rediscoveries of the 1960s that Black poets made was that *people* are poems. There's a peculiar quality of Damas, I think, which made him more easily able to identify with the younger poets than some of the other people of his generation were able to do. He had what I would call the blues spirit—that particular way of looking at the world and seeing the contradictions, making fun of the contradictions, being utterly serious, yet living fully and sensuously in them and yet having a means for dealing with the contradictions. There was his wit—his mockery of the personal, the social, and the political foible. As I said, he was a poem, and of course, one raises the question, "What is a poem?" It's the verbal organization, I'd say, of experience into beautiful forms. But the most enduring kind of poetry is the poetry that deals with truth; and this is what makes poets dangerous. There are people who don't like poetry, there are people who don't like poets. Because poets make us uncomfortable at the same time that they please us. But the poem is not only an organization of experience, the poem is a blueprint. And the syntax of a poem, the aesthetic syntax, the linguistic syntax, is just a step away from, or the other side of the political syntax, the syntax of political action. The poem is a time machine. Damas's time has not really come yet. We haven't really begun to deal with that.

Many of the problems that were addressed by the Negritude Movement were partially addressed by the so-called Black Consciousness Movement of the sixties. Many people are writing it off as being dead. It's not dead. We are engaged again in a very important struggle. We learned from Damas that culture is important. The definition of culture is important. For people of African and non-Western descent, ethnicity is important. The analysis of it is important: that one can be both fair and universal in whatever he or she is ethnically. And Damas the Negro—he knew that. And he realized that our Institute is interested in that. He realized that it is important for Howard University to retain its historical ties with all the great spirits that have moved among us. And his legacy to us is his life, his model, and his incomparable spirit.

BLACK POETRY

THE CONTINUING CHALLENGE

Paper presented at Melvin A. Butler Poetry Festival,
Southern University, Baton Rouge, LA, Apr. 30, 1979.

In the 1960s, there was an enormous outpouring of Black creative energy, conditioned in part certainly by the events and personalities, the conflicts, the confusion, the dangers, and the excitement of those days. Now as we approach the new decade of the 1980s, we naturally pause to assess ourselves, our standing, our accomplishments, our failures, our promise. It is characteristic of human nature to do so. How did we fare in the intervening years? How are we faring in the 1970s? What is our prospect for the future?

Our concern during this festival is poetry—the poetry of Black people in general, of Black Americans in particular. And it is proper and fitting that this is so, for of all of the literary creativity of the sixties, the most outstanding work accomplished was in poetry.

Yet, sad to say, that work remains to be seriously considered not only by the general literate population but also by the Black readers for whom it was intended. And although many of the poets continue to write, others apparently have gone silent; have turned their attention, and even at times, their loyalties to other concerns.

So that body of work which we have called the "new" Black poetry still stands as a challenge to us all—a challenge to our social and political understandings and to our aesthetic and spiritual growth.

What is the nature of this challenge? As I see it, the challenge lies in three parts: (1) the challenge of the cultural base, i.e., of the folk and popular roots of the poetry; (2) the challenge of the tradition, i.e., the tradition of Afro-American poetry and of other traditions which may have influenced it; [and]

(3) the challenge of the modern world, which impacts upon us all in both a positive and a negative manner.

(1) *First the cultural base*. I essentially here refer to the fact that the sixties poets drew heavily upon the resources of Black speech and Black music in their work, and unless one were well acquainted with that speech and music then much of the poetry, sometimes entire poems, would be unintelligible. Conversely, if one *did* understand the speech and the music, in *context*, subtle and beautiful meanings were often apparent. I have written and spoken of this at length elsewhere. So, I shall not repeat myself except to say that in this poem by Carolyn Rodgers, for example, there is an assumption that we know the music that she refers to. The poem is entitled "How I Got Ovah / It Is Deep II." It tells of her conversion. Her mother has "commanded" her to attend church with her. She was secure in the knowledge that she had "escaped" God. She was not prepared "for the Holy Ghost," or to "drink the water turned to wine." So she went back another day: "and so I went back another," etc. In order to feel this poem, to sense it in its fullness, one must know not only the hymn but something of the feel of the Black Church service. It is a simple but subtly moving poem.

Other poems are more intricate in their use of cultural materials as I have pointed out in my anthology *Understanding the New Black Poetry*. What I didn't emphasize in the anthology, though, is the fact that there are poems which go behind the folk tradition to the cultures of Africa. Among the writers employing these materials are Henry Dumas, who is in the anthology; Jayne Cortez, Ishmael Reed, and the Caribbean poet Edward Brathwaite. One of Reed's first published poems, and still one of his best known, is "I Am a Cowboy in the Boat of Ra," in which he displays a detailed knowledge of Egyptian religion. [Lorenzo Thomas has written an essay on this aspect of Reed's work.] Jayne Cortez and her husband, sculptor Mel Edwards, are both immersed in African religion. Mel's work in welding iron is rooted in his knowledge of the tradition of Yoruba iron workers' secret society whose spiritual head is the god Shango. In her book *Mouth on Paper*, for example, Jayne Cortez writes praise poems in the African manner for Christopher Okigbo and Henry Dumas, both of whom died at an early age, Okigbo at 35 (1969) and Dumas at age 34 (1968). She writes a praise poem, too, for Mrs. Alberta King, the mother of Martin Luther King Jr., who was murdered by a young Black man in the very church where her husband and son preached. In these poems, Cortez uses surrealistic images to unify the African and the Afro-American roots of our culture. Some of its richness can be seen in the following: "Alberta / spirit with waist beads / of ebony clay // Alberta / with brass face bells // Alberta / womb of red and purple masks // Alberta

/ in a secret society of tears Alberta." And in that secret society are Harriet Tubman, Betty Shabazz, Coretta King, and Myrlie Evers.

Another aspect of the cultural base which I did not emphasize was the visual. Some, of course, is apparent in the imagery. What I have in mind now, though, is the printed or written language arranged for visual effect. Although this seems to be a modern invention, it is not. It not only goes back to Greek poetry, as I did point out, but back to the picture writings of our ancestors who lived in Egypt and what is now known as Nubia. [Tradition has it that the Yoruba, for example, came to Nigeria from the North—i.e., from Egypt.] Black poets emphasized their inspiration from Black music during the sixties. But the music also inspired Black visual artists, and the challenge of *their* work to the poets, and the possibility of cross-fertilization is fantastic.

(2) *Let us consider next the challenge of the Afro-American literary tradition*, especially that of the poetry. The essential challenge is to discern the patterns of continuity, from Lucy Terry's "Bars Fight" (1746) to the present. I have tried to suggest some of these patterns. Obviously, there were others. Much work needs to be done. There are works to be published, works to be collected, biographies and autobiographies to be written, and critical studies to be made. The objectives and aspirations of poets need to be understood and appreciated, their influences need to be studied. Comparisons, though objectionable to some writers, need to be made also.

Some of this work is beginning to appear. Theodore Hudson, Kimberly Benston, and Werner Sollors have written important works on Amiri Baraka. James Emmanuel, and others have written on Langston Hughes. George Kent is writing on Gwendolyn Brooks, and I have published several essays on Sterling Brown. Jean Toomer, of course, is a perennial favorite of the college professors.

Still the main work appears neglected, or is slow in coming, and the only full-length study to date is Eugene Redmond's "critical history" of Afro-American poetry entitled *Drum Voices*. Jean Wagner's *Black Poets of the U.S.* deals with poets from Paul Laurence Dunbar to Sterling Brown.

Other aspects of the tradition which need examination include the influence of white poets on Black poets and vice versa, the question arising out of the "performance" of poetry, and the whole sticky network of thoughts embodied in the Black Aesthetic discussions.

(3) *Finally*, there remains the most difficult challenge of all—the challenge of the modern world. It affects our poets and their work in both negative and positive ways. I have already implied, now I shall state, that our poets and our poetry must have adequate support if they are to survive and flourish. We no longer have to wonder whether we are capable of producing great

poetry. We have already done so. What we need now then is to develop the support systems which our poetry, and indeed, all of our arts need. These systems are as follows:

(a) Craft—these include workshops, festivals of this type, writers' conferences, and the like.

(b) Publications—since the demise of *Black World* and Broadside Press, since "Black" went out of style with the white press (indeed, it was never really "in"), we have many poets who are unable to get their work published. Fortunately, however, we have the *Journal of Black Poetry* still, *First World*, *Soul Book*, *South & West*, edited by Pinkie Gordon Lane, *Energy Black South*, *Black Collegian*, and other heroic publications. Other small presses also accept Black poetry. And, of course, many poets publish their own works, with their own funds.

(c) Reviews and criticism—these, obviously, are dependent on the publishing scene, and reflect that scene. Scarcely anybody's poetry is reviewed nowadays, for various reasons ranging from lack of space/time to racial and cultural arrogance. In order to get around this we can assign new poems/recent poems in our classes in composition and literature. Make them the subject of term papers and theses and dissertations. But most especially, we need to develop three or four publications which are exclusively devoted to the review of literature, with emphasis on recent poetry.

(d) All of these functions can take place easily, though not necessarily in our schools and colleges which are logical places for them to take place in. Here with inquiring young minds and creative and challenging teaching, the groundwork for a unified support system can be laid. This festival, which is now in its eighth year of existence, is testament to that. Let us multiply the idea. Let us spread the good news. Let us take up the challenge again. We have the will, we have the way. Paradoxically, the way leads us back to and through the first challenge, the challenge of the cultural base, for the greatest challenge of the modern world is fragmentation and spiritual death. I need not tell you about it. T. S. Eliot called his age, this modern age, "a wasteland" and his contemporaries, "the hollow men." And though he was describing the Western psyche of the post–World War I generation, he may as well have been speaking for the Western psyche of 1979. Except that since Eliot wrote, the world has lived in nuclear terror and mass murder and starvation, the death of God, spiritual dry rot, and streamlined madness. And critics and poets no longer consider value in poetry, except the value of innovation. And no longer consider any audience but other critics and poets. And no longer consider morality as relevant. Or political concerns. After all "a poem causes nothing to happen," a famous poet said. And so, amid all of this, Black poetry which was written by Black people for Black people, to liberate them from bondage, is to these critics a curious outdated exercise. But we know better. We know that all of the world's greatest poetry, all the world's greatest art, and its greatest music is deeply rooted in moral systems and the life of the spirit. And if we don't know, then we should know, *that* our poetry at its best, is rooted in our music and our religion, and the voices and spirits of our ancestors, who earned their faith in life and their wisdom in the real world; who survived the Middle Passage, and four hundred years of segregation and discrimination; who invented spirituals and the blues; who invented a music which is at once specifically ethnic and universally elastic—this Black music of jazz—this mechanism of the spirit which is capable of reconciling the most shattering contradictions of personal history and historical confusion. In our poetry, rooted in this music, rooted in the *moral* character of this music we have invented a way of speaking which, when the world one day listens, will fill it with astonishment. Meantime, let us do our own work, in our own time, the work nearest to hand. Let us say the poem. Let us speak the truth to the people.

INTRODUCTION TO THE IMAGE OF BLACK FOLK IN AMERICAN LITERATURE CONFERENCE

Introductory remarks to The Image of Black Folk in American Literature conference, Institute for the Arts and Humanities, Howard University, Washington, DC, May 1979.

We have recently emerged from one of the most challenging and productive periods in the history of American culture, the period of the 1960s, and a crucial aspect of those years was the political and creative energy embodied in the civil rights movement and later in the Black Consciousness Movement. Those movements brought to intense focus many of the central problems in American life, those involving the definition of national consciousness, national values and priorities, and power relationships. Black Americans challenged virtually all of the important national institutions and many of the values on which those institutions are predicated. These challenges eventuated in significant changes in American society ranging from the end of formal segregation in public accommodations and public schools to a reassessment of the methodology and content of education itself. The strategies and energies of the civil rights movement, the analysis, the rhetoric, and stances of the Black Consciousness Movement both helped to shape and to fuel the anti-Vietnam [movement], the free speech movement, the women's liberation movement, the gay liberation movement, the American Indian movement, and other aspects of that turbulent era. The sixties and early seventies also saw a quickening of artistic sensibility—in music, in art, and in literature. In Black communities, music ignited the other art forms, especially literature. There was a creative outburst of poetry and drama and of forms wedding the two. There was significant fiction. There were ritual dramas by Amiri Baraka, Ed Bullins, Ron Milner, and Barbara Ann Teer. There were the fantastically inventive novels of Ishmael Reed, and, above all, there was the poetry, much of it pedestrian, much of it ephemeral, but a surprisingly large amount of it both intellectually challenging and verbally brilliant. And it was the poetry in particular that aroused the most hostile response from those not sympathetic to the liberation movements or to the technical strategies and assumptions of the writers.

These issues first came to a head in the Black community with the formulation of the concept of a "Black Aesthetic," which meant for some a blueprint for writing "liberation" literature, for others, an exploration of the manner and modes of expression which are historically and culturally associated with Blacks. From the beginning, there were intense debates, contradictions, recantations, denials, and confusion. Some of this resulted from rigid, dogmatic statements by some of the better-known writers, and some came from the reactions of older writers and students of Black American history who saw in the concept a negation of the kind of open society which the civil rights movement had promised. Some saw in it a provincialism and a return to the separatist spirit of Marcus Garvey and Martin R. Delaney. Others saw it as a joke, and wrote off the entire literary phase of the movement as merely political, merely polemical, and, at best, merely pathetic.

But the writers themselves, though not uniformly of the opinion that there is a "Black Aesthetic," or that Black writers should employ it if there were, were more often than not aware of a special role which they had to play in the definition of their people's history. In the fall of 1974, then, from November 8-10, at Howard University, the newly formed Institute for the Arts and the Humanities held a national conference of Black writers to assess the state of Black American writing and the concerns of Black American writers. The theme was "The Image of Black Folk in American Literature." All of the best-known writers and as many of the others as could be identified were invited to attend. Novelist John O. Killens served as conference director. Killens was writer in residence with the Institute, Haki R. Madhubuti was poet in residence, and Clay Goss was playwright in residence. Killens had held two writers' conferences at Fisk University when he was in residence there in the late sixties, and Rosey Pool, editor of *Beyond the Blues*, had held a conference at Alabama A&M College when she taught there. So there was a precedent for the Howard conference. There was even a precedent for the theme of the conference, Sterling A. Brown's seminal work "Negro Characters as Seen by White Authors" (1933) and *The Negro in American Fiction* (1937). Brown was senior research associate at the institute at the time of the conference, over forty years after the publication of the initial essay, at a time when the question of self-definition was again uppermost in the minds of Black intellectuals, and his presence reminded them that their task was greater than showing off the good qualities of the race and becoming respectable to the majority. And they knew their task. They knew that image making was more important than respectability. They knew that in the modern world of television and movies and communications satellites, image making was, among other things, a political activity. They had, after all, witnessed the Little Rock showdown, the Montgomery march, the Kennedy assassinations, the moon landings, the Vietnam War, the King funeral, and the Watergate hearings on television. They too were bombarded by "blaxploitation" movies and mindless commercials in blackface. They knew the power of the media to magnify or to diminish. They knew that in the modern world the image was more than icon, the image was a lever for controlling reality. And, from Killens's welcoming speech to the dynamic challenge of Ossie Davis, to the reminisces of Charlie Russell, writer after writer spoke of the need to wrest control of the Black image from its exploiters and to employ it for the liberation of the people.

The thirty odd participants invited to discuss "The Image of Black Folk in American Literature" were divided into six panels, on nonfiction, young readers, playwriting, poetry, fiction, and screenwriting. There were three panels on each of the first two days. There were also receptions where writers could socialize and a marathon poetry reading where young students' work was read along with that of some of the participants. The morning of the third day was devoted to a business meeting, where there was an attempt to organize a congress of Black writers, and the afternoon was given to a writers' workshop held at Lorton Reformatory in Virginia. There the main impact was created by novelist Piri Thomas, who had served six years in prison himself for armed robbery and who had made a moving presentation the day before on the Howard University campus. But there were deeply affective statements by the others, Haki Madhubuti, to be sure, whom all the inmates knew, but also by Killens and young Clay Goss. The greatest surprise, though, was the fiery elegance of the women writers Alice Childress and Mari Evans. *They got over.*

This book represents a part of the total experience of the conference. Although most of the papers were delivered from written manuscripts, some were delivered from notes. And there were extended riffs and improvisations even on the written papers, but I have printed the manuscripts in the writers' original form whenever possible. I have also tried to preserve some of the excitement of the presentations, some of the colloquial, informal eloquence which is traditional in the Black community, by reproducing with the least amount of editing the turns of thought, the slips of the tongue, the spontaneous insights which characterize oral composition. Ossie Davis's speech "The Control of Images as an Aspect of Power" was delivered from an outline, but the effect was stunning. Maya Angelou, Piri Thomas, Ron Milner, Charlie Russell, Lonnie Elder III, and George Davis spoke from notes also. In fact, one must say that Maya Angelou *performed* her presentation, for she not only spoke, she acted in her inimitable way, and she *sang*. So, the transcribed account which appears here merely suggests the flavor of her effort.

There was a strong undercurrent of excitement and tension present and it comes through in some of the oblique comments that some writers make. It appears more directly in other places. In his statement of the conference theme, for example, John Killens isolates the failings and confusions of Black writers who mistake verbal violence and romanticization of ghetto life with revolutionary writing. Quincy Troupe will pick up this theme later when he speaks of poets who "murder-mouth" white people. Killens mentions other concerns, most of which are addressed by the other writers. The question of the treatment of Black women by both Black and white writers, for example, is addressed directly by Joyce Ladner Carrington and Paule Marshall. Maya Angelou, in her "The Black Southerner as Inspiration to Black Writers," addresses one of the paradoxes of Black writing of the sixties, the failure to deal adequately with the Southern scene, although most of the actual change occurring in the country was taking place there. Others had different answers, of course, and attributed the lack of attention to the Southern scene to the bias of editors and writers who are located "up South" in the North. Those readers familiar with the current state of Black writing will realize that these last two concerns have grown significantly since 1974, as witnessed by the appearance of regional publications such as *South & West, Callaloo, The History of the Free Southern Theatre*, the Hoo-Doo Black series, and writing by Kalamu Ya Salaam, Tom Dent, Jerry Ward, Pinkie Gordon Lane, Charles Rowell, Arthenia Bates Millican, and Ahmos Zu-Bolton. Another aspect of this phenomenon is the rediscovery of Zora Neale Hurston, stimulated by Robert Hemenway's biography, the exploration of Black folklore in the work of Toni Morrison, and the novels of Alice Walker. On the image of the Black woman, the emergence of Ntozake Shange, Gayl Jones, and Audre Lorde suggests the recent developments on the subject. In fact, the present scene in Black writing is virtually dominated by women.

A crucial question which animated the conference was whether the Black revolution of the sixties was a myth. What had it really accomplished? And wasn't the writers' movement elitist? These questions were being raised because writers who had formally considered themselves Black National-ists had now turned to Marxism-Leninism, as Joyce Ladner Carrington and John Henrik Clarke observe. The questions were also being raised by writers who identified culturally with the "Third World," and had never considered themselves Nationalists. At any rate, it was a sensitive point, and both Askia Muhammad Touré, in his "Towards the Consolidation of an African-American National Literature," and Ron Milner, in his "The 60s: Myth or Reality" address the issues involved here. On another, more personal level, Haki Madhubuti responds to charges from someone in the audience that certain important figures from the sixties, particularly Amiri Baraka, had been deliberately excluded from the conference.

It was important that these questions be raised publicly, for, as the failure to create a national Black writers congress shows, there was and is a great deal of diversity among Black writers, even when they agree on basic notions such as the identity of the enemy or the task of the writer. Since that time some of the writers attending the conference have moved even further away from the idea of a *national Afro-American literature* and of themselves as having a special function as Black writers. Others, however, have not found any contradiction between Marxism and their identification with the Black community. Still others have gone beyond a superficial identification with Africa and have begun to explore the imperative developed by John Henrik Clarke in his "The Black American Writer in Crisis," or the example of Henry Dumas as stated in Quincy Troupe's "Henry Dumas and the African Continuum."

Several writers concentrated on the representation of Blacks in the work of both white and Black authors. Pointing out the negative features of these images as well as the need for realistic characterizations, these writers examined works from a variety of genres, including the movies, children's books, theater, and poetry. Samuel F. Yette states that "there are too few *varieties* of Black heroes. This lack of diversification limits the leverage of Black folk in the image struggle." Lorenz Graham calls attention to the pioneering essay by Sterling Brown "Negro Characters as Seen by White Authors" (1933) and indicates how the preconceptions by editors about the intellectual capacities of Blacks caused them to refuse his books. June Jordan points out the "deadly perspective" of American greed, overconsumption, and waste which wages warfare against nonwhite children. She calls upon her fellow writers to "write stories that preserve the living, struggling, needful spirit from its extinction." And she suggests specific ideas for such stories. Sharon Bell Mathis indicates the concerns which writers of children's book should have, and she discusses some models which she has found to be worthwhile. In the area of adult fiction, Kristin Hunter Lattany and Paule Marshall complement one another's presentation, Lattany dealing essentially with the Black male image and Marshall with that of the Black woman. Both statements are made with insight and verve.

The political dimensions of image making engage the concerns of Mari Evans in her "Poetry as Political Force." She calls upon fellow writers to seek clarity of vision and excellence in craftsmanship. The other poets take up the theme of political obligation, and both Kalamu Ya Salaam and Haki Madhubuti explore the issue. Quincy Troupe takes a different stance. He criticizes the shortcomings of the Black Nationalists without attacking them, and he cites the work of Henry Dumas as an indication of the directions that Black poetry can profitably take and remain true to its traditions and obligations.

Richard Wesley gives a detailed but compact account of the development of recent Black theater, the problems and the opportunities. He indicates that because of the nature of dramatic presentation, the Black playwright is involved with a machinery of production which constantly pushes him toward compromise. The same thing occurs in film and television, and Ossie Davis considers this in his opening statement, as do Charlie Russell in his "On Writing for the Screen" and Lonnie Elder in "My Involvement with the Film Industry." George Davis and Ishmael Reed discuss these economic problems from the viewpoint of the fiction writer. Reed's essay is particularly illuminating not only for the precision of his observations but for what it reveals of the professional pragmatic side of his personality.

In sum, then, this set of statements should prove useful to students of recent American writing and, particularly, to students of Afro-American literature. All the writers represented here continue to be productive. All have something important to say about the portrayal of Black people in the literature of the recent past and the special problems of the Black writer. Most of the problems and issues which they address have grown more complicated and intractable in recent years. As a result, it should be noted that the writers' conference has become established at Howard University and, to date, four have been held on themes of both practical and theoretical concern to Black writers and those who read and study their works.

Finally, I wish to thank everyone who has helped with this publication. I wish to pay special thanks to Virginia A. Blandford, Institute secretary, for typing the manuscript. I wish to thank Harold Burke for taping the original conference sessions and Juliette Bowles for transcribing and editing one of the speeches. Since the staff of the Institute has changed considerably since 1974, and since that original staff also contributed to the conference and this publication, I have listed their names on the following page along with those of the current staff.

THE HEAVY BLUES OF
STERLING BROWN

A STUDY OF CRAFT AND TRADITION

Published in *Black American Literature Forum* 14, no. 1 (Spring 1980): 32–44.

Sterling Brown's poetry may profitably be studied, and his achievement precisely assessed, by implicating his work in the stylistics of the Afro-American culture in which it is saturated. There are, of course, aspects of the poetry which can properly be studied within other parameters—the formal Anglo-American tradition found in "Vestiges," for example, or the tradition of [Robert] Frost and [Edgar Lee] Masters, [Carl] Sandburg, and [Edward Arlington] Robinson. But it is within the dimensions of Afro-American expressive culture that one may perceive most clearly the originality and subtlety of Brown's work.

Of the varied forms of Black expressive culture, music is indisputably the most dramatic, moving, and pervasive; and of the many forms which the music takes, the most typical, the most potently charged is the blues. At one end of the spectrum the blues are sensual ditties of lost love and hard times. At the other end they resonate on the same frequency with the spirituals, but in a somewhat different space, where the burden of salvation is equally weighty but the hope comes chiefly from self. The blues, then, are a music and a poetry of confrontation—with the self, with the family and loved ones, with the oppressive forces of society, with nature, and, on the heaviest level, with fate and the universe itself. And in the confrontation a man finds out who he is, a woman discovers her strengths, and if she is a Ma Rainey, she shares it with the community and in the process becomes immortal.[1]

The hallmark of Sterling Brown's poetry is its exploration of the bitter dimension of the blues, which he links with a view of humankind that he shares with writers like Sandburg, Frost, and Robinson. Their influence helps to catalyze the poet's work without diluting it, and he extends the literary range of the blues without losing their authenticity. When he employs other folk forms such as the ballad, the "folk epic," the "lie," and the song-sermon, he does so with complete confidence, not only in his skill but in his models, both the literary and the folk. The literary models merely confirm what he already knows from the folk: that these forms embody a way of life that is valid and valuable.

Although most of the poems in *Southern Road* are not blues as such, they are suffused with the blues tradition.[2] Indeed, one can make the case that the entire volume is an extended treatment of the blues mood and spirit, that each of the sections of the book presents facets of the Black Experience which evoke the worldview and feel of the blues. Even the last section of the book, "Vestiges," so named because it contains poems written in the poet's earlier manner, in the formal measures of the English poets, is caught up in this spirit by virtue of its placement and its elegiac tone. Earlier in the book, however, there are a number of poems which suggest a significant range of the blues spectrum, although they are not written in blues form.

"Kentucky Blues" is an example. It is blues-like chiefly in its aphoristic imagery and its vernacular verve, as in the following stanza:

> Women as purty
> As Kingdom Come,
> Ain't got no woman
> 'Cause I'm Black and dumb.

In a poem like "Riverbank Blues" the emphasis is on the blues mood rather than form. The mood is established in the first stanza:

> A man git his feet set in a sticky mudbank,
> A man git dis yellow water in his blood,
> No need for hopin', no need for doin',
> Muddy streams keep him fixed for good.

And the entire mood of seductive indolence is created through a description of the riverbank. There is an undertone of threat and danger which one associates with blues about the forces of nature:

> Towns are sinkin' deeper, deeper in de riverbank,
> Takin' on de ways of deir sulky Ole Man—
> Takin' on his creepy ways, takin' on his evil ways,
> "Bes' git way, a long way . . . whiles you can."

Two things stand out about this poem which justify its title: the mood created by the description, and the reaction of the persona. Blues, I observed earlier, are a music and a poetry of confrontation, and here the challenge to the persona is despair, which the poet presents in the personified river, where the persona

> went down to the river, sot me down an' listened,
> Heard de water talkin' quiet, quiet lak an' slow:
> "Ain' no need fo' hurry, take yo' time, take yo' time . . ."
> Heard it sayin'— "Baby, hyeahs de way life go."

The entire poem is related to traditional situations and imagery in blues poetry, as in the following:

> I'm goin' to the river
> I'm gonna buy me a rockin' chair
> If the blues overtake me,
> I'm gonna rock away from here.

But the crucial thing is the reaction—the heroic underpinning of the blues which so appeals to Brown and which merges in his poetry with the theme of the common man in the tradition of [Walt] Whitman and [Mark] Twain. As the man watches the slowly rolling river, something beside him

> rared up an' say,
> "Better be movin' . . . better be travellin'. . .
> Riverbank'll git you ef you stay."

"Riverbank Blues" serves to remind us that the blues are not only a music, but also a complex of emotions and a certain way of looking at life; thus, the poet here is justified in titling the poem as he does. There, of course, was ample precedent in the music profession itself. One might observe that Langston Hughes also followed this practice, his poem "The Weary Blues" being just one salient example.

Hughes was able to evoke the blues feeling in a sharp vignette that sometimes consist of no more than two or four lines:

> I wish the rent
> Was Heaven sent.

Brown too has this ability to capture the pithy precision of folk speech and poetry. In "Rent Day Blues," which first appeared in *Folk-Say IV: The Land Is Ours*, Brown's special brand of humor appears in a variation on the blues form—a sort of blues ballad.[3] The poet omits the second line from the typical three-line blues stanza in "Rent Day Blues," making two lines, which he then breaks up into four. Langston Hughes, by comparison, often wrote the stanza as six lines. The short lines move swiftly, tersely, with snap. The opening stanza retains the effect of a couplet in the statement about the rent:

> I says to my baby,
> "Baby, but de rent is due;
> Can't noways figger
> What we ever gonna do."

The woman answers:

> My baby says, "Honey,
> Dontcha worry 'bout de rent;
> Looky here, daddy,
> At de money what de good Lord sent."

The pivoting of the voice on the word "baby" in the first stanza and the enjambment of the last two lines help establish the sense of a couplet, mentioned above. With the second stanza, however, with the words "honey" and "daddy," the rhythms of Black speech demand a prolongation, an emphasis, which establishes the quatrain for the ear as well as the eye. The resulting ballad movement of the poem thus carries something of the flavor of a compressed blues stanza. Amplified by the typical blues situation, this handling of the poem's rhythm and movement is a further indication of Brown's skill.

"Long Track Blues," which also first appeared in *Folk-Say IV*, is closer to the tradition of blues composition, in terms of its dramatic situation and mood.[4] Note, however, that this poem too omits the second line for conciseness, although the poet sometimes supplies it when reading in public:

Went down to the yards
To see the signal lights come on;
[lines 3–6 from "Long Track Blues"]
Lawdy, let yo' green light
Shine down on that babe o' mine.

For specificity of detail and evocative power, this is one of Sterling Brown's finest poems. Its ease is deceptive. In order to appreciate fully his achievement here, one must acquaint oneself with the body of blues and other songs which deal with railroads and trains, with leavings and heartbreaks, particularly with the cluster of songs in which the lover rebukes the train for taking his babe away, as in "Mean Ol' Frisco," perhaps the most famous:

Say, that mean Ol' Frisco
And that low-down Santa Fe
Come and stole my baby 'way—
Better blow her back to me

And Sterling Brown consciously deepened the meanings and multiplied the implications of a Black American folk base, to paraphrase James Weldon Johnson, by his skillful selection and synthesis of the imagery which often appeared in songs of quite different types. Thus, the signal lights in Brown's poem not only call up the "train with the red and green lights behind" but also a related image found in many blues: "If I could shine like the headlight on some train." Grading into this image, one finds the "gospel train" and the "little Black train of death." Other related images of light and trains are found in hymns, gospels, and spirituals. These associations are not at all gratuitous, as we shall see later in the discussion of "Memphis Blues."

Let us return now to *Southern Road* and look briefly at "Tin Roof Blues," which is written in classical blues form. It is a marvelous distillation of both blues method and substance. Echoes from traditional blues appear in the very first line:

I'm goin' where de Southern crosses top de C. & O.

One, of course, hears the undertone:

I'm goin' where the Southern cross the Yellow Dog.

And one probably hears it in Bessie Smith's voice. The third line, too, is a distillation of hundreds of blues songs, and it is especially poignant since it stands as the second clause:

> I'm goin' down de country cause I cain't stay here no mo'.

This theme of leaving so typical of the blues appears in lines like:

> I'm going to Chicago, sorry but I can't take you.

Or:

> I'm going, I'm going, pin up Black crepe on your door.

And:

> I'm going down this road feelin' bad, baby.

And:

> I'm going where the weather suits my clothes.

And what is the wanderer in "Tin Roof Blues" looking for? He's looking for a place where people are friendly, honest, and down-to-earth, where they take control of their own lives as best they can, where they don't wait for fate to give them a lucky hit on the numbers. The poem closes with delightfully compressed imagery:

> I'm got de tin roof blues, got dese sidewalks on my mind,
> De tin roof blues, dese lonesome sidewalks on my mind,
> I'm goin' where de shingles covers people mo' my kind.

One might compare these lines from "Freight Train Blues," by Thomas Dorsey and Everett Murphy (1924):

> Got the freight train blues. I've got the box cars on my mind.
> [repeated 1x]
> I'm gonna leave this town because my man is so unkind.

Notice, first of all, the subtlety of Brown's variations in the second line of his last stanza. The omission of the first two words of the first line ("I'm got") gives the second some of the shorthand quality of sung blues lyrics, in which the instrument may carry the second line, or a grunt or a deliberately muffled approximation of the words as originally sung. And one would certainly expect a skilled blues singer to take such liberties with the formally repeated lines in the "Freight Train Blues" text. The variation which Brown makes at the beginning of the line also makes it possible for him to augment the mood with the adjective "lonesome." This kind of emotional augmentation approximates the musical practice. The "I'm goin'" of the third line is a clever resolution of the syntactical ambiguity (with reference to so-called Standard English) of the expression "I'm got." It forms a visual and aural parallel to the "I'm got" of the first line, but is more precisely a clarification which allows the imagery and the final statement to speak for themselves without obtrusion. And here, certainly, Brown achieves the kind of language which James Weldon Johnson spoke of some years before. Again, notice the compression of the lines, the economy characteristic of folk poetry. From "freight train blues" to "box cars on my mind" the jump is much shorter, less imaginative—with a tendency toward the pathetic—than the imaginative leap from "tin roof blues" to "dese sidewalks on my mind," which realistically evokes the wanderlust of Black blues living. With the last line of the "Freight Train Blues" stanza, "I'm gonna leave this town because my man is so unkind," commercial glibness, which is characteristic of so many so-called "classical blues" songs, intrudes upon the achievement of the first two lines. In contrast, the last line of Brown's stanza serves to draw the whole poem together, thematically and tonally, for here the word "shingles" is set against the tin roofs of the city—wooden, honest wooden shingles "covers people mo' my kind." So, the poet accepts the challenge of suggesting the spontaneity of improvisation, although he carefully controls his effects in a manner which the commercial song writer would be unable to do, and which he would find unnecessary, since his text would be in effect a pretext for the singer to do his or her own thing in the first place.

The theme of wandering is a powerful one in folk literature and occupies a prominent place in the blues and the ballads and tales which nurtured the art of Sterling Brown. There is a well-known historical matrix of this wanderlust and leaving, which includes the migration of Blacks after the Civil War—the northward and westward migrations which peaked during the two world wars, and the movement from rural to urban areas even within the South itself. This is, to be sure, not strictly a Black phenomenon, but the effect which it had upon Black life was profound. The examples cited above are fairly self-sufficient on a literal level. On a deeper level, the theme of wandering or leaving is concomitant with the notion of the blues as a poetry/ music of confrontation. The confrontation is frequently with a loved one, though often it is with one's enemies or with specific unhappy conditions in society, or with oneself. And the resolution comes through sexual triumph, or through violence, an assertion of one's manhood/womanhood, or through a bitter acceptance of the harshness, even the absurdity of life, expressed with cunning humor and with wit, or irony. The final confrontation, of course, is with death, and here the motif of the wanderlust takes on a special irony. The folk expression for it is "You can run, but you can't hide." And the blues poet knows this. It is an ultimate knowing, but one which requires a lifetime of repetition. A man may run away after committing a murder, for example, but he can't run away from himself. ("Cain't nobody hide from God.") He may try to run away from confrontation with the self, but eventually life forces him to make decisions which reveal who he is. Characteristic of Sterling Brown's figures is the heroism which the confrontation reveals, even in the case of a Joe Meek. In "Georgie Grimes," one could hardly call the character heroic, but he has his pride, and our grudging respect. He has just killed his woman. With his red suitcase in his hand he "sloshes onward through the rain," he "remembers hot words, lies, / The knife, and a pool of blood." And he remembers her sightless eyes, and he knows that fear will follow him for the rest of his life. As he stumbles through "the soggy clay," muttering to himself, "No livin' woman got de right / To do no man dat way," we realize a bitter, brutal dimension of the folk, and the blues, experience.

The three poems on Big Boy Davis which open *Southern Road*—"Long Gone," "When de Saints Go Ma'chin' Home," and "Odyssey of Big Boy"—explore three stages, as it were, of the wanderlust theme. All of these poems are blues-like in tone and language, though not in overall structure. "Long Gone" depicts a typical footloose man who leaves his woman despite his mixed feelings. In "When de Saints Go Ma'chin' Home," the poet's first published poem, Big Boy, the wandering songster, plays music which progresses from "the bawdy songs and blues," "the weary plaints," to his mother's favorite song, with which he ended all of the concerts for his middle-class friends. As persona, Big Boy, in effect, asserts through the shape of his concert the unity and meaningfulness of his life. Technically, the "concert" section of the poem is a microcosm of the musical tradition; and, further refined, the second section, with its series of portraits evoked by the music, is an emblem of folk society framed by the consciousness and craft of the poet.

Big Boy Davis's concert also illustrates the mingling of the religious and the secular in Black music and Black life,[5] and although that fact is now well-known, one must still realize that the means for achieving that mingling or fusion are rather more complicated than substituting "baby" for "Jesus" in a song based on gospel tunes or chord progressions. Brown learned this quite early in his career, and expressed it with subtlety and power not only in "Odyssey of Big Boy" but in poems like "Ma Rainey" and "Memphis Blues." The wanderlust motif or feeling is an important ingredient in the blues universe and in the notion of *Soul* as the embodiment or essence of Black lifestyle.

In "Odyssey of Big Boy," one of Brown's finest and most characteristic poems, there is a classic statement of wanderlust as Soul. Big Boy envisions the final confrontation after years of wandering. He outlines his history in comic-heroic terms. He has been a mule skinner, steel driver, tobacco harvester, coal miner, farmhand, roustabout, short-order cook, and dishwasher. And he has had his good times with the women, running the gamut from a "Creole gal" to a "stovepipe blond." He continues:

> Done took my livin' as it came,
> Done grabbed my joy, done risked my life;
> Train done caught me on de trestle,
> Man done caught me wid his wife.

So, when his "jag is done," there is no room for complaining. He has lived his life and taken the risks, and the confrontation has produced a clear self-knowledge and a view of the moral order of the world, where he, indeed, is bone and flesh of John Henry and the archetypical brother, the embodiment of Soul.

Although the outstanding feature of Sterling Brown's blues is their somber outlook, the poet's treatment of the blues material ranges from emphasis on mood and character, to a focus on the sociological, to an accent on the philosophical. Sometimes, as in "Odyssey of Big Boy," all three elements are present in the same poem. In "New St. Louis Blues," however, the sociological emphasis is almost clinical. The poem is a kind of blues suite, consisting of three separate but related poems entitled "Market Street Woman," "Tornado Blues," and "Low Down." All three are written in the three-line blues stanza, but there is a scientific detachment from the subjects which recalls the proletarian literature of the 1930s. One can't easily imagine these poems as songs, as in the case of "Tin Roof Blues," for example, or "Long Track Blues," which Brown recorded with piano accompaniment for Folkways Records.[6] In other words, "Market Street Woman" and "Low Down" are case studies of social oppression.

Even in "Tornado Blues" protest against oppression is the central theme, for although the "Black wind" from "de Kansas plains" has caused the initial destruction, the suffering which preceded it and which surely follows is man-made, the result of an oppressive social and economic system. It was mostly "de Jews an' us" that the tornado ruined. "Many po' boys' castle done settled to a heap o' dus." The "Newcomers"—destruction, fear, death, and sorrow—"dodged most of the mansions, and knocked down de po' folks' do." And this is what they found:

> Foun' de moggidge unpaid, foun' de insurance long past due,
> Moggidge unpaid, de insurance very long past due,
> All de homes we wukked so hard for goes back to de Fay and Jew.

Technically, the achievement of "New St. Louis Blues" lies in the adaptation of the strict blues form to precise sociopolitical statement, and the organization of the three separate but complementary poems into a tonal whole. But the achievement goes beyond isolated technicalities or social protest. Certainly, protest is an important part of the blues tradition, but it is an implicit protest, as Albert Murray observes. The crucial thing is that Brown goes beyond the social protest writers of his time and finds in the blues a philosophical position which is compatible with his own. It is this position, this attitude, this tone which most clearly sets him apart from others who employ the folk idiom. This "grim" perspective, to use the poet's own word, has some of its roots, at least, in the blues. There is, to be sure, a dimension of the blues which is unmistakably tragic, even fatalistic, in which human activity is pitted against the overwhelming forces of nature, depicted at times as impersonal, objective, or indifferent, at other times as the embodiment of a malevolent teleology. It appeared in the "blues suite," for example, in lines like these from "Tornado Blues":

> De Black wind evil, done done its dirty work an' gone,
> Black wind evil, done done its dirty work an' gone,
> Lawd help de folks what de wind ain't had no mercy on.

In the down-home blues tradition, Furry Lewis of Memphis sings:

> Wind storm come, an' it blowed my house away,
> Wind storm come, an' it blowed my house away,
> I'm a good old boy, but I'm ain' got nowhere to stay.

And Mississippian Son House sings of a devastating drought in "Dry Spell Blues":

> The dry spell blues have fallen, drove me from door to door.
> Dry spell blues have fallen, drove me from door to door.

The dry spell blues have put everybody on the killing floor.

The language in the song moves from the literal to the symbolic as the singer establishes a landscape worthy of [T. S.] Eliot's *The Waste Land*, as it moves from references to parched cotton and corn, the price of meat against that of cotton, to a description of the world as a powderhouse where all the money men sit in their coil. With that range of language in mind, then, how lyrically right becomes the line "Let your rain come down, and give our poor hearts ease." Even the cliché of the second clause is restored to its pristine sincerity.

In a symbolic landscape, the precocious Robert Johnson sang of a veritable blues storm, through which he stumbled much like Sterling Brown's Georgie Grimes. Johnson's imagery, however, is at once biblical and hallucinatory, in the manner of the old sermons:

> Blues fallin' down like hail, blues fallin' down like hail,
> And the days keep on worryin' me, for a hell-hound on my trail,
> Hell-hound on my trail, hell-hound on my trail.

But Johnson and other blues people lived and sang in the real world, not in a symbolic landscape, and that world was harsh and oppressive, and dangerous. There were floods and droughts and tornadoes, and a merciless social order, built on the Black man's subjugation. Even in times of natural disaster Black folks seemed singled out for special punishment. Such a time was the great flood of 1927 which left an indelible impression on blues literature. Paul Oliver, the blues historian, has a highly compressed account which warrants quotation:

> No one had anticipated the full horror of the 1927 floods. Houses were washed away with their terrified occupants still clinging to the rooftops; the carcasses of cattle and mules floated in the swirling, deep brown water; isolated figures whom none could rescue were last seen crying for help as they hung in the gaunt branches of shattered trees. Dresses and table-tops, clothes and toys were caught in the driftwood and floating timbers, to twist madly in a sudden whirlpool, and then sweep out of sight in the surging, eddying, boiling waters which extended as far as eyes could see.

From the town of Cairo, one could accurately judge the extent of the flooding at the towns farther down river. A rise of fifty feet above minimal level indicated that a severe flood was imminent. Oliver continues, "In 1927 the water had risen to 56.4 feet—nearly two feet above the previous highest reading." And at Vicksburg,

> the level had risen some sixty-five feet and with such a tremendous volume of water that the devastation was on an immense scale. Branches—or "crevasses"—in the levees were recorded in fifty places and twenty-eight thousand square miles of land were under water. Whole townships were engulfed and the frightened people—largely Negroes—made for the hills at Helena and Vicksburg.

Some six hundred thousand people "were rendered completely destitute," and Blacks were at the mercy of white landlords who exploited a corruptly administered relief program. Total damage to the region was assessed at more than 350 million dollars.[7]

Many songs were written about the 1927 flood, but surely the best known was "Backwater Blues," which received majestic treatment by both Ma Rainey and Bessie Smith and moving treatment by others.

Sterling Brown had seen Ma Rainey in his youth, and her voice and her dignity had made a tremendous impression on him. Although he hadn't heard her sing "Backwater Blues," he had met someone who had, and he fused that account with his own impressions, his own knowledge of the people and the region and the music into one of the finest evocations of Black life that anybody has ever written, his poem "Ma Rainey." Sterling Stuckey calls it "perhaps *the* Blues poem,"[8] but to be precise, it is not a blues poem at all, in terms of structure, the way that "Tin Roof Blues" is, for example. It is, instead, a consummate dramatization of the spirit and power of the blues and their historic role as ritual in Black life.

The poem is divided into four stanzas which function in effect as movements in a musical sense. In the first, the tone is light and festive, capturing the excitement of the singer's personal fame:

> Folks from any place
> Miles aroun',
> [lines 5–6 from "Ma Rainey"]
> Flocks in to hear
> Ma do her stuff.

It's a holiday when "Ma hits / Anywheres around." Quickly the poet has established not only Ma's fame but the geography of the backwaters as well—Cape Girardeau, Poplar Bluff, all the way "fo' miles on down / To

New Orleans delta / An' Mobile Town." In the second stanza the pace changes as the line lengthens and the focus is closer, tighter. People come "from de little river settlements," from "blackbottom cornrows and from lumber camps." The lens zooms in, as people "stumble in de hall, jes' a-laughin an' a- cracklin', / Cheerin' lak roarin' water, lak wind in river swamps." The high feelings and the good times and the joking keep going in the "crowded aisles." But others wait for a deeper reason. Then Ma makes her entrance, flashing her famous smile, and "Long Boy ripples minors on de Black an' yellow keys." And the poet in stark dramatic terms speaks with the voice of the people. It is the communal voice, the response of the ancient ritual pattern, the answer to Ma Rainey's call to "deir aches an' miseries": "O Ma Rainey, / Sing yo' song; / Now you's back / Whah you belong." The expression "Sing yo' song" is still current in the Black community. People say it spontaneously when they are moved by someone who appeals to their deepest concerns, whether a gospel singer or Aretha Franklin singing about hard times in love. And they compliment her by saying, "Sing your song," because the song is theirs too. Brown continues, "Git way inside us, / Keep us strong . . . / O Ma Rainey, / Li'l an' low; / Sing us 'bout de hard luck / Roun' our do'; / Sing us 'bout de lonesome road / We mus' go."

She gives them back themselves and they return the love and the truth: "Now you's back" with us, "whah you belong"—and now with *this* kind of singing, you're affirming our truth. And the language resonates on the mythic level, for the singer is priestess and, before that, the surrogate of the gods. This was her role, in that time before time. But here it is compressed, transubstantiated into song, personal commentary transmuted into communal statement. And they know, they understand the ultimate tragic truth of human experience, and they accept it and thereby transcend it. Hard luck is irrational, but there it is. Call it fate, call it mischance, it is still there. And it will remain. "So sing yo' song," and "sing us 'bout de lonesome road / We mus' go."

One would think perhaps that the possibilities of the poem had been exhausted at that point, but the poet moves into a different perspective and amplifies his effect by letting the *blues* speak for themselves. In stanza 4, then, he returns to the narrative mode of stanza 2. Here the point of view changes to that of a single persona:

> I talked to a fella, an' the fellow say,
> "She jes' catch hold of us, somekindaway."
> [lines 41–50 from "Ma Rainey"]

Dere wasn't much more de fellow say:
She jes' gits hold of us dataway.

The communion is complete. Even song now is unnecessary, and Ma Rainey, the priestess, is spent—the spirit has left her, the spirit is loosed and surrounds and hollows them all. It is like the end of a sermon, or a baptism.

Technically, there's one final touch as the persona picks up the language of the "fellow," which had been enclosed in quotes, as an account, and repeats it, compressing and melding the account, the reminiscence, the historical flood, and the present into an acknowledgement of his oneness with the people and the experience. "Dere wasn't much more de fellow say: / She jes' gits hold of us dataway." Not "somekindaway" but the way you have just experienced it—"dataway."

Just as Sterling Brown celebrates his people's health and sanity and their heroic confrontation with adversity, he attacks anything which oppresses or corrupts them. The vehemence of his attack is proportionate to his outrage and his sense of the people's loss. In "Children's Children," he directs a stream of elegant sarcasm at an unfaithful generation bent on abandoning its heritage. But in "Cabaret," one of his most important poems, the target is larger—it is nothing less than the prostituting of Black life by the large society and the capitalistic system. Here he not only dramatizes the struggle of man against nature, but the conflicts between Black and white, the powerful and the powerless, the overlords and the underlings, and the complicity of Black people in their own degradation. The enveloping event of the poem again is the great flooding of the Mississippi in 1927, but whereas "Ma Rainey" demonstrates the heroic resiliency and philosophic maturity of the people through an authentic blues ritual, "Cabaret" becomes a complex vehicle for devastating satire and all that is false and parasitical in the American way of life. It is thus a poem on the antiblues spirit, the dialectical opposite of "Ma Rainey." Just as "Backwater Blues" provides the emotional mainspring for "Ma Rainey," the banal Tin Pan Alley song "Muddy Water Blues" provides the basis of the satire in "Cabaret." The words of the song, drifting in and out of the narrative flow, help to shape it by providing a chronological base for the action, which is amplified in the event of the poem proper, a floor show at the Black and Tan Club of Chicago, in 1927, as we learn from the poem's subtitle. The two events which govern the poem may be viewed as two concentric circles, the larger one symbolizing the outside world with the conflicts between man and nature, overlords and underlings, powerful and powerless, white and Black—the sociopolitical conditions

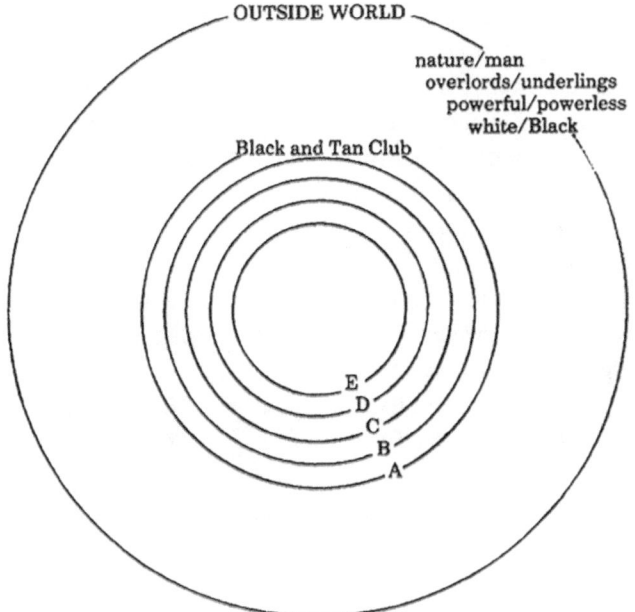

OUTSIDE WORLD

nature/man
overlords/underlings
powerful/powerless
white/Black

Black and Tan Club

E
D
C
B
A

Figure 1

of the Mississippi Delta, and the country itself. The smaller circle, symbolizing the event of the club, is a microcosm of the world outside. But here there is a suspension of real time, historical time, so to speak, and substituted for it is the time of the floor show, a hollow ersatz art. The poem itself is a verbal construct which mediates between the two "events." The reader is guided through a set of interlocking levels of perception and commentary, which may themselves be viewed as subevents of the action in the club. The historical event of the flood is refracted through various modalities, which we perceive as levels of feeling or meaning, as voices, or angles of perception and commentary. The first level, "A," is the narrative. The poem opens here with a scene of the rich "overlords" and their "glittering darlings" (ll. 1–10). It occurs also at ll. 14–16, 20–24, 26–31, 33–34, 44, 58–63, and 76–81, for a total of thirty-five lines. The other voices/levels are as follows:

"B"—Sardonic #1. Here are reactions to the behavior of the participants in the club event—the band, the chorus, the waiters, and the overlords. It occurs at ll. 11–13, 25, and 45–49, for a total of nine lines.

"C"—Music/Chorus. Lyrics of "Muddy Water Blues" sung by the chorus of "Creole" beauties provide a chronological base for the action. Along with voice/level A, this level provides the main structural lines of the poem. It occurs at II. 17–19, 32, 35–36, 50–52, 57, 68–69, 74–75, and 82–83, for a total of twelve lines.

"D"—Sardonic #2. This voice/level provides reaction to the club event by the juxtaposition of images of toil, suffering, destruction, and death resulting from the Mississippi floods. The sociological tone shades into the naturalistic and the fatalistic. It occurs at II. 37–42, 53–56, 64–67, 70–73, and 84–86, for a total of 23 lines.

"E"—Music/Instrumental. This voice/level is represented through onomatopoeia as the music is left to speak for itself in a manner comparable to the quotation of "Backwater Blues" in "Ma Rainey." It occurs at II. 43 and 87, at the midpoint and the end of the poem.

Let us return to the poem itself. It opens with "Rich, flashy, puffy-faced, / Hebrew and Anglo-Saxon / The overlords sprawl here with their glittering darlings." Then "the jazzband unleashes its frenzy." Up to this point the action of the poem is presented on level A, narrative; but suddenly we encounter a sardonic voice, printed in italics, which comments on the band, trained "doggies" performing for the overlords. We are on level B:

> *Now, now,*
> *To it, Roger; that's a nice doggie,*
> *Show your tricks to the gentlemen*

When we are returned to the narrative level, A, the band is depicted in pathological images:

> The trombone belches, and the saxophone
> Wails curdlingly, the symbols clash,
> The drummer twitches in an epileptic fit

At level C (II. 17–19), we hear the voice of the chorus singing the obscene banalities of the Tin Pan Alley song about the flood. We remember, of course, "Backwater Blues" and Ma Rainey singing her song. But the chorus sings: "Muddy water / Round my feet / Muddy water." Back on the narrative level, A (II. 20–24), we are informed that "the course sways in," and in an aside, we are told that they are not really "Creole Beauties from New Orleans," as billed, but come from almost everywhere else—Atlanta, Louisville, Washington, Yonkers. And on level B (I. 25), the Sardonic Voice #1 exclaims with mock preciousness:

> *O, le bal des belles quarterounes!*

The narrative voice creates a picture of mock romantic sensuality as it describes the "shapely bodies" of the chorus and their pirates' costumes, and it reflects the sarcasm upon the maudlin images of river life conjured up by the dancing, the music, and "the bottles under the tables" (II. 26–31). And it reminds us of Lafitte, the real pirate (II. 33–34), and his modern counterparts, the "overlords" themselves. There is a rich interplay of voices, tones, and perspectives at this point in the poem as the voice of the chorus (C) surfaces—"Muddy water, river sweet" (I. 32)—and the narrative voice (A) refers us to Lafitte's "doughty diggers of gold" (II. 33–34). The words of the chorus become unbearably unreal as they sing of the "peace and happiness" of the Delta (C, II. 35–36) in 1927. Sardonic Voice #2 (level D) crashes in, distinguished by parentheses, its grim tone, and its naturalistic depiction of the sociology of the flood. First, there is the virtual slavery of the Black convicts who have been pressed to work on the levees (II. 37–42):

> *(In Arkansas,*
> *Poor half-naked fools, tagged with identification numbers,*
> *Worn out upon the levees,*
> *Are carted back to the serfdom. . . .)*
> [lines 42–43 from "Cabaret"]

Amplifying these lines, in the music of the period, one finds Leadbelly singing "Red Cross Store Blues" and Big Bill Broonzy who sang:

> You'll never get to do me like you did my buddy Shine;
> You'll never get to do me like you did my buddy Shine;
> You worked him so hard on the levee till he went stone blind.

On the deepest level/voice, E, the drummer makes a break which the poet captures in terms that anticipate Langston Hughes's rendering of bebop sounds in his *Montage of a Dream Deferred*. In fact, the term *bebop* itself as a name for the music probably had its origin in onomatopoeia, and just as "bop" singing tended toward the use of wordless "lyrics," the heart of Brown's poem demonstrates the tendency of Black musicians to employ the instrument as an extension of the voice. In certain situations, in the scat singing of Dizzy Gillespie, for example, the result is a teasing expression of the antirational, Dadaistic impulse. And so the drummer plays (I. 43): "Bee-dap-ee-DOOP, dee-ha-dee-BOOP."

As "the girls wiggle and twist" to the music (A, I. 44), Sardonic Voice #1 (B) offers them at auction (II. 45–49). They, like the musicians, are ordered to go through their paces for the "gentlemen":

A prime filly, seh,
What am I offered, gentlemen, gentleman

The song continues its phony sentiment (C, II. 50–52), interrupted by Sardonic Voice #2 (D), which now asks without bitterness (II. 53–56), "What is there left the miserable folk?" In reply, the voice of the chorus chimes in (C, I. 57), "Still it's my home, sweet home," as the poet emphasizes the falseness with the "moans and deep cries for home" coming from the "lovely throats" of these displaced "Creoles." And the alcohol heightens the illusion they create (A, II. 58–63).

In the real world of the Mississippi Delta (D, II. 64–67), "The Black folk huddle, mute, uncomprehending" the ways of "the good Lord." They have no "shelter / Down in the Delta," as the song goes (C, II. 68–69). On the level of Sardonic Voice #2 (D, II. 70–73), the heavy-bellied buzzards fly low over the Yazoo, "Glutted, but with their scrawny necks stretching, / Peering still." This counterpoint of images is striking, this interweaving of voices and levels, the commercial song moving in and out of the real world of the Delta, that make-believe of the cabaret, all of it held in dynamic suspension in the world of the poem. As the song, as the event for the interior scene comes to a close (A, II. 76–81; C, II. 82–83; D, II. 84–86; E, I. 87):

The band goes mad, the drummer throws his sticks
At the moon, a papier-mâché moon,
The chorus leaps into weird posturings,
The firm-fleshed arms plucking at grapes to stain

The final notes of the trumpet and the final line of the poem ("Dee da dee D A A A A H"), if one must seek a literary comparison, or the equivalent of [Ernest] Hemingway's "Nada" in "A Clean, Well-Lighted Place," in which the writer parodies the Lord's Prayer with the Spanish word for "nothing." And again, one must note the anticipation of bebop and the Dadaist element in it, especially in the singing. However, in characteristic style, Brown has arrived at this position through essentially realistic means. On the sociological level, the political level, and the moral level, there is a powerful indictment of modern slavery, in the exploitation and prostitution of the musicians and their music. They are, in effect, no better off than the poor victims of the flood, or the convicts; and if they were aware of their condition, they could ask, *"how come the good Lord / Could treat them this a way."* These are the heaviest blues of all, and the poet has presented them to us through an elegant indirection.[9]

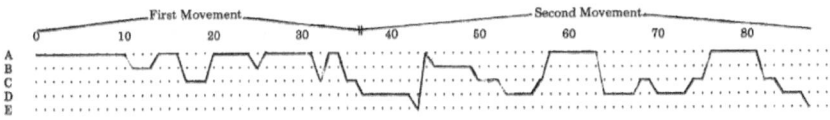

Figure 2

To appreciate Brown's craftsmanship, it would be useful to study the relationship between the various voices/levels of the poem both as they fit together in a thematic scheme, as in figure 1, and as they produce a pattern left by the poem itself as its action moves through the "time" of the poem, as in figure 2. Here the "time" is indicated by the lines of the poem, perpendicular to which appear the levels/voices which I have just enumerated.

We now have a kind of grid on which we can trace the movement, the action, and, indeed, the geometry of the poem, its essence summed up in an action that flows like an arpeggio of downward-turning blues. At a glance, we see the movement to the various levels, the duration of the stay, and the intervals between jumps, which vary from the dramatic movement from E to A (II. 43–44), after the descending pattern begun at I. 34, to jumps of a single level, as from A to B in II. 44–45. If we check the text at the movement from E to A, we discover that here at the midpoint of the poem the drummer has just played a break which makes a frivolous and ironic comment on the preceding level, D, which had just introduced the real world into the poem. In its frivolous ambiguity, the break is a dramatic introduction to the second movement of the poem at the same time that it propels the movement along as "the girls wiggle and twist." We may note also that, at the last time at this level of the poem (E, I. 87), the trumpet unmistakably echoes the words "MUDDY WATER" from level C, I. 83, commenting in its Dadaistic way on the nothingness of life. One notes too, by way of structure, that the first instrumental appearance seems to be the drums; the second, the trumpet. Finally, level E represents an onomatopoetic extension and intensification of level C, thus faithfully following the tradition in Black music of employing the voice as an instrument.

If the poet presents the blues through indirection in "Cabaret," in "Memphis Blues" he presents them through the matrix of the oral tradition which helped to shape their growth. The poem partly draws upon the traditional notion of "preaching the blues" found in both music and oral literature, but significantly it is not a parody of the sermon but a brilliant exploration of the song-sermon form in which the blues are historically and formally grounded. Its A-B-A form is a common song pattern and is shared by jazz and the sonata form. It is also the pattern which typical sermons take—text, development and application, repetition.[10] In the poem the enveloping sections are historical parallels to the present: "Was another Memphis / Mongst de olden days, / Done been destroyed // Like de other Memphis in / History." That is the warning of apocalypse, the sign of the Judgment. The poem is a blues sermon on the Last Judgment. The language evokes the hymns of Blind Willie Johnson, the Texas preacher who sang and played in blues style and tonality:

> See the sign of the Judgment
> Oh, yes, my Lord,
> Time is drawing nigh!

And the stage is set. The long middle section of the poem consists of six stanzas, each posing the ultimate question in the life of a Christian: Where will you be on the day when God sends down Judgment? It is the *Dies Irae*—Day of Anger, Day of Judgment, and a central theme of Western literature and art. One recalls the medieval plays *Every Man* and *The Castle of Perseverance*, and the other moralities which address the theme in a form comprehensible to the common man in fourteenth-century England. One remembers, too, Marlowe's Dr. Faustus imploring the heavenly spheres to cease and bring time to a halt. And who can forget the peal of the *Dies Irae* as it strikes fear and repentance into the heart of Goethe's Gretchen?

Most of the old-time preachers were probably ignorant of Goethe and the Faust legend, but they knew the Bible fairly well, especially the book of Revelations, and the most gifted of them knew enough history to draw lessons from it and to incorporate them into their sermons. Their knowledge was matched if not surpassed by superb rhetorical skills. The love of language was rooted in their culture. They sang: "Run, sinner, run and find yourself a hiding place." They admonished their congregations to work on the "building" for the Lord. They warned the gambler, the dancer, the drunkard, the "cussin' man," and the whoremonger to work on the building too, for the day was coming when "God's gonna separate the wheat from the tares." They questioned the sinner in his headlong flight: "O whar you runnin', sinner?" They asked him: "Sinner, what you goin' to do / When de devil git you?" And there would be nowhere for the sinner to go, for "there's no hiding place down here."[11]

Brown builds the middle section of his poem on the pattern of these songs of the Last Judgment, a pattern which is also used in the sermon. That pattern is reinforced by a smaller rhetorical pattern of concentrated and compressed Black cultural experience, a mascon, and in choosing it the poet goes to the ambivalent heart of the Black man's Christian heritage. He is both Christian and Black. He is a child of God, yet not a man. There are contradictions, and conflicts, but one kind of resolution is found in the blues. However, the blues that lie outside the church are the devil's music. Still the blues came out of the church, as the singers themselves say. Thus, there is no contradiction in the development of the poem. The first person to be addressed in the "Judgment Day pattern" is the Preacher Man—

> Watcha gonna do when Memphis on fire,
>   Memphis on fire, Mistah Preachin' Man?

And the Preachin' Man replies:

> Gonna pray to Jesus and nebber tire,
>   Gonna pray to Jesus, loud as I can,
>   Gonna pray to my Jesus, oh, my Lawd!

This is correct Christian behavior and the language and sentiments echo the Judgment Day spirituals cited above. Had the poet continued in this vein, the poem might have ended with a tonality and structure akin to the sermon-poems of James Weldon Johnson. But the poem is to be an experiment in blues tonality, as the title suggests, and we are not disappointed. Something remarkable and subtle begins to happen with the introduction of this answering refrain. For one thing, the poet has established perhaps the most characteristic pattern of Black oral/musical tradition, the call-and-response, and both parts of the pattern take delightful variations of rhythm, tone, and diction as the poem proceeds. Each variation in the "call" is like a chord change, which is developed by the "response."

Although tonally and thematically the first response recalls the spirituals, the rhythm is jazzy as in gospel music. In addition, a closer examination will reveal that the call-and-response pattern is enhanced by the familiar mascon qualities of the call and the anaphora of the response. The pattern also contains an artfully concealed extension of the blues form in which the two lines of the call constitute, in effect, the first two lines of a blues stanza, while the response is a rhetorical elaboration of the third line. However, instead of the quick turn or the punch line of the blues stanza, the response stretches out into a kind of jazz melody.

Although each "change" is distinctive, we remain in the same key, as it were, as the calls are made in sequence to the Preachin' Man, the Lovin' Man, the Music Man, the Workin' Man, the Drinkin' Man, and the Gamblin' Man. Each responds in his own way, in his own rhythm and accent, but all end up with the refrain "oh my Lawd!" first spoken by the Preachin' Man. This expression not only links the personal together, it allows for ironic variation of tone from the religious somberness of the opening section. In effect, the "Lawd" of the spirituals is subtly transformed by the "Lawd" of the blues.

The call also is a kind of blues riff which is not only found in blues songs but in other areas of the oral tradition. Thus, Big Bill Broonzy sings a song called "Honey O Babe" in which these lines appear:

> Whatcha gonna do when the pond goes dry, honey, honey?
> Whatcha gonna do when the pond goes dry, babe, babe?
> Whatcha gonna do when the pond grows dry?

And the response is:

> Sit up on the bank and watch the poor things die,
> Honey, O babe o' mine.

Novelist John O. Killens recalls a chant which children of his generation sang in Americus, Georgia. The first line is the call; the second, the response:

> Watcha gonna do when the world's on fire?
> Run like hell and *holler*, "fire!"

And Blind Lemon Jefferson sang, when John Killens was a little boy:

> Watcha gonna do when they send your man to war?
> Watcha gonna do—they send your man to war?

It is important, then, to realize that the call is a fundamental feature of blues style, and this particular call is one of the most deeply engrained in the oral tradition. This realization helps us to understand the structure of "Memphis Blues" and the reason that the title is justified. Each individual call, we may note further, is a kind of compressed blues experience, for the blues are a poetry of challenge and confrontation, and this fact is reflected in the poem's thematic concerns and its structure—its stanzas, its imagery, its rhythm, its diction, its overall shape.

In Memphis, Furry Lewis sings:

> Whatcha gonna do, your troubles get like mine?
> Whatcha gonna do, your troubles get like mine?

The wordless response comes ringing in from the guitar, but one ever-present possibility occurs in the response of another song:

> Get a handful of sugar and a mouthful of turpentine.

Again, diagrams help one to appreciate the poet's skill in the construction of "Memphis Blues."[12] Each of the six stanzas of the middle section possess the following structure. First is the *call*, which is a kind of riff that may be diagrammed as follows:

Mascon	Challenge
Challenge (repeat)	Persona

Next is the *response*, which may be diagrammed thus:

Anaphora —————	————— Statement
Anaphora —————	————— Intensification
Anaphora —————	—— Elaboration and refrain

As these diagrams dramatically demonstrate, the call is rather rigid, with a kind of singsong rhythm, characteristic of certain ritual language and of children's song. That quality is heightened by the repetition of the challenge. Variation is achieved and the poem is activated by changing the specific challenge in each call and, of course, by addressing a different persona. So we may list these elements in order: (1) "Memphis on fire," Preachin' Man; (2) "tall flames"—a variation—Lovin' Man; (3) "Memphis falls down," Music Man; (4) "de hurricane," Workin' Man; (5) "Memphis near gone," Drinkin' Man; and (6) "de flood roll fas'," Gamblin' Man. We may note that the poet achieves coherence in the call by specific mention of Memphis in calls 1, 3, and 5, and by citing the destructive forces of nature in 2, 4, and 6.

It is the response, however, in which we best see the skillful work in the poem. The anaphora builds up a driving, jazzy pattern which the second part of the line develops into a series of brilliant explorations of the melodic variety of Afro-American speech. In the first, the preacher's voice reaches a tender intensity when he prays to "my Jesus," with the initial fillip of "oh, my Lawd!" In the second, the Lovin' Man in a sensual stammer of alliteration is "gonna love my brownskin better'n before," and the emphasis is not on his being a "do right man," but on the miracle of "my brown baby," which parallels the language of the preacher. One of the most felicitous of the responses is the third, in which the poet sets up a rocking rhythm that suggests the piano's bass line, then suddenly shifts into a lovely scattering of treble notes. Here is the entire stanza:

> Ain' no skin
> Off de n[*****]'s back. All dese cities
> Ashes, rust. . . .
> De win' sing sperrichals
> Through deir dus'.

When questioned about the hurricane, the Workin' Man in the fourth stanza makes a heroic personal response which is crucial to an appreciation of the tone and significance of the entire poem. He will not give up, and he will not be content with praying. He'll put the buildings back again, to stand, and he takes pride in his energy, his will, and above all in his style: "Gonna push a wicked wheelbarrow, oh, my Lawd!" Even the Drinkin' Man will go down in style with his "pint bottle of Mountain Corn," and the stopper in his hand. Finally, we come to the Gamblin' Man:

> Flood roll fas', Mistah Gamblin' Man?
> Gonna pick up my dice fo' one las' pass—
> Gonna fade my way to de lucky lan',
> Gonna throw my las' seven—oh, my Lawd!

At this point we realize that the language of the poem in these six blues vignettes reflects Black life's emphasis upon style. That emphasis is at times overlooked and frequently misunderstood although it has attracted considerable attention from the media as well as the scholarly community. In effect, the style or the styling is an assertion of meaningfulness, not of frivolity or illusion, although there are, of course, assertions which may be so classified. An examination of the last response, then, is in order. The Gamblin' Man is not going to panic and fall down on his knees and beg God for mercy. That would be the coward's way. It would also be very "unhip." Death is final, but he meets it with a gambler's nerve, which is a kind of courage. He's not going to the Promised Land, but to the "lucky lan'," which he has created out of his own life, his own experience and values. He does not live in illusion and he takes responsibility for his life. The same thing applies to the Drinkin' Man, probably the most unsavory character of the group. Even he is going out in style: "Gonna get a *mean* jag on, oh, my Lawd!" These are not poor, benighted, superstitious foundlings in the hands of Fate, as Jean Wagner, for example, interprets Sterling Brown's characters,[13] but ordinary blues people, heroic in their own way. As for the Drinkin' Man, we understand him better when we recall Bill Broonzy's words: "I'm gonna keep on a drinkin' / Till good liquor carry me down." Note that it's *good* liquor and "Mountain Corn," made by experts for virtuoso drinkers. And lurking behind the response are the immortal lines: "I got the world in a jug, the stopper's in my hand." So sang Bessie Smith.

These last stanzas of the group prepare us for the return to the somber theme of mutability in the final section of the poem: "Memphis go / By Flood or Flame; / N[*****] won't worry / All de same— / Memphis go / Memphis come back." What warrants attention here is the loaded ambiguity of the last two lines, which one can read as an equation of the spirituals with the moaning of the wind, or as an existential projection of human value upon "objective," impersonal nature. And the songs are spirituals, not the blues, nor yet the songs of Tin Pan Alley, and the people have made them out of the substance of their lives, bleak though they might have been. An affirmation is made out of their courage, their strength, and their resilience, but equally out of their faith in themselves and their style. So, when one reexamines the poem with the haunting lyricism of its enveloping sections and the artful mastery and development of folk resources in the middle, one wonders why it has not received its critical due. And one has to conclude that some of the fault, at least, can be attributed to a patronizing attitude toward the folk themselves, whom the poem celebrates.

In this brief assessment of the "blues" poetry of Sterling Brown, I have tried to demonstrate that a closer examination of the work reveals that he is, indeed, a skillful and careful craftsman, but a full appreciation of his achievement is dependent on a knowledge of and a feeling for the dynamics of the folk culture, some aspects of which have only begun to receive serious and systematic attention during the past fifteen years. Failure to appreciate these dynamics leads on one hand to the casual snobbery of a usually judicious critic like Nathan I. Huggins, who writes after a brief look at "Memphis Blues": "Such poems of Langston Hughes's and Sterling Brown's defy criticism because they lack pretension. They do not ask for academic acclaim; thus, they are exempt from its contempt. In truth, Hughes was not writing to be approved as a literary poet (Brown sometimes did)." He continues, asserting that Hughes "expected his poems to be taken on the simple and unpretentious level on which they were written." By adopting folk forms, Huggins states, Hughes, and presumably Brown, obtained a freedom which while important in itself "deprived him of the control and mastery that might make each (or indeed any) of his poems really singular. Langston Hughes avoided the Scylla of formalism only to founder in the Charybdis of folk art."[14]

On the other hand, failure to respect the dynamics of the folk base also leads to distortions, and misinterpretation of the thematic aspects of Brown's art. In this regard, Jean Wagner—despite Robert Bone's citation of his "capacity for empathy" and his ability to "surmount linguistic and cultural barriers"[15]—manages to cramp the blues nuances of Brown's poetry into a rather mechanical universe of foolish faith and stoic endurance.[16] That Brown's view of life as expressed in the poems is tragic there is no doubt, but that view is expressed in terms which grow naturally out of the blues perspective, and, at times, the blues form in its many permutations. Brown's achievement, like that of the blues themselves, is a special kind of synthesis. Brown is not a folk poet, but a poet in the folk manner, who cunningly conceals his craft in the stylistics of the tradition itself. He not only mastered the academic studies and sources of his people's lore but the principles undergirding the lore itself. Thus his remarkable ability to render the sounds of speech, its nuances of rhythm and texture and meaning, was nourished not so much by his thorough knowledge of the literature written in dialect as by his immersion in the actual flow of the oral tradition, in the country homes of his students, in the barbershops and cafés of the South—Lynchburg, Atlanta, New Orleans—in all the varied places where Black folks gathered and talked and told lies, screamed at children, and sang the blues, or moaned the spirituals. He understood the contradictions in the people and in himself, and he did not sentimentalize them. He treated them roughly in his analysis, as Wagner indicates, but no rougher really than they treated themselves, not only in the dozens but in the whole range of the tradition, because survival and affirmation were their implicit objectives. If he is cynical at times and despairing, so are they. But the cynicism of the blues is ultimately cleansing. It sets limits and reinforces them—the blues allow for hope, for endurance, and, above all, for the very control that Huggins speaks of, but control of a deeper sort—moral control. Big Bill Broonzy, for example, recalls working deep in a hole under a city street. As he glanced up, he noticed another, earlier level where workers used to stand. He laughed to himself at the irony.

Here he was a Black man "lookin' up at down." And he wrote a song about it. Memphis singer Furry Lewis, still alive at this writing, once sang about his misfortune: "My shoes done got thin. / I'm back on my feet again." So much for progress. And even before the Depression, long before then, someone sang, "I been down so long it seems like up to me." And we link up the insights with Sterling Brown's poetry, in which the heavy water blues absorb the "chilling" social analysis and transmute the elegiac vestiges of his youth into a unique testament of the human will to endure.

NOTES

1. On the blues as a poetry of confrontation, see S. E. Henderson, "Blues for the Young Black Man," *Negro Digest*, Aug. 1967; S. E. Henderson, "*Southern Road*: A Blues Perspective," *New Directions*, July 1975. See also Albert Murray, *Stomping the Blues* (New York: McGraw-Hill, 1976), 250–52. Note, too, Murray's caption to the photos of dancers at the Savoy Ballroom, which reads, "Saturday Night pas de deux uptown any night, Confrontation . . . improvisation . . . affirmation . . . celebration." Ibid., 12.

2. Sterling A. Brown, *Southern Road* (1932; repr., Boston: Beacon Press, 1974). All references are made to the 1974 edition.

3. B. A. Botkin, ed., *Folk-Say IV: The Land Is Ours* (Norman: University of Oklahoma Press, 1932), 252 ff.

4. Botkin, *Folk-Say IV*, 251 ff.

5. For further discussion, see Murray, *Stomping the Blues*, 23–42, esp. for the important distinction made between the "Saturday Night Function" and the "Sunday Morning Service." See also James H. Cone, *The Spirituals and the Blues* (New York: Seabury Press, 1972), esp. chap. 6; Paul Oliver, *Conversation with the Blues* (London: Cassell, 1965); William Ferris Jr., *Blues from the Delta* (London: Studio Vista, 1970). Commenting on the "unity" of Black music from the viewpoint of jazz musicians, Donald Byrd states, "When I use the term jazz, I speak of all Black music." Donald Byrd, "The Meaning of Black Music," *Black Scholar* 3, no. 1 (Summer 1972): 30. Max Roach takes a different approach: "They are misnomers: Jazz music, rhythm and blues, rock and roll, gospel, spirituals, blues, folk music." Max Roach, "What 'Jazz' Means to Me," *Black Music* 3, no. 10 (Summer 1972): 6.

6. *Sixteen Poems of Sterling A. Brown Read by Sterling A. Brown*, produced and ed. Frederic Ramsey Jr., Folkways Records FL 9794, 1973.

7. Paul Oliver, *The Meaning of the Blues* (New York: Collier Books, 1963), 263, 266, 267.

8. Sterling Stuckey, introduction to *Southern Road*, by Sterling A. Brown (1932; repr., Boston: Beacon Press, 1974), xxvii.

9. On "elegant indirection," see Stephen Henderson, *Understanding the New Black Poetry: Black Speech and Black Music as Poetic References* (New York: William Morrow, 1973), 33–41. Cf. Murray, *Stomping the Blues*, 214: "The preeminent embodiment of the blues musician as artist was Duke Ellington, who, in the course of fulfilling the role of entertainer, not only came to address himself to the basic imperatives of music as a fine

art but also achieved the most comprehensive synthesis, extension, and refinement to date of all the elements of blues musicianship."

10. The repetition may be obliquely expressed or expressed through nonverbal means. In either case, the completion is recognized by the congregation. In an unpublished doctoral dissertation, "The Performed African-American Sermon," Gerald L. Davis develops a model of the sermon from intensive field work and a study of recordings. He provides a close critique of the scholarly literature, especially the work of Bruce A. Rosenberg and Albert B. Lord. Gerald L. Davis, "The Performed African-American Sermon" (PhD diss., University of California, Berkeley, 1978).

11. Howard W. Odum and Guy B. Johnson, *The Negro and His Songs: A Study of Typical Negro Songs in the South* (1925; repr., Hatboro: Folklore Associates, 1964), 72, 77. Citations refer to the 1964 edition.

12. The diagrams, especially figure 3, are intended chiefly to show the location of structural elements, not their function.

13. Jean Wagner, *Black Poets of the United States*, trans. Kenneth Douglas (Urbana: University of Illinois Press, 1973), 483–90.

14. Nathan I. Huggins, *Harlem Renaissance* (New York: Oxford University Press, 1971), 226–27.

15. Robert Bone, foreword to *Black Poets of the United States*, by Jean Wagner, trans. Kenneth Douglas (Urbana: University of Illinois Press, 1973), xiii.

16. See Wagner's entire discussion of Sterling Brown, especially his discussion of the poem "Southern Road" and the section entitled "The Inanity of Faith." Wagner, *Black Poets*, 489–95. Wagner misses the nuances of Brown's position and, apparently, much of his art.

ONE MORE TIME

THE BLACK AGENDA REVISITED

Paper presented at the Institute of the Black World, Atlanta, GA, 1982.

There are two related themes in this presentation. The first is a somewhat personal statement about my relationship to the Institute of the Black World [IBW] and the Atlanta University Center and my present work at Howard University. The second is a "challenge for the 1980s."

Since this is a kind of homecoming, let me begin with the personal. I came back to Atlanta in 1962. I had previously been a student at Morehouse College in the late forties and I came back to Atlanta because of the civil rights movement and the intellectual ferment in the city. I remained in Atlanta until 1971 after we had established the IBW. I went to Howard University that fall and now I return once again in 1982. Twenty years is a long time, twenty years out of your life. I name the years—1962, 1963, 1964, 1967, 1968—and immediately one perceives the rush of historical and cultural events that gather about and define the personal. Here in Atlanta around 1963 and 1964, to begin with, there was a growing awareness of cultural developments in the nation. I hold in abeyance now the death of Medgar Evers; I am not talking about the March on Washington, or the Voting Rights Act, or the Vietnam War, but they are presences and forces. I am talking about cultural activity. Specifically, I am talking about *Dasein Magazine* at Howard University in 1962, one of the pathbreaking student productions in the country at that time. There are a group of students calling themselves the Howard Poets who laid the groundwork for some of the major discussions of aesthetics that developed in the seventies. The first issue of *Dasein* was in 1961. In 1962, in New York City, another group of young artists, including persons like Ishmael Reed and Tom Dent, published a periodical called *Umbra* that is highly significant in the history of the period. By 1967, a group of students at North Carolina Central University were publishing a journal called *Ex Umbra: Out of the Shadows*. It was also very important. By 1965 there was a journal coming out of New York called the *Liberator*. The cultural editor was Larry Neal. By 1968, *Black Fire* appeared, an anthology which was, and still is, a monument to that period relative to the history of Black American literature and Black American culture. *Black Fire* was published and edited by LeRoi Jones [Amiri Baraka] and Larry Neal. The crucial thing about the book was the fact that it began with an ideological position, and gathered together some of the most radical politics, and some of the best writing of the time.

Here at Atlanta University in 1967, Bernice Reagon, Dennis Jarrett, and I presented a program called "Soul Roots" in Sale Hall Chapel. One of the most important aspects of the experience was the fact that Dr. Benjamin Elijah Mays contributed $2,000 to the program. That was a *very important* crossing of generational lines for me because Dr. Mays knew exactly what we were trying to do.

What we were trying to do was to bring to this academic community something of the fervor, something of the spirit, something of the poetry of Black people that we took for granted. And what that program signified to us was the unification of Black people across class and generation lines. We brought these students face-to-face with their mothers and their fathers, their grandfathers and grandmothers, with the bridge that took them across.

That was an event for Sale Hall Chapel. That was an event for Morehouse College, for 1967 was the centennial of Morehouse College and Howard University, and we showed them the bridge that had taken them across. Babe Stovall from New Orleans was a bridge; so was Bernice Reagon, who had discovered him for us. And Babe Stovall played "When the Saints Come Marching In," and tore the place up. And the gospel music made the ceiling ring—the Free for All Baptist Choir and David Whitfield's Grace Gospel Singers at Clark College, the fabulous Thurman Specials. And there was Bernice herself and there was Liz Spraggins. And what happened in essence was that the whole space was transformed.

And that idea of transformation is one of the ideas, one of the aspects of sensibility, that reached lovely fruition in the 1960s and the 1970s, the idea of creating a space of your own for your own. The idea of creating a space, to humanize that space, to take over a conventional structure and transform the relationships between speaker and audience because here, for example, we're standing above you, and so forth. Bernice has powerful feelings about that. At any rate, that same person is now at the Smithsonian Institution where she has introduced some of the models that were developed right here and in other stations of the civil rights movement and the freedom struggle including the idea of shaping a space to include the vibrations and thoughts of the people.

Relative to this point was a series of concerts in late 1966 that involved the Atlanta University Choir during which Dr. Willis Lawrence James introduced African music for the first time. At the 1966 Christmas concert there was the expected variety of songs, some with traditional arrangements, some with more modern harmonies, and some from other cultures, and refreshingly, there was a gospel-like song. At first the response, conditioned by the architecture and the tradition, was demure, but Liz Spraggins, the soloist, took a little trill to her voice, a gospel turn, and immediately a nervous laughter, a kind of holy laughter went through that audience with a thrill. That was the antecedent of "Soul Roots," for in 1967, we pulled out all of the stops. There was a "Soul Roots" concert again in 1968, but 1967 was the miracle year. In 1967 also, a group of poets sponsored by the Woodrow Wilson Foundation visited Morehouse and other Southern colleges, two white poets and two Black poets, Donald Finkel, Paul Blackburn, A. B. Spellman, and Jay Wright. The two white poets read first and then Spellman said, "We arranged it this way because I want to make a statement." And he spoke about the political and cultural importance of Black poetry. That statement made a link between the campus and the national community beyond. It was a manifesto that signaled a radicalization both of consciousness and curriculum. As far as I can recall, there were just two courses in Black literature (or Negro literature as it was called then) being taught in the entire Atlanta University Center. One was taught at Spelman and the other at Morris Brown. But things were changing, and perceptive students and faculty were starting to question everything, not least of which was the curriculum. These then were the beginnings of what was later to be called the Black Curriculum, the initial framework that led to the creation of IBW and its agenda. So, the Black Curriculum was an important presence here, and is, in effect responsible for your presence here today. We are still discussing curriculum because the Black Curriculum is still relevant, to use that vintage word from the period. The Black Curriculum and the cultural movement were aspects of the same phenomenon. In Atlanta, by the summer of 1967, the Atlanta University Center Council of Presidents had approved a proposal that was submitted to them from the committee of faculty and students that they had appointed to study the various curriculum offerings here and to make recommendations for change. And all of us went through that analysis, including the students who came from northern universities to participate in the project. Finally, we wrote a proposal that furthered the movement toward meaningful change.

That movement was toward both personal and institutional liberation. In the summer of 1967 then, an institute in Black Culture was conducted at Spelman College under the administrative direction of Dr. Melvin Drummer, which helped establish a nucleus of personnel and ideas around which a coherent set of courses would whirl in a little Black cosmos of their own. Amazingly, the instructors themselves found a measure of liberation for the talents and knowledge that the existing curriculum did not allow them to express. A single case in point is Dr. Wendell Whalum, a distinguished scholar and choir master who, we discovered, was an unsung authority on gospel music, which is one of the most fertile of Black musical traditions. Had there been no "Soul Roots Festival" had there been no Black Curriculum movement, we might never have known this aspect of his musical gifts. But in 1967, at Spelman College at the Summer Institute in Black Culture, Wendell Whalum delivered a series of absolutely fabulous lectures on the history of Afro-American music.

The Black Curriculum idea was to overlap other ideas, first that of Black Studies, then of the Black University. Around the time that the Black Curriculum idea was circulating in the South and in the North, the Black Studies idea had clearly emerged in the North and in the West. As the two started to overlap, there was a broadening and a mutual reinforcement. The Black Studies idea seemed to take hold immediately, and shortly after, about 1968, there evolved the concept of the Black University. All of this was happening in a period of about a year and a half to two years. This rapid growth and dissemination of ideas resulted from two main factors, the forums provided by Black periodicals like *Black World*, *Soul Book*, *Ebony*, *Liberator*, and others, and the proliferation of conferences on Black affairs on both Black and white campuses. By 1970, there was a conference on the Black University at Howard University organized by Acklyn Lynch and designed to debate the idea of a Black University. In 1970, the AHSA (African Historical Studies Association) Conference was also held at Howard University. And at Jackson State College in the same year, Margaret Walker held a major conference on Black Curriculum. The death of Martin Luther King Jr. two years earlier had radicalized the entire movement, and in the report of the Atlanta University Curriculum Development Committee, there is a sudden right-angle turn as the academic discussion suddenly runs into political reality. That reality was addressed by the Black University which embodied at once the Black Curriculum and the Black Studies idea, and both of these ideas were very controversial. Even Vincent Harding was bothered at first. And he wrote his now famous open letter to the Northern students to call their attention to the problems of logistics—Who was going to teach these courses?—and the problems surrounding the survival of Black colleges in the South.

The ideas were controversial because they demanded radical change. The Black University, Black Studies, and later the Black Aesthetic were all part of a more fundamental concept, a sociopolitical concept, essentially a political concept, the idea of the Black college. And it's difficult to talk about these things because one can begin almost anywhere and go in any direction. Take for example, the concept of oratorical style, and place it in the context of Martin Luther King Jr., H. Rap Brown, and Stokely Carmichael, or Amiri Baraka, and you immediately realize what happened. The quality of the change resulted from the strategy of the change, and the strategy was both political and aesthetic.

This was so because a fundamental assumption of the emerging ideology was that aesthetic structures and mechanisms needed grounding in the mores, in the life patterns of the people. Rap Brown wasn't called Rap for nothing. He was called Rap because he could "rap." Rapping was a kind of poetry but Rap was not a poet. Stokely was not a poet. The point is, LeRoi Jones [Amiri Baraka] was. Haki Madhubuti [Don L. Lee] was. There should have been no wonder then that this was a time when there was a tremendous efflorescence of Black poetry, a phenomenon that has scarcely been touched. When it is finally and sympathetically examined, I think we will find that this period was just as great as the Harlem Renaissance ever was. But the analysis should be not merely for its own sake but to extrapolate from the concrete situations the life-giving patterns, the life-sustaining patterns of our people.

At the IBW, I worked on some wonderful curriculum ideas with Chet Davis, and later with Howard Dodson. We were compiling a volume of statements and case histories on Black Studies that was designed as a guide to the directors of those programs. The range of our attempt and ambition astonishes me today. We did not complete the work, but had we done so the whole course of the movement might have been different. Fledgling administrators, under enormous pressures to perform impossible tasks, would have found some of the moral support and practical advice that they needed, but ideological diversions held up the project. At any rate, we began 1970 with the idea of curriculum in mind. That fall we held a conference and retreat at Idlewild, Michigan. Our aim was to bring together the best minds, the most successful and most innovative people in the Black Studies movement to help us plan a Black agenda for the 1970s. Later the idea of a Black agenda was taken up on the national level. I don't know how many people realized our role in it, but at IBW we knew that we were studying ideas in motion and challenging the existing leadership.

All of us had our position papers to present and I read a paper entitled "Black Saturation: A View of the Humanities." The chief ideas from that paper are, in my view, still worthy of attention. That is why this present attempt is titled "One More Time: The Black Agenda Revisited." Now before that, on the committee here at Atlanta University in 1968, I presented a paper which contributed to the final statement entitled "Course Saturation in the Black College." I mention this in order to show that the most crucial idea in my theoretical statements about Black Culture—the idea of saturation—derives directly from my encounters with students, faculty, and administration during those years from 1967 to 1971. As early as 1967, one of those students came to me and raised questions about the course content and emphasis at Morehouse and the other schools in the Atlanta University Center. Why, he asked in sum, why don't we deal with the Black Experience in our courses? I had mulled over the idea and I was thinking of putting into the period courses all of the Black Experience that "should" be there. But the student said to me, "No, you don't put anything into the period, you pull something out of it." And I realized that he had moved me from mere pedagogical principles to those that were political and philosophical and moral. The truth, then—that's what saturation is about. Coming here today I went back in my mind over the idea of saturation to see just what it was that I was trying to say over ten years ago. I thought of the people who had met with us at Idlewild and I thought about the Black University debates. I thought especially about those pragmatists who had enabled structural changes to be made at their institutions. One such person was Andrew Billingsley, who was then vice president of Academic Affairs at Howard. In my Idlewild paper, I spoke of his social awareness, what he had done. I said:

> This kind of awareness cannot be left to chance, if we are to survive. The experience of Blackness, in all of its dimensions, cannot be left to a handful of students who specialize in literature, or art, or history. It must be an integral part of any serious attempt to prepare our children and our youth to live and to flourish and to prevail in this country. On the level of formal education it means a total involvement—to the point of illumination, commitment, and action—in the life of the Black community, by whatever means the structures and mechanisms from the school can provide us.

I saw this as part of the Black University and the traditional Black college as well. I continued as follows:

I am not speaking about indoctrination. I am speaking of *saturation*, which means, again, simply absorbing as much of the Black Experience as one can, as much as one needs to find out who he is and what he must do to go where he must, with his people, for without them there *is* no identity except the one which the West has foisted upon us and which we know all too well. Again, *saturation* is reached when the Black man in America understands, accepts, utilizes, and celebrates his Blackness, then becomes as unselfconscious about it as his brothers are on the ancestral continent. He and his community are one and move together, for as we discover who we are, we realize what we have to do, and we exert our energies toward the acquisition of the proper skills and techniques.

Thus, *saturation* can be spoken of as: (a) a condition or goal, specifically a kind of total health or well-being; (b) a mechanism or process in attaining that condition or goal. With specific reference to education, *saturation* can be viewed as the end product of the Black University replacing the outworn concept of the "well-rounded man," the "Victorian gentleman" of John Henry Newman, who seems to be the model in theory for so many of our colleges and schools.

I was talking specifically about our courses in the humanities because they very obviously affected the development of the value system of the students and because this was an area where we had accumulated substantial scholarship from previous generations to build upon. In sum, out of this notion of saturation in a curricular sense I have tried to develop the idea of saturation in others, particularly the aesthetic. Thus, the concept itself comes out of a great educational need, one that certainly is with us still.

Although my paper at the Idlewild conference was entitled "Black Art and Culture in the 1970s," it was rooted in the Black Curriculum and Black University debates of fifteen years ago. Since fifteen years is a big chunk out of one's life, it is not just a little unsettling that we should be addressing the same issues in the 1980s. Notwithstanding, I call attention once again to the profound importance of Black Culture in any appraisal of Western and, indeed, world civilization. And today as then, I believe that the revolutionary and liberating potential of Black Culture is simply the truth itself. The truth of Africa. The truth of the daughters and sons of Africa. If Black people really passionately felt that truth and acted from it, they would free themselves.

First, however, there were four major sets of problems which had to be addressed in systematic fashion. As far as I can see, those problems still exist, but in 1970 they were so vast and their solutions so urgent that I felt that an institute, fully staffed with our brightest scholars and artists should be established to work exclusively on them so as to affect fundamental changes in the way we view ourselves and our destiny. With the IBW experience in mind, I was projecting an institute that particularly addressed problems of the humanities and the arts.

Fortunately, Dr. Billingsley was attending the conference and had been seriously thinking about the role of the Black University. He brought institutional structure and substance to many of the ideas that others merely debated. So, in 1971, Howard University received a grant for the establishment of an Institute for Advanced Studies in the Humanities. I was eventually brought into that activity, but the main point is that the proposal and the subsequent development of the Institute for Advanced Studies in the Humanities relied substantially upon some of the things that happened at the Idlewild conference, not the least of which, perhaps, was an acceptance of the idea of saturation and the classification of certain problems that exist in reference to the humanities. This institute blueprint eventually produced the Howard University Institute for the Arts and the Humanities. Thus, we can plainly see how certain ideas, generated in the Atlanta University Center, and tempered by historical events, were shaped by various IBW conferences and made accessible to others. Notwithstanding these modest successes, nowhere, to my knowledge, does there exist the kind of center that I had in mind. The problems that existed in 1971 still exist today, for the artist, the scholar, the activist, and the teacher. They are:

(1) Problems of incomplete knowledge
(2) Problems of discontinuous knowledge
(3) Problems of distorted knowledge
(4) Problems of apathy and inferiority feelings about Black art and culture

Let us look briefly at them as they apply to the study of literature and art.

1. *Problems of incomplete knowledge.* These are essentially problems of scholarship. In literature, for example, they include knowledge of persons, canons, periods. The period which seems to attract the greatest attention is that of the 1920s and 30s, variously called the Harlem Renaissance, the Negro Renaissance, or the New Negro Movement. The writers who seem to attract the greatest attention are Langston Hughes and Jean Toomer. More recently some attention has focused on Sterling Brown, who denies the existence of a "Harlem Renaissance." The generation that matured in the 1940s is beginning to attract serious attention and major work has been done on some of them. Among them are Gwendolyn Brooks, Ralph Ellison, and especially Richard

Wright. But work needs to be done on Robert Hayden, for example. However, writers of the sixties who created some of the most moving literature of their time have scarcely received any critical or scholarly attention at all. Often their work has not even been reviewed. We can't, of course, evaluate their work if we don't know about it. We can't project extensions from it if we don't know it, or take it seriously. Among the 60s writers who have received book-length examination, the only two that I know are Haki Madhubuti and Amiri Baraka. Others are obviously deserving of attention—in books, theses, dissertations, and critical articles. These studies can and should take many forms, from the bibliographical to the interpretive.

2. *Problems of discontinuous knowledge.* By this I mean the lack of knowledge which connects smaller bodies of information into larger "wholes"—the individual anecdotes and memoirs, the shared experiences that enable us to speak of a "Harlem Renaissance" or a "*Dasein group*" or an "*Umbra group*" or a "Harlem Writers Guild." Projects that address these problems are often of long duration, and require dedication and skill, sometimes the dedication of a lifetime, as in John Lovell's forty years of work on the spirituals which eventuated in *The Forge and the Flame: The Story of How the Afro-American Spiritual Was Hammered Out.*

Relevant to the sixties and to any projection for the 1980s, of course, are the relationships among the various Black literatures which have developed around the world—literatures which Janheinz Jahn called "neo-African." The 1960s and early 70s were a period of "Pan-Africanism" where everyone read [W. E. B.] Du Bois and [Frantz] Fanon; when Black Americans became aware of the modern and traditional literatures of Africa and the Caribbean. The groundwork is now being laid for meaningful comparative studies, just as in the world of the creative artist a cultural cross-fertilization has taken place as evidenced in the poetry of Keorapetse Kgositsile, Kalamu ya Salaam, Jay Wright, Jayne Cortez, and Ntozake Shange to name a few. Among the important works are Wilfred Cartey's *Whispers from a Continent*, O. R. Dathorne's *The Dark Ancestor*, and the bibliography on Black Caribbean women, compiled by Maurice Lubin and Janet Sims.

These "problems" of criticism and scholarship are perhaps the most interesting of all because they challenge the critic and scholar to create seedbeds of ideas, force fields of possibility that help propel the creative writer and artist into even more daring exploration.

Other interesting work in this area includes Lorenzo Thomas's essay in *Obsidian*, "The Crowns of Thoth," written on Ishmael Reed; Houston Baker's *The Journey Back*; and Robert Stepto's *Afro-American Literature: The Reconstruction of Instruction.*

3. The *problems of distorted knowledge* are the result either of ignorance or political decision. They must be approached, then, through education. When properly perceived, decisions regarding education, whether one's own, or one's community, are political. They must be approached, therefore, with a clear assumption about the truth of the situation, that is a workable model of the truth. It is unnecessary to fight all of the negative responses to Black literature and art; but it is necessary to fight on all levels of the responses—the pedagogical, the critical, the scholarly, the creative. And one must be willing to examine positions that are antithetical to one's own, for even in these one might find something useful. A good deal of the critical talk and writing of the 1960s dealt with these distortions. As late as 1974—the Institute for the Arts and the Humanities devoted an entire conference to "The Image of Black Folk in American Literature." The conference director was then writer in residence at Howard University John Oliver Killens. That kind of battle unfortunately will have to be continued into the 1980s and probably beyond, for the central truth is anathema to the Western world—that truth is our awareness of Africa as the cradle of the human race and of human civilization.

Our heritage is evoked by the life work of dedicated persons like W. E. B. Du Bois, William Leo Hansberry, John H. Clarke, Cheikh Anta Diop, Vincent Harding, and Margaret Walker Alexander. More recently, we have had to add a fine young scholar from Rutgers University, Professor Ivan Van Sertima, author of *They Came before Columbus: The African Presence in the New World* and editor of *Journal of African Civilizations*. Here is potentially the most revolutionary idea of all. It is so threatening to the Western nations and cultures that they have expended billions of dollars and destroyed millions of lives in order to suppress it. I speak, to be sure, not merely of the slave trade and the regenerative effect of Alex Haley's *Roots*, but of the American educational system, and the French, the British, and the Dutch. I speak of the publishing industry; of the media. I speak of national immigration policy vis-à-vis Haiti. Attitudes toward modern Africa, and for that matter, toward the entire Third World. I speak of the deadly impotence of a country whose leadership is caught in a web of electronic signals, which "primitive" countries have learned to master. I speak of the confusion of appearance and reality. I speak of the stuff that constitutes both art and civilization when all is said and done—energy and ideas and decisions, values and spirit. I speak of Walter Cronkite as candidate for president and Ronald Reagan as president. I speak of Dr. Strangelove and Newspeak. I speak of the secret in the Black psyche embodied in a "cliché" blues line, "You can read my letter but you sure can't read my mind."

4. The last group of problems still abide, unfortunately with us. If you have any doubt, just examine at random a group of textbooks of American literature of the 20th century. Look at the patterns. Examine the books at Black schools and white schools. Is there much difference? Examine the curriculum. Examine the theses and dissertations proposed on Black writers—at Black schools. One must conclude that the *apathy and feelings of inferiority* are still there. A proper addressing of the first three groups of problems would help to eliminate them.

On the most elementary level these are problems of education, problems, if you please, of curriculum building, as well as the scholarship that supports such curriculum. They will not be solved by this generation, and neither will they be solved by the next because they are built-in problems, structural problems, that, eventually call for a reordering of society. That, too, is our task. Let us do our part, then, in our time, so that the struggle may continue.

MODERNITY AND OTHER DIRECTIONS IN AFRO-AMERICAN LITERATURE

REFLECTIONS ON THE PAST TWO DECADES

Published in *The Next Decade: Theoretical and Research Issues in Africana Studies,*
edited by James E. Turner, 109–20. Ithaca: Cornell University Press, 1984.

Our task—an examination of Black literature of the past two decades—is complex and challenging. Part of this complexity stems from the literature itself, part from the times which produced it, part from the proximity to it, and part from the nature of its reception.

Notwithstanding these problems—and they are difficult, some probably insoluble—we are all aware not only of the considerable quantity of that literature, but also of its peculiar vitality and, more recently, its neglect.

The topic of this panel, "Modernity and Other Directions in Afro-American Literature," contains several terms which merit attention. The first is "modernity" by which the framers of the conference signify the "immediate present" of the writers and their work. The second is "other directions," which implies movement in a discernible pattern or path toward a consciously or unconsciously assumed goal. Thus, the topic assumes a pattern, however complex or obscure, in Afro-American literature, a movement (or complex of movements) towards these goals. In other words we ask ourselves, where has Black literature been heading over the past twenty years? Where is it presently headed?

Such questions beg other questions, of course, and in order to avoid this fallacy, as much as possible with my limited knowledge, let me say that it is foolhardy, wasteful, and misleading to speak about the "direction" of Black literature without attempting to establish some bearings, some sense of logical and historical location. As readers, consumers, students, and ideally, as cocreators of literature, we quickly perceive our limitations. We must have organizing principles and categories to work with; but we are so close to the literature that such organization is difficult and deceptive as categories coalesce and assume unwieldy size or fragment themselves in bewildering numbers. And thus, we are left with two basic things, a set of problems, which may be addressed in systematic fashion; and a set of perceptions and impressions. They are, perhaps, two sides of the same coin. The *problems*, as they appear to me are situations which require the assistance of scholarship. They are:

(1) Problems of incomplete knowledge
(2) Problems of discontinuous knowledge
(3) Problems of distorted knowledge or misinterpretation

These problems may occur in any period of Black literature, or of any literature; however, quite obviously they are affected by other considerations, some of which are mentioned at the beginning of this paper—the nature of the literature itself, the times which produced it, its reception, and our proximity to it. To repeat, there are problems and challenges to the scholar and critic. As we shall see later, the creative writer has another set of problems, some of which are related to these and some which are peculiarly the artist's, in this case, the Black writer.

At any rate, both the scholar/critic and the creative writer are involved, consciously or not, in this business of "direction." The latter may want to do his or her "own thing"—make a personal statement—which may turn out to be from the scholar's perspective a "typical direction," a typical impulse, style, ideology of a given period or set of parameters. It should not be difficult, then, to see how "incomplete knowledge" of what others are doing, or of a given subject/theme may result in the differing kinds of evaluations suggested above. An example of this would be the poems on the Black matriarch which were so popular in the 1960s, although there were excellent earlier treatments of the theme/subject by Owen Dodson, Sterling Brown, and others. Thus, Don L. Lee [Haki R. Madhubuti] in a poem to his grandmother is certainly making a personal statement, at the same time he is also making a "typical" statement of the 1960s, exploring a typical topic of Afro-American poetry.

To elaborate somewhat, problems of incomplete knowledge include knowledge of persons, canons, and periods. The period of Afro-American literature which seems to have attracted the greatest scholarly interest is the 1920s and 30s, variously called the Harlem Renaissance, the Negro

Renaissance, or the New Negro Movement. Writers who have attracted the greatest attention are Langston Hughes and Jean Toomer. More recently, some attention has focused on Sterling Brown, who pointedly denies the existence of a "Harlem Renaissance," and Zora Neale Hurston. The following generation that matured in the 1940s, including such writers as Gwendolyn Brooks, Margaret Walker, Robert Hayden, Ralph Ellison, and especially Richard Wright, is gradually attracting attention. For the 1950s, the interest has largely centered on James Baldwin.

Meantime, the Black writers of the 1960s and early 1970s who created some of the most moving and challenging literature of their time have scarcely received any critical or scholarly attention at all. Often their work has not even been reviewed, and even when it has been, the result is often cursory or superficial. We cannot evaluate their work, of course, if we don't know about it. We certainly can't project extensions from it if we neither know it nor take it seriously. But even honest, well-intentioned efforts run headlong into the problem of incomplete knowledge, which in the case of recent and contemporary writers is formidable. Many of the writers who came into prominence in this period are still fairly young—in their middle 30s or early 40s—and have not completed their canon, so to speak, although we have no way of ascertaining this, since a writer's canon may be closed long before the end of his or her life. In addition, a writer's published work may indicate a small fraction of the "canon." Fortunately, there have been some salutary moves, to correct this situation, prominent among them being the example of Random House in the publication of the works of Henry Dumas, under the editorship of Eugene Redmond. Another prominent example is the *Selected Plays and Prose of Amiri Baraka / LeRoi Jones* and *Selected Poetry of Amiri Baraka / LeRoi Jones* which represent a kind of interim report on his impressive talent.

But there are many others, so numerous, in fact, that they are easily overlooked, especially if they published only a few works or were not "widely anthologized," as the cliché goes. How is one, then, to organize all of that information? How is one to find it in the first place? I would say through the traditional methods of research, to begin with, and then by employing the most sophisticated and efficient means that are currently available. Indeed, the beginnings of that work are emerging. And as examples, I cite the following: Eugene Redmond's *Drum Voices: The Mission of Afro-American Poetry* [1976]; A. Johnson and R. Johnson, *Propaganda and Aesthetics: The Literary Politics of Afro-American Magazines in the 20th Century* [1991]; Barbara Christian, *Black Women Novelists: The Development of a Tradition, 1892–1976* (1980); Janet L. Sims, *The Progress of Afro-American Women: A Selected Bibliography and Resource Guide* (1980).

These studies can and should take many forms, from the bibliographical to the interpretive. Those cited above are merely examples of the kind of necessary spadework which remains to be done. This is chiefly the work of the professional scholar; and since the task is so enormous and its achievement so important, the role of institutions like the Africana Studies and Research Center is crucial although all of us, of course, can play our part, however modest, in addressing the "built-in" problem of *incomplete knowledge*.

The writers themselves have a special obligation to the resolution of this problem which they can fulfill as they see fit. First, they should organize and preserve their literary legacy of notes, MSS [manuscripts], both published and unpublished, their memorabilia, their autobiographies, etc., and make those materials available to a Black institution, either in stages or in toto, as a bequest. Atlanta University, for example, has some MS poems of Gwendolyn Brooks from her early work. The writers can help us also by publishing collections of their topical work, as in Ishmael Reed's *Shrovetide in Old New Orleans*, or their autobiographies, as in Addison Gayle's *Wayward Child* and Julius Lester's *All Is Well*. And in addition to autobiographies, interviews are vital sources of information. To be sure the problem of incomplete knowledge will always be with us, since there is no consensus of what "complete knowledge" should be, or even whether it would be attainable; notwithstanding, we obviously need a base of information about our literature and our culture, especially during this period, upon which we can erect the political and aesthetic structures necessary for our future well-being.

Discontinuous knowledge is to incomplete knowledge as "coherence" is to "unity" in the older rhetoric. A composition, we were told, must have a beginning, middle, and an end—unity. It must have all of its parts. Its several parts must also relate harmoniously and flow logically from one level to the next. By conditioning we seek such unities in other aspects of our lives. But the problems of discontinuous knowledge are the purview of the specialist, who assembles smaller bodies of information into larger meaningful "wholes" such as the individual anecdotes and memoirs, the shared experiences which enable us to speak of a "Harlem Renaissance," a "Dasein group," an "Umbra group," or a "Harlem Writers Guild."

E. Ethelbert Miller, Theodore Hudson, John O'Neal, Ishmael Reed, Tom Dent, Barbara Smith, Eugene Redmond, and others have produced or are producing work on "Black literary communities," to use Miller's evocative term. This kind of endeavor is absolutely essential to an understanding of Black literary accomplishment during the past two decades, and one may venture to say that an analysis of their several histories may have important lessons for us, from a programmatic viewpoint, as we try to assess the recent

past and prepare for the future. Briefly, Black literary communities are primarily and most obviously *regional* and may center around an individual
or institution such as a museum, a workshop, or a university. Thus, some
examples are the Studio Museum, the Harlem Writers Guild, the Institute of
Positive Education, Reed and Johnson Publishing Company, Karamu House,
and the Ascension Poetry Series.

The regional quickly shades into the intellectual and the ideological, especially where a publication is involved and some examples are the Institute of
Positive Education and *Black Books Bulletin*; OBAC [Organization of Black
American Culture] and *Black World*; the Howard Poets and *Dasein* and so on.

Complicating matters are the relationships between the various communities, characterized by some of the same behavior patterns that exist
between elements in the larger nonliterary communities. Two of these are
as follows: (a) *Regionalism and/or parochialism.* There are some positive
aspects of the former, e.g., in the contemporary Southern movement,
embodied in *Callaloo.* There are negative aspects also as in the urban-
vs.-rural syndrome characteristic of some writing of the 60s, which
looked down upon or ignored the Southern heritage. Another aspect
of this syndrome was the idealization of things Southern. (b) *Migration
of writers between communities, formation of new ones.* Some indication
of the importance of this phenomenon can be seen in the movement of
significant New York writers, like Ishmael Reed, David Henderson, Joe
Johnson, Jayne Cortez, and Quincy Troupe, and Alice Walker in California. Of further interest is the fact that Walker is originally a Southerner
with strong cultural ties, who is rapidly maturing as a politically sensitive
spokesperson, and Reed, Henderson, and Johnson were part of the Umbra
group. They have all done important work, of course, in their new context.
Their migration in effect was a kind of cultural transplantation. Questions
for the scholar would involve analyzing the earlier work of these writers,
comparing it with the more recent, and determining if possible, whether
the change of environment had anything to do with the evolution of the
new work. Two other Umbra writers can be mentioned, Tom Dent and
Askia M. Touré, the former Rolland Snellings.

Since returning to New Orleans, Dent has become a major force in the
Black Southern literary cultural movement and is a founder of *Callaloo* along
with native Mississippian Jerry Ward and native Alabamian Charles Rowell.
Touré spent a brief period in Atlanta before returning to the East, where he
is politically active in Philadelphia and New York.

To return to the South briefly, one must note the presence in Atlanta of
two major figures, recent immigrants—Toni Cade Bambara, who is here

today and who has recently published her first novel, *The Salt Eaters*, which, unlike her previous work, is set in the South, in Georgia, in fact. Also, a part of the Atlanta community now is another conference participant, Hoyt W. Fuller, editor of *First World*. The interesting thing here is that Fuller was born in Atlanta. Although he is not a Southerner, and *First World* is an "international journal of Black thought," he is also a catalyst in the Atlanta community. And Atlanta is the chief focal point—meeting point, in intellectual and institutional terms of the "Black Southern cultural movement."

These examples certainly do not exhaust the notion of Black literary communities or the effect which the migration of writers has upon them. One hopes, indeed that an examination of these "communities" in historical perspective will be assumed by students of the literature and certainly by the writers themselves.

Before we leave the topic, however, we should mention a special kind of "migration," that of the Caribbean or African writer who spends extended periods of time in the United States, or who takes US citizenship, and produces work in the adopted country. That is one of the most fascinating cases for the student of the literature. One can't easily forget the special voice of [Keorapetse] Willie Kgositsile, for example, or the early Michael Thelwell. And Thelwell himself tells us that Chinua Achebe influenced the writing of *The Harder They Come*.

Thelwell also promises in an interview to write a novel on the civil rights movement. This perspective should open vistas. One mentions also Dennis Brutus, Wilson Harris, George Lamming, Sylvia Wynter, Joan Cambridge Mayfield, Ayi Kwei Armah, Ivan Van Sertima, Leroy Clarke, Ed Brathwaite, and others who stretch their hands toward us from across the seas, Gideon Mutiso from Kenya, among them, and young scholars like Mariame Sy of Senegal. Here is the fusion, the melting, the spiritual bonding, here is the seedbed of the new literature, here is the new dimension. Here is the new culture—the consolidation of the old, the future of fragmentation.

The new culture must be struggled for, otherwise its evolution will be determined essentially by the forces which determine the rest of society. The critic's/scholar's orientation provides him/her with the system and the vocabulary to describe the struggles. On the most basic level, however, we already know it. The developments of the past two decades are replete with it, and the present situation is certainly fairly clear to most of us. But quickly, we may point out struggles between individuals and organizations; individuals within organizations; rivalries between organizations and the use of their publications as ideological forums. This is as it is, perhaps as it should be. Black writers have no monopoly on it.

But they do have an obligation, or if the word offends, an opportunity. At the Institute of the Black World, we saw the involvement of the Black artist and intellectual as "the struggle to define the struggle," and Lerone Bennett once made the observation that "it is finally not so important that we love one another but that we confront one another." And so the struggle continues.

With struggle there is drive; without it, there is drift. And in our attempt to make sense, to find pattern and direction in this literature of the recent past and the present, we must realize that we are now dealing with another category of problems, *problems of distorted knowledge and/or misinterpretation.* That is the endless struggle, an essential outgrowth of the first two sets of problems, when it is not their corollary. There is nothing more to say here except that in the final analysis what is needed goes beyond scholarly accuracy, philosophical insight, ideological correctness, or intellectual clarity—what is needed is courage.

This lack of courage may even be perceived as another pervasive set of problems—a kind of endemic self-doubt, a moral apathy, a cultural entropy. But we leave it here. If we are serious about our presence here, in our concern for our literature and our artists, about our future in the 1980s and beyond, then we play out the role which best suits us.

There are challenges on all levels and there are heroic possibilities for all—for the writer, the editor, for the reader in any of his/her various roles. We begin with the editors of the past two decades who made the movement possible—individuals who published their own work in mimeograph form, Carolyn Rodgers and others; single heroic figures like Dudley Randall; others with their own brand of heroism—Hoyt Fuller, Ishmael Reed, and Joe Johnson, to name but a few. The campus publications on Black campuses and white. These were movements toward struggle, and finally toward a tentative unity, as the struggle moved on. Today a handful of Black editors of differing perspectives still exert major influence on our literature—Toni Morrison comes to mind naturally, Marie Brown, Phil Petrie, Hoyt Fuller, Haki Madhubuti [Don L. Lee]. They are essential, as long as they confront us and themselves. They will play a major role in signaling directions that the literature will take. If they do not confront us, we must confront them.

For the writers themselves, there are hard choices and heavy challenges. They too must confront their individual selves and their communities and their previous work. They must decide, if they haven't, their relationship to the community, the hows, the whys—they must consider, and many, I assume, have already considered their relationship to their own work. They must confront the work of others. I see their situation as a set of three challenges: (1) the challenge of the folk base; (2) the challenge of "tradition"; (3) the challenge of the modern world.

Reactions to these challenges may be conscious and deliberate or they may be unconscious. A writer, to begin with, may consciously ignore the challenges. It is his/her prerogative. Such a writer, however, is likely not to consider himself or herself a "Black" writer. I speak of those who have no such reservation.

But even "Black" writers may not consciously see the challenges that I have listed. That doesn't make them any less Black, especially if they write about "their immediate present." But I suggest that if the literature is to grow and develop, then we must be conscious of the challenges of the culture—the cultural imperatives. The challenge that was most enthusiastically embraced in the past two decades was that of the folk base. Indeed, the folk resource has attracted our writers almost from the very beginnings of our American stay. I have merely to mention a few names: Edwin Campbell, Paul Laurence Dunbar, James Weldon Johnson, W. E. B. Du Bois, Langston Hughes, Robert Hayden, Sterling Brown, Margaret Walker, Zora Neale Hurston, Richard Wright, Gwendolyn Brooks, James Baldwin, Ralph Ellison. From the past two decades, Amiri Baraka, Henry Dumas, Vertamae [Smart-]Grosvenor, James Forman, Ahmos Zu-Bolton, Rikki Lights, Larry Neal, the *Dasein* group, the *Umbra* group, Sarah Fabio, Julia Fields, Jayne Cortez, Jodi Braxton, Toni Morrison, Thulani Davis, the *Callaloo* writers, and others.

Notwithstanding this involvement, the challenge of the folk base is enormous. Glimmerings of new models appear in such works as *The Salt Eaters*, in the lonely and neglected work of Julia Fields, in her poem "Mr. Tut," for example; in the New Hoodoo syndrome of Ishmael Reed and others; in Henry Dumas's work, both poetry and prose—in "Shall the Circle Be Unbroken?" These works, and indeed the challenges of the folk base, go beyond the picturesque and the nostalgic to an exploration of pre-Western lifestyles and modes of thought. The folk base is amenable to as many different approaches—ideological and aesthetic—as the writer has the courage and the imagination to apply.

By "tradition" I mean the larger patterns of literary production that affect the writer, here the Black American writer. The writing of the past twenty years reveals the fact that Black writers are well read not only in their own tradition, but in that of others as well, the Euro-American tradition, the European, and in particular, the so-called Third World writers, who range from Mao Tse-tung, to [Frantz] Fanon, Nicholas Guillen, [Wole] Soyinka, and Léon Damas.

Even the work of the 1960s was clearly and explicitly affected by this worldwide production. Closer to home, one could easily discover, for example, the influence of an E. E. Cummings. And Sonia Sanchez even wrote a deliciously bawdy parody of that "American master." Sonia and other poets wrote haiku and tantras and other formal works based on Eastern models.

Essentially the movement was away from "Western forms." It was movement in an important "direction," and it occasionally produced some startling and original work. Some of us tried to describe the work and suggested ways to appreciate its originality. Those efforts, though partly successful, have met with a mixed reception which ranges from dismissal resulting from simplistic misreading or ideological difference to alternative analysis resulting from a reassessment of the data presently available.

Still the movement away from Western forms has not really ended, if only for the fact that so-called Western forms themselves are harder to define in the modern world. And it is precisely a lack of tradition which characterizes the modern world, modern aesthetics. So, the "immediate present" by which the framers of the conference designate "modernity" is also a fundamental ailment in the concept of "Modernism," which in literary history signifies the work of such diverse writers as Gertrude Stein, James Joyce, T. S. Eliot, and others, and seeks, in effect, to write a kind of permanence in art, in ritual, and myth. It has been succeeded by other styles and fashions, not only in literature and the other arts, but also in the accompanying scholarship and criticism. I do not pretend to any mastery of this knowledge. I am not sure that it can be mastered. Nevertheless, one key to a grasp of the problem, at least, lies within Afro-American culture itself. We have produced a cultural paradigm in Black art, especially in Black music that enables one to focus the discontinuities and disjuncture of the modern world. I have spoken about that at some length on other occasions. Now, I shall merely quote Larry Neal and say, "The answer is in our music." Our music, at its best, has always addressed the problem of continuity and change, fragmentation and reintegration. The music is analytical and probing and unafraid. It is engaged and involved. It is problem-solving—in a technical as well as an emotional sense. The music is not afraid of new philosophies or new technologies or old philosophies and technologies, for the music deals with time filtered through the pulses of African sensibility. So no ideological hang-up should prevent Black poets from writing "sound poems," especially with the model of Bob Kaufman, and Ella Fitzgerald, Louis Armstrong, and the moaning of the Baptist preacher. The answer is in the culture. We must *study* the culture, not take it for granted.

There is an encouraging recent development in our literature which I shall mention in closing. It is perhaps the most important development since the 1960s. I speak of the prominence, the achievement, and the promise of Black women writers. I have already named a few of them. They have always played a significant role, and certainly made major contributions to the literature of the 60s and 70s; however, the new prominence demonstrates that the bearers of the culture and its essential creators have also accepted the challenge of the modern world—the challenge of disunity and fragmentation. We shall all be the stronger for their primal vision.

"Turn the face of history to your face," says the poet June Jordan in a poem dedicated to her mother. That after all is the only important direction.

TAKE TWO—LARRY NEAL AND THE BLUES GOD

ASPECTS OF THE POETRY

Published in *Callaloo* 23 (1985): 215–39.

Larry Neal was one of the most imaginative and talented writers and theorists of the generation of the 1960s, the generation that created the Black Arts Movement and the New Black Poetry. A complex person capable of holding in his consciousness contradictory elements in a state of high tension, he was at once enormously attracted to the achievements of the Modernist artists and to the revolutionary ideology of his age as embodied in [Frantz] Fanon, [Karl] Marx, Mao Tse-tung, [Amílcar] Cabral, and Malcolm X. He believed in the absolute necessity of historical analysis as a basis for revolutionary action at the same time that he knew that the true spirit of the revolution lay in the forms of Black Culture, especially Black religion and Black music. On one hand, he felt that art was the handmaiden of political change; on the other, he knew that art was an instrument of prophecy and a vehicle of transcendence. Although conversant with the exciting achievements of the New Music, with [Max] Roach and [John] Coltrane, Sun Ra and [Ornette] Coleman, he had a special place in his thought for [Duke] Ellington, [Billie] Holiday, [Charlie] Parker, Lester Young, and Miles Davis. And beneath it all was the blues, the men and women of the blues. Like [Langston] Hughes and [Sterling A.] Brown and [Ralph] Ellison before him, he recognized the great synthesizing power of the blues, and in a manner more specific than theirs he recognized the spiritual and religious connection between the blues and the African past.

The important thing about all this is that Neal sought to bring order out of his apparent contradictions. That effort one perceives until the very end in a considerable part of his work and the record of his struggle is one of outstanding accomplishments of the movement which he helped to create and to explain.

For the purpose of this essay, I have chosen to examine Neal's two collections of poetry, *Black Boogaloo* and *Hoodoo Hollerin' Bebop Ghosts*, in order to ascertain his changing perspectives and the technical means by which those changes are affected. *Black Boogaloo*, subtitled *Notes on Black Liberation*, was first published by the Journal of Black Poetry Press in 1969 and is dedicated to his wife, Evelyn. A preface by LeRoi Jones [Amiri Baraka], "Sound for Sounding," reinforces the subtitle. This book, Jones says, is a harbinger of things to come. It is a post "literary" book because the poet and his generation are *men* first then writers. The poems are functional. They are "sound for sounding." In the first instance, the reference is to the break with tempered scales, chord progressions, tonal centers, and the like that one associates with modern jazz as it incorporates more and more "sound" into its constructions. It is an assertion of freedom, of liberation from the dead hand of the past, from the oppressive patterns of a bankrupt culture. Although poets like Larry Neal were often inspired by the musical model, the musicians themselves as well as the writers and general audiences were well aware of the orality of Black music throughout its manifestations. In *Black Boogaloo*, this connection appears in "sounding," a technique of satire akin to the dozens, which is translatable into music and which has appeared historically, in the blues and throughout the authentic manifestations of jazz—in the dirty tones and the blue notes, in the smears and riffs and inspired dissonances, in the tension between rhythm and harmony. Although "sounding" is less severe than the dozens, according to Geneva Smitherman, noted authority on the language of Black Americans (*Talkin and Testifyin*, 120), it is nonetheless rooted in the same attitudes and behavior. Perhaps Jones also has in mind the fact that eventually one has to confront the enemy on far deeper levels than the verbal. But for the time being this level is critical:

> These words
> are to be spoken. These songs are to be sung. Sound. They are
> sound. Real. Make (it to & with) sense (1)

Jones is more explicit at the end of the preface: "All the world is around us, and looking . . . to be changed. It is / the Black Artists . . . the soldier poets who will change it." He thus concludes the preface:

> Go'n Larry Neal,
> with yo' bad
>
> Self (ii)

And Neal goes forth, the soldier poet of this volume.

The poems are grouped into four "sets," the term coming from jazz performance. There is also some thematic movement in the first three sets, which tend either toward the historical or the topical aspects of the struggle of the race for freedom. In the poems in set 1 listed below, this movement is apparent in the titles but more specifically, of course, in the poems themselves. Let us note a few random examples. "Love Song in Middle Passage" opens with a graphic description of carnage in "the westward pull of death" as "slick white knives slit Black throats." Therefore, the Blacks must learn to kill, even though they are life itself, in order to defend and preserve themselves. Neal writes:

> even though we are the sun's song,
> the rear, the surge, the rhythm and poetry;
> [lines 44–45 from "Love Song in Middle Passage"]
> we must destroy
> to live. (11)

In fact, the poet implies, in order to confront a heartless blood-drinking enemy, Blacks must become *efficient* killers: "We must become stone-cold killers, / panther-spirits, invisible men, // while thrusting the blade into the beast-heart." From that revolutionary violence there will emerge a new man:

> sucking in the meaning of your discovery,
> sucking in the liberated wonder of the cosmos,
> expanding until the world is filled with
> a vibrating Black light.

The violence is not only physical but symbolic, spiritual, and psychological. It destroys the old self that wallowed in the values and white ways of the West, that are still overwhelming in their power. We catch glimpses of the New Man. He is adumbrated in the ancestral past as well as in the revolutionary present. He is sensual and spiritual, mackman and prophet, railroad worker and musician, the Seventh Son of the Seventh Son. He is "descended from Drum / from that which first formed." He is Original Man, at times in touch with primal powers, but he is caught between mythic memory and the cruel lessons of history, the fractured wisdom of Africa and the oppressive technology of the West. So, the task of the revolutionary, the soldier poet, is to speak to the collectivity, to raise their consciousness, to show them their greatness, to preach the glory and necessity of struggle. One of the poems which focuses on the topical dimension of that struggle is "The Slave," dedicated to LeRoi Jones [Amiri Baraka]:

> Along the streets
> > the stores are barricaded,
> black upheaval,
> > what moves is ours.

And Neal concludes with:

> > clear the air good
> their ashes would even contaminate
> > confusing our rhythms
> now we are slaves for ourselves. (38)

It is in set 4, however, that we get the most direct and explicit statements on revolution and the building of a new people and a new society. It consists of ten poems which develop variations on the theme of revolution and bring the volume to a smashing crescendo. Only one of the poems in set 4, "Orishas," appears in *Hoodoo Hollerin' Bebop Ghosts*, and there it occupies a different position and weight in the "symbolic landscape" of that book. In set 4 it serves as a kind of coda which links the theme of revolution to its Afro-American cultural context. "Neglphics: Or Graffiti Made Respectable," the first poem in the set, is a collection of "found" poems and slogans employed in the Marxist manner, but it is a technique suffused by Black oral tradition, particularly the dozens. The targets are national and international figures including integrationist Blacks. Two examples are:

> Wilkens got scabs on his head from scratching so much!
> Hoover hangs out in the men's room of the D.C. "Y." (40)

Graffiti as positive statement appears in the following:

> Shine says: "Unite or Perish."
> and   Black Power
>   Every Hour (40)

Lines of pure poetry occasionally intermingle with the slogans:

> a lifting Spirit, be reincarnated
>   in a Coltrane solo.
>   * * *
> Destroy the imperialist and their lackey
>   running dogs. (41)

"Black Boogaloo," the long poem that gives the book its title is a prescription for action, and as such it was printed as a poster and widely distributed. An ambitious construction employing slogans, raps, and other revolutionary rhetoric, it opens with a call for unity.

> BROTHERS AND SISTERS UNITE! BROTHERS AND SISTERS UNITE!
> Form small groups,
> study the enemy. Organize carefully know yourselves and those.
> [lines 4–6 from "Black Boogaloo"]
> Prepare for a war of national liberation. (42)

The call is immediately followed by three subsets of Boogaloo notes, or, as it were, three choruses based on the "BROTHERS AND SISTERS UNITE" introduction or "head." To the question that he rhetorically posed in one of his essays—What does boogaloo mean?—he gives specific answers and instructions. First to the poets:

> Blow Black. Blow Black Love. Kick some ass, poets. Kick some jive poet's ass. Take over the Urban League's offices. Kick Whitey Young's ass. Then read him a poem telling him why you did it, as if he doesn't know. The same for roy wilkens. (42)

Then the notes for the painters with *their* specific instructions:

> TAKE OVER THE POSTER BOARDS IN THE BLACK COMMUNITY.
> WAKE UP ONE MORNING BIG BLACK FACE STARING US IN THE
> EYES. BIG BLACK FIST CLENCHED IN THE POWER SIGN. PAINT
> [lines from 18–23 from "Black Boogaloo"]

BLACK LIFE. BLACK LOVE. DEATH. (42)

And the notes are followed by an ecstatic riff on the validity of "revolutionary death" and the "validity of struggle."

Pointed instructions are given to Black musicians, exhorting them to take what they need and ending with a call to all Black people that echoes Baraka's famous poem "SOS." Even amid the practical, however, there is the rap raised to the level of poetry: "Boogaloo, dance / the Ali Shuffle, / dazzle the Beast with footwork. / Power dance" (43). Following this set of notes is a "bridge" announcing the beginning of revolution: "It's on. / It's on. / It's on. The shit is on." The leaders are introduced:

SUN RA FOR PRESIDENT. RAP BROWN FOR VICE PRESIDENT. KENYATTA FOR MINISTER OF DEFENSE. THE PEOPLE THE PEOPLE, THE PEOPLE. THE COLLECTIVE. THE COLLECTIVE. THE COLLECTIVE. ORGANIZE. ORGANIZE. (43)

Following this is an apotheosis of Malcolm X:

MALCOLM LIVES. MALCOLM LIVES. MALIK EL HAJJ SHABAZZ LIVES. (43)

There is a return to the opening theme of unity, but this time with the focus on Black students:

RENAME YOUR SCHOOLS: NAT TURNER UNIVERSITY. CHARLIE PARKER INSTITUTE. LUMUMBA COLLEGE. KICK JIVE NEGRO PROFESSORS IN THE MOUTH.

The effect of lines like these upon a live Black audience in the 1960s and 1970s was simply devastating, as anyone who witnessed Neal's readings during that time can attest. The poem ends with a call to a meeting: "COME TO THE MEETING AT 360° SOUL STREET . . . SOUL CITY . . . NOW IS THE TIME" (44). What is especially noteworthy here is the manner in which the poet touches the main levels of the Black Experience and brings them to bear on the demands of the time, the call for struggle and revolution. History is mingled with ideology and the popular and folk traditions are analyzed and exploited for their revolutionary energy.

Some of the remaining poems address specific problems, opportunities, or obstacles facing the revolution. Sometimes the ideology dominates the poetry, sometimes the ideology itself is ambivalent. A case in point is

"Brother Pimp," where the poet's romantic admiration for the style of the "Life" clashes with the socioeconomic realities of the oppressed. The pimp is addressed thus:

> you are the roots of our Black power,
> would-be brother.
> you are the essence of style, that which
> we gleaned from the raw underbelly of the city. (46)

But it is self-contradictory and somehow naïve to ask the pimp to destroy his livelihood, as in the following exhortation:

> take control, brother pimp, of the streets
> convert Black whores into Black women.
> rise build, rise build, organize.
> rise build, rise build, organize. (46)

The futility of the plea becomes even more apparent in the postscript. The poet describes a woman "being ripped / by raving beasts, dripping gore and death-smell." She dies "an ecstasy-death, the body betrayed by weak n[*****]men" (46). Although the pimp is responsible, the poet still senses some good in him and invites him, "brother pimp, would-be warrior," once again to join the revolution:

> like her we are waiting for you to join
> the Black thing.
> we are waiting. join us.
> ALL PRAISE IS DUE THE BLACK MAN. (46)

"Poem for Revolutionary Night" is a multidimensional evocation of the voices of revolution contrasted with the quiet and mysterious fog that hangs over Harlem. The voice of conscience, indicated by italics, directs him to the spiritual and historical destiny of revolution.

> *Where the street turns, there is a man, he will tell you where to go.*
> *Will tell you where to lay down your life, and how.*
> *Will destroy your life to give life eternal* (47)

There is no escaping destiny. The Nationalist who wants to go back to Africa is killed, as well as the integrationists symbolized by Roy Wilkins.

Other perspectives are shown, for instance, that of the old man who warns of the dullness of revolutions. The poet/persona is encouraged by the "contact," who urges him on. But his mind crowds with other possibilities, including escape from responsibility. Nevertheless, there must be revenge and redemption, and subsuming it all is the need for rebirth, which he realizes in epiphany:

> rebirth is acceptance of the shortness of our lives
> is acceptance of the endlessness of our spirits

And in a rather theatrical conclusion the poet shouts defiance at the "bitch of sorrows" and hails the revolution.

A much better poem and more convincing evocation of the spirit of revolution appears in "Jihad," where the poet appears to draw on the allegories of the Whore of Babylon, from the Bible and from English literature, commencing the poem: "From the East, we marched, the Armies of Jihad, speaking a New / Tongue, the Language of the Jihad, the Holy Tongues merged into One." The following passage is similarly reminiscent of [Edmund] Spenser's description of the monster "Error" and [Jonathan] Swift's description of the spider representing the Moderns in *The Battle of the Books*:

> Charging the Whore. The Bitch of Babylon dispensed army after army,
> weapon after weapon. The air spun, a whirling sound that made the
> Bitch rock in pain. agony-fire. all manner of beasts and symbols
> oozing out of her sores. (50)

Noteworthy here in addition to the borrowing of the Islamic concept and doctrine of the jihad is the poet's constant expressing of political and ideological concepts and concerns in the language of religion and mythology. Noteworthy, too, is the range of the allusions and symbols, from West Africa, Egypt, and the Middle East. The symbols are free-associated with images drawn from the urban West accented by the language of the streets.

> And I could see too behind the haze of the Bitch, behind the mountain
> of flesh rising into the haze in which she now sits, the All Seeing
> Eye pervading the confused landscape; the Eye persisting through
> the haze; while her armies poured out of her hole. (50)

The second book, *Hoodoo Hollerin' Bebop Ghosts*, stands in crucial and self-conscious relationship to *Black Boogaloo*. Where the latter is highly polemical, openly and intensely ideological, and frequently topical; where it addresses the Black collective whose consciousness it seeks to raise; where often it is incendiary and explosive and "functional," the former is more personal and polished, more varied technically and artistically more ambitious. Despite these changes, however, there is no loss of vitality in the second book, but rather a maturing of the sensibility and craft which promised an even higher level of attainment.

The author's note on the book jacket reveals important clues to his development up to this point. He states:

> Just wanna slip in a personal note about these poems. They represent a rough cross section of my most publishable poems that were written somewhere between 1964 and 1973. If the tone of some of them seems rather polemical, it is because my literary sensibility was forged essentially in the context of the ideologically intense sixties. However, I have tried to select poems for this volume in which the polemic and poetic merge into an organic, *personal* statement.

It is important to note several things here—the poems are a representative sample of his best work. They were written between 1964 and 1973, thereby overlapping the poems of the *Black Boogaloo* collection, and some of them may seem polemical in tone. Finally, the author chose for this volume poems "in which the polemic and poetic merge into an organic *personal* statement." One notes the emphasis, as the author explains the origin of the polemical tone and spirit in the influence of his father, Woody Neal. A brief account of his mother's literary and musical influence is also given, as well as the tantalizing fact that he attended St. Elizabeth's Catholic Church as a child. Speaking specifically about the poems, the author states that their "overall symbolic landscape" is "Pan African." He continues:

> It should go without saying that the work also owes something, perhaps a great deal, to the rich tradition of Western poetry. However, the work's essential energy, metaphor, iconography, and symbology are primarily derived from the history, mythology and oral traditions of Afro-America, the Caribbean, and West Africa. What happened was that round about 1963–1964, Charles Fuller, the playwright; Jimmy Stewart, musician-poet, and I arrived at the conclusion that the Afro-American poetic spirit was essentially trapped in the iconography of the West, and that it was time for another kind of poetic orientation to assert itself. You can make of this whatever you choose.

Let us make of it what we must. First, it gives some clue to Neal's intellectual relationship to fellow Philadelphia artists, as well to pockets of contemporaries in New York, Washington, Los Angeles, and other places. It links them, in turn, to Black artists of earlier generations—Langston Hughes, especially, and Sterling A. Brown, but the vision, the energy and the drive of the latter period exceed in scope almost everything that preceded it. And one has to go to Langston Hughes's poem "In the Quarters of the Negroes" (*Ask Your Mama*) to approach the sweep of the younger writers.

When we turn to the text of *Hoodoo Hollerin' Bebop Ghosts* itself, we begin to discover how the poet develops the "organic, personal statement" "in which the polemic and poetic merge." We should be aware, however, that other elements are also present, such as the historical, for example, and the mythical. In fact, we must note in *Hoodoo* a more subtle and effective handling of these elements, especially the latter.

In comparing the two books, we find that *Hoodoo* contains 58 poems over against the 32 in *Black Boogaloo*. Of the 58 poems, 18 appear in one form or another in the earlier volume. These 18 "crossover" poems must somehow have been considered by the writer as some of his "most publishable poems that were written between 1964 and 1973." They must also have been considered as useful contributions to the personal statement that he wished to make. If we take the word "personal" to mean "individual" and "private" in contrast to "group"/"collective" and "public"; if we take the word in that sense rather than an autobiographical or confessional sense, then we have the latitude to acknowledge the lyrical daring and excellent workmanship of the poems.

When we consider the poems that were omitted from *Hoodoo* we discover that some of the most violent and bloodthirsty are gone—such as those in set 4, "Neglphics: Or Graffiti Made Respectable," "Black Boogaloo," "Poem for Revolutionary Night," or "Jihad," for example. Notwithstanding, among the 18 that are retained, there are some that are unmistakably revolutionary in theme, such as "Orishas" with its "Oath" section, and the short and powerful "The Slave." At any rate, there was no need to repeat *Black Boogaloo*. It had done its job, had made its contribution to the cause.

When we consider the totally new work, the "work in progress," the Shine poems, we realize that although the tone had changed somewhat, and the form; although the "message" was "deeper," more cosmic, more mythical, it was still Black and still revolutionary. But we must examine in detail some of the changes, some of the adjustments that Neal made as he elaborated his statement, as he reworked and refined the materials of his poems. In this regard, he was like a musician obsessed by themes and structures and the oblique spirituality of sound. And we learn this essentially by comparing this work with the "crossover" poems, touchstones both for the *Black Boogaloo* volume and *Hoodoo.*

Generally speaking, the changes that appear in the *Hoodoo* version of the "crossover" poems, may be classified as follows: (a) typographical, (b) grammatical, (c) dictional and tonal, (d) a recasting of original imagery, (e) a rearrangement and/or recasting of original elements. Some of the changes are slight, especially the typographical, and may merely involve changes in punctuation which do not affect the integrity of a given line or phrase. But other changes in punctuation do affect rhythm and tempo, as in "For *Our* Women," where semicolons are changed to periods or periods to commas, or commas omitted altogether. As we shall see, too, changes in punctuation occasionally reflect attitudinal changes.

Other typographical changes involve the manipulation of type space so as to affect the length or the shape of a line. This concern with the visual frequently appears as an attempt to clarify phrasal and other syntactical patterns. A good example of this kind of change occurs in "Libations for Olorun" (4–13), which, largely rewritten, also serves to illustrate other kinds of emendations. The critical point, though, is that there is a greater reliance on established visual patterns and established typography in *Hoodoo* and less on the purely auditory imagination of the reader, as was the case in *Black Boogaloo.*

There are also grammatical changes and/or corrections in the new book. A case in point is "Woody and the Reading Railroad," where we find these lines:

> My old man mumbling in the morning
> after mom,
> mumbling weariness, jamming his self
> into those work-boots
> [lines 5–7 from "Woody and the Reading Railroad"]

Among the few changes in the poem we find the semicolon in 1.1 becoming a dash, making for a less formal appearance. In 1.8, "railroad-man" becomes "railroadman" and "travelling" becomes "traveling" with no discernable effect on the poem. In the passage quoted above, beginning line 11, "mom" is capitalized in 1.12, and in 1.13, "weariness" becomes "weary" in the second version and perhaps loses some of its original force. In the same line the original "his self," which has considerable evocative power becomes self-consciously correct—"himself." Inasmuch as both texts contain slips of spelling and other lapses that a good copyeditor should have caught, and inasmuch as Neal reveled in the ambiguities and tensions that exist between so-called Standard English and Black vernacular, one can only guess that grammatical self-consciousness rather than aesthetic refinement motivated such changes. At any rate, without manuscript texts it would be virtually impossible to ascertain the motive or reason for a particular change.

With regard to tone, I realize that almost any element in a poem may contribute to that quality and therefore the distinction that I am making may seem arbitrary. What I wish to emphasize here, then, is the difference in tone that results from word choice, or diction. In "For *Our* Women," for example, most of the changes involve punctuation and chiefly affect the tempo of the lines, but an attitudinal change can also be noted in line 3 (both takes) where "these women wrapped / in the magic of birth" becomes "those women wrapped / in the magic of birth." The net result is a more formal perception, distanced by time, legend and myth, an effect which, it is safe to say, characterizes the changes that the poet makes in the second volume. A related example occurs in "Kuntu," one of the most interesting poems in the group, showing as it does, the poet's deep interest in African/Afro-American religion and his attempt to develop a unified philosophy and aesthetic based upon them. Recall that the poem deals with the Self and its relationship to the Cosmos and the Creator, to the processes of Creation, to the questions of ontology. The poem opens thus:

> I am descended from Drum
> I am descended from Drum
> from that which first formed
> from that which first formed

He is descended from the original pulse that formed the Word which informed the Universe:

> Drum's words informed us, giving us flesh
> and flesh shaped the Word
> I say, and flesh shaped the Word

The ecstatic knowledge of divine origin and human essential immortality is reminiscent of transcendental thought and Eastern religions, but the main point here is that in the original version of the poem the knowledge links the revolutionary fervor and deeds of past times to the present, where Drum "informed the flames" and pushed us back into "our most powerful time" (*Black Boogaloo*, 19). Drum speaks to the revolution:

> Drum running down some mean shit
> to all the Brothers and Sisters
> all the Brothers and Sisters
> listening to Drum, my Old Man.

Note those last words, "my Old Man." Here the poet as Son of God, as prophet, speaks in the Black vernacular, in the best Black Power rhetoric and manner. By contrast, in take 2, the father is distanced and, absorbed into the new structure of the poem, becomes "my Mighty Father / the heart of it all" (*Hoodoo*, 75). That is a considerable leap from the vernacular and the hip tone of the original. Not that the second version is any less effective than the first, but there is a conscious change of tone which is reflected in the diction and, as I shall point out, in the larger structure of the poem. There are a number of such changes in the "crossover" poems.

Although once again two categories overlap somewhat, I have called them for the sake of convenience "the recasting of original imagery" and the "rearrangement and/or recasting of structural elements." Briefly, the recasting of imagery takes place both in obvious and in subtle ways. The image of the father is changed chiefly through the diction which is more elevated and formal and charged with biblical associations. But more explicit in the same poem is the compression of the historical images in section III of take 1, where some 17 lines are reduced to five. Here is the original version of the third section:

> [lines 38–44 from "Kuntu"]
> Drum running down some mean shit
> to all the Brothers and Sisters
> all the Brothers and Sisters
> listening to Drum, my Old Man.

The entire poem leads up to this statement. Structurally it is prepared for by a lovely lyrical passage at the end of the preceding section:

> No wonder we float so lightly in Summer
> we float high, drifting on the rhythm of Drum,
> do air-dances O so lightly,
> the Drum informing our lives, our wars.

In take 2, the reference of revolutionary violence, to armed struggle, are more controlled, more literary, more oblique, and this control is effected through a major structural change in the poem. Since section II is truncated at the end of the main philosophical statement, section III now begins with a modification of the lyrical passage quoted above. These lyrical elements are further developed, analyzed, and explored for mythic possibility rather than for links with the revolution. The passage is amazing in its mixture of African and Western imagery, with "the all-slithering hiss" and "serpentine ropes" perhaps invoking Damballah while the "bull-churned stars" suggest Osiris, the bull-roarer of Mithra, Zeus, and the like. At any rate, the emphasis is shifted away from the struggle, the historical references compressed by the syntax and muted by the wordplay, the punning of "Vassa, Massa" and "Harriet, chariot." We have thus almost another creation, one where the Drum calls not to action but to contemplation, with the poet as historian, not soldier, reflecting upon his own time.

What do these changes signify? we may ask. Some are largely stylistic but may embody a reworking of thematic concerns, both for aesthetic and for ideological reasons. With regard to the latter, one could reasonably conclude that in the revisions, as in *Hoodoo* as a whole, there is a freer expression of the poet's preoccupation with technical and philosophical concerns and less direct involvement with the rhetoric of revolution. There is no real desire or need to destroy the "white aesthetic" now. He merely appropriates what he needs from it while developing the possibilities of Black indigenous styles. This may appear as a contradiction—perhaps it is, but a rereading of the essays indicates, at least, that the possibility was there from the beginning. What happens then is a shift of emphasis from history as the handmaiden of revolution to history as the precursor of myth. That was a dangerous shift in the context of the times to be sure, and perhaps contributed to accusations that he had abandoned the struggle. I leave the argument to the historians and the political thinkers, who will evaluate the man and the period when more is published about both.

For the present it is clear that *Hoodoo Hollerin' Bebop Ghosts* is an extended exploration of themes and motives found in *Black Boogaloo* and, indeed, in Neal's essays. The "crossover" poems are key structural elements in the new work and, to some extent, they may be looked upon as thematic embodiments of the energy that fueled the earlier work. Among the problems that arise, however, is getting the earlier poems to fit into the new scheme, or the new flow. Somewhere in his mind, Neal held fast to his favorite musical model, and this is apparent not only in the subject matter and style of the poems but also in the orchestration of the two books. Remember that he organized *Black Boogaloo* into four "sets" and in addition refers to the structure of *Hoodoo* in musical terms. "The last movement of the book," he states in the note on the dust jacket, "is entitled 'Shine.' These poems are excerpts from a work in progress." The statement of intent creates problems even for the determined reader, for unlike *Black Boogaloo* the "movements" are not set forth, either explicitly or implicitly. There are seven poems on Shine which close the book along with two other works, "The City of Zar" and "Colloquies." One could make the case that they constitute a "movement," but it would be easier to argue for the continuity of everything preceding it than to try to find the other hypothetical "movements." Still the fact remains that Neal seems to have conceived the book in that fashion, and stated, moreover, that the last movement was part of a work in progress. We do not know expressly what that work was but he speaks of it in an interview with Lisa DiRocco, of *The Drum*, published in 1978, four years after the publication of *Hoodoo*. There Neal refers to the work in progress as "a book of poems," "a suite," "a series," a "slender book," and discusses the significance of the figure Shine as the embodiment of the blues spirit. These comments indicate that he still had the musical model in mind, and, moreover, was still greatly involved with the folk matrix of the culture. Speaking of the book, Neal states that it will be "about Afro-American folk figures," about the "permutations" of the legendary Shine. In addition, Shine himself will be reincarnated at various periods:

> I've been working with reincarnation a lot, and in that series there will be a lot of reincarnation moments, cyclical moments. The poem, as I've always thought of it for myself, begins in the heart of the sun; and then it goes through time, and various reincarnations of this figure called Shine. (11)

The idea of Shine's reincarnation dovetails with Neal's interest in folklore, which appears in *Hoodoo* as poems about "ghosts, mysteries, voodoo gods, other worlds," but more fundamentally it results from his adoption of the African view of the dead into his philosophy and his aesthetic:

> I'm trying to deal with the world of the dead. The African world view is that the dead are not dead. The dead are really all around. So, those poems are trying to be informed by those ghosts. The ancestors are ever present, because that's one of the functions of ghosts.

Furthermore, the blues provide impulse, power, and mechanism to affect these reincarnations, whether as Shine or Lester Young or Billie Holliday. In two of his best poems, "Lady Day" / "Lady's Days" and "Don't Say Goodbye to the Porkpie Hat," Neal demonstrates the potency of these ideas and reveals the underlying unity of his thought. In both poems, the changes emphasize the mystic and religious infrastructure of Neal's art and philosophy. In both, the revisions are extensive.

In the Billie Holliday poems, Neal, in effect, has written two closely related poems, one clearly derived from the other. Even the titles suggest the change of focus as "Lady Day" becomes "Lady's Days." Both poems recount the singer's appearances in "hick towns" on the way to gigs in Baltimore and Washington, DC. They describe travel conditions and reflect on Billie's life. In the first, "Lady Day" evolves, as persona, from woman to "spring goddess." The narrative voice is that of "Prez" as reflected in epistolary form. In "Lady's Days," the singer appears as the existential embodiment of the blues, and the narrative voice is that of a lover, or a persona for the poet. The heart of both poems is the ritualistic interaction of audience and singer in a manner recalling Sterling Brown's "Ma Rainey," not to mention real life. Described as "hicks and squares come to hear the Lady sing," their faces remain in the memory, "the soft and the hard." "A lot of these negroes had scars on their faces." Lady understands her role, her purpose, her power.

> She left
> them moaning, wailing for more of the song, digging the Gardenia
> bit she had going, digging the song as it turn(ed) soft in her mouth,
> as the mouth turned softly in the song, they dug. (26)

She presents them with the beauty in the pain of their own lives. The healing power of the song derives from the real pain and suffering of her own life, which included a childhood rape and prostitution. In life transmuted into song, in the poem, the pain is transmuted into myth:

> Billie
> beautiful, the raped child. the spring rape of the goddess. early
> pain. and when they worshipped, the rape lingering even after
> a hot bath at the end of the night.

The first poem concludes with a lament for the dead goddess whose truth was too strong for the people to bear. "Lady's Days" concludes more ambivalently with Lady realizing and accepting her fate as enduring vessel of sorrow and pain, as ritual celebrant of ancestral blues, "the holy blues," to use Willie Dixon's term, that makes us strong.

Neal extends the ancestral connection in the second poem by describing the audience in a compressed, impressionistic manner that signals the symbolic, and he omits the myth of the spring goddess and focuses instead on a specifically African ritual and linguistic gesture. Compare the following two passages:

> Yeah, she left them crying for more. they faces twisted in
> her pain, their pain, the slow power of the blues she
> said once. (*Black Boogaloo*, 26)

And:

> Faces. the pain rides them
> more pain
> their pain
> ghosts ride them (*Hoodoo*, 66)

In the second passage, the pain becomes an orisha, in indirect reference to the blues god. Here, too, via memory and ancestry the present moment repeats the African view of the world. In effect, the original poem is deepened, as reportage and easy manipulation of myth give way to the existential insight characteristic of the blues. The insight is technically enabled by a shifting of Billie's expression to the end of the second poem, where it receives a greater weight and emphasis:

> Slow power of the blues, you said.
> you said, you said that it had to go
> down that way; honey, ain't gotta be no
> reason for towns, faces, moans. (67)

Neal's fullest poetic expression of the blues experience appears in "Don't Say Goodbye to the Porkpie Hat," a spiritual odyssey with a mythic substructure. It is the most extensively revised of all the "crossover" poems. The original version appeared in *Negro Digest* in September 1967. Dedicated to Langston Hughes, who had recently died, it nevertheless was written for Lester Young, who had died in 1959. The second version of the poem, dedicated to the spirits, the powerful ghosts, of "Mingus, Bird, Prez Langston, and them," apparently first appeared in *Hoodoo Hollerin' Bebop Ghosts*. Although the second take is just 23 lines longer than the original, and retains the basic structure, there are many differences that range from a recasting of imagery to the omission of older lines and the addition of new ones. Typical of the minor changes are the following: The hat, magical in the folk tradition of Billy Lyons and Stackolee and first described as "swirling in the sound of sun saxes," now takes on cosmic power, "swirling in the sound of the sax blown suns." Where the "musicians move in and out of this gloom" in take 1, in take 2 we read "Musicians heavy with memories / move in and out of this gloom." The reference to memories, the raw material of history, enables the poet to load the succeeding lines with a wealth of sociological detail that he merely hinted at in the original poem in the reference to a musician as "an obscene riff repeating lynch scenes." Among the major changes, Neal omits some forty lines which deal with a mixture of legend and the biography of Lester Young. He replaces these with a long, admirable new passage of jazz history which evokes the period from the late twenties through the early fifties. This account and the reworked conclusion are not mere virtuoso displays, however, but a structural grid, if you please, which deliberately, through "tonal memories," through the evocation of the blues, recounts the resurrection of the Blues God and the reincarnation of Shine.

Most poets of the period, it must be noted, stuck to the contemporary scene, with references to [John] Coltrane or James Brown and the like. Neal, on the other hand, is passionately involved with the symbolic and ideological import of the entire history, and he gives us Jelly Roll Morton, Fats Waller, and Willie "the Lion" Smith. He values the power of these old, dead musicians. He values the power of the African view of the world:

> in blue
> [lines 42–53 from "Don't Say Goodbye to the Porkpie Hat"]
> There was Jelly Roll Morton, the sweet mackdaddy,
> hollering Waller, and Willie The Lion Smith—
> some mean showstoppers.

Don't say Goodbye to the Porkpie Hat, because he is the essence of jazz, of blues, of Black Spirit. He resurrects Himself from the energy of the horns, and reappears:

> skimming the horizons, flashing bluegreen yellow lights
> and blowing Black stars
> and weird looneymoon changes.

In the hip zoot suit of life, the porkpie hat is "a vision for the world." And a vision for our time and our future. But first the earth must be cleansed. The earlier version of the poem is explicit and topical, as it addresses the 1960s. Here is Neal's famous account of the horns of destruction:

> Sounds drift above the cities of Black America:
> all over America Black musicians are putting
> on the porkpie hat again, picking up their axes,
> preparing to blow away the white dream.

In the second version, the account is less polemical, more reflective, but still full of vitality. The musicians "prepare to blast the white dream" with "crisp and moaning voices / leaping in the horns of destruction, / blowing death and doom to all who have no use for the spirit." Then follows a long lyrical extension, a kind of solo flight that addresses the music itself. We go on, he says, "wailing on into star nights, / rocking whole worlds, unfurling song on song / into long stretches of green spectral shimmering," and "talking some lovely shit and do / to the Blues God who blesses us." Here is the complete apotheosis of the blues. There is no corresponding line in the earlier version, although the concept appears even earlier in the essays.

In the ecstatic conclusion to take 1 we see the deification of the great jazz musicians as it emerges from their immortality. For example,

> Bird lives
> Lady lives
> Lester leaps in every night

The blues live as sound, as spirit living in sound, an idea that fascinated Neal, one which he repeats over and over in his work. In the new version of the poem he develops the ideas more fully. Note the substitution of the "Blues God" for Shango in the earlier version and the introduction of "the cosmic Trane," John Coltrane, as the take-off point in the ecstatic epiphany:

> [lines 126–31 from "Don't Say Goodbye to the Porkpie Hat"]
> the Blues God lives
> we live
> live
> spirit lives

He borrows a riff from his poem "Black Boogaloo" and compresses and accelerates it:

> Dig. Dig Black. be. be. be. be. be.
> Be. Be. Be. Be. Be. (*Black Boogaloo*, 43)

It becomes the driving force behind the final flight:

> dig the cosmic Trane
> dig be
> [lines 144–55 from "Don't Say Goodbye to the Porkpie Hat"]
> take it again
> this time from the top

In this poem a considerable segment of the poet's thought is presented—the apotheosis of the Blues God, the spiritual unification of the African and the Afro-American experience, and their unification with the East; the resurrection and transformation of gods and men, reincarnation, Eternal Return. This was the pattern that he might have extended in the Shine poems. At any rate, it was an important pattern in his thought and his art. He had given us the blueprint in his outline "Some Reflections on the Black Aesthetic," where he synthesizes notions of history, art, and political struggle. In *Hoodoo Hollerin' Bebop Ghosts*, he repeats it again and again, as in the opening poem, "My Lord, He Calls Me by the Thunder," and the closing poem, "Shine and the Lady Girl." And these two poems, which encompass the book, as it were, are symbolically and thematically connected by the image of a bird, a songbird at the end, and a fabulous singing hawk at the beginning. The bird in both poems zooms into the eye of the sun, where "there is peace," and where the poem originates. And that is where the blues people live, the children of the sun, embodied in the epical Shine, that is where they live, clothed in immortality. Neal said in the DiRocco interview: "The poem, as I've always thought of it for myself, begins in the heart of the sun; and then it goes through time, and various reincarnations of this figure called Shine" (11). As for the blues, "The blues god is an attempt to isolate the blues element as an ancestral force, as the major ancestral force of the Afro-American." And despite his appreciation of what others had said about the blues, he claimed the Blues God for his very own: "—the blues god—it's not nobody else's metaphor. It's mine" (12). Really, it was much more than that. It was a major conceptualization, a quantum jump in the ideology and iconography of Afro-American cultural history, an achievement as significant as the Black Aesthetic itself, a new syncretism on the level of myth.

WORRYING THE LINE

NOTES ON BLACK AMERICAN POETRY

Published in *The Line in Postmodern Poetry*, edited by Robert Frank and Henry Sayre, 60–82. Urbana: University of Illinois Press, 1988.

In its most distinctive expression Black American poetry of the 1960s and 1970s turned self-consciously toward music and oral tradition for inspirations and model, at the same time it struggled with stylistic and thematic concerns inherited from the larger body of American and Western poetry, toward which it reacted with both approval and rejection. This interest in tradition coupled with the influence of the prevailing literary climate affected the way the poets wrote and how they were received.

In its historical relationship with the early body of American work, Black "literary" poetry has generally followed the models established by the white literary community. Thus, Lucy Terry wrote "Bars Fight" in octosyllabic couplets, while the more talented Phillis Wheatley wrote in the manner of [Alexander] Pope and the leading lights, both English and American, of her century. Similarly, Paul Laurence Dunbar reflected the American local colorists and humorists in his dialect poems, and the late Victorians in verses such as "Ere Sleep Comes Down to Soothe the Weary Eyes" (Hughes and Bontemps 43). Before Dunbar, Albery Whitman wrote under the direct influence of the Romantic and Victorian poets and their American counterparts. His relevance here lies in his determination to prove that Negro poets could master any of the verse forms that others had employed. And in the 1940s, 1950s, and 1960s, Melvin B. Tolson attracted the attention of poets like Allen Tate and Karl Shapiro with his adaptation of the high Modernist mode, as he proceeded, perhaps half ironically, to "outpound Pound." Known first as LeRoi Jones, Amiri Baraka frankly acknowledged his debt to William Carlos Williams, [Federico García] Lorca, [Ezra] Pound, Charles Olson, and [T. S.]

Eliot. In addition, he speaks with enthusiasm about contemporaries like [Philip] Whalen, [Gary] Snyder, [Robert] Creeley, [Allen] Ginsberg, and others (Donald Allen, *The New American Poetry* 425). To repeat, throughout its history Black American poetry has reflected the stylistics of the white community, even when that community portrayed the Blacks in their midst in unflattering terms such as the "coon" jingles which reappear in James Weldon Johnson. When one examines a number of poems published by Black poets of the 1960s and 1970s, of the Black Arts Movement, one easily recognizes the general American patterns and technical concerns. Consequently, many of the problems of lineation, both for critic and poet, appear in Black American poetry as well. Notwithstanding, there are special problems generated by the ideological and aesthetic concerns of the Black Arts Movement which may be illuminated by a consideration of their specific reaction to lineation.

Since there is so much variety in the New Black Poetry of the sixties and seventies, some clarifying statements are necessary. First, the term "New Black Poetry" was popularized by Clarence Major in his anthology *The New Black Poetry* (1969) modeled on Donald Allen's *The New American Poetry*, which included only one Black poet, LeRoi Jones [Amiri Baraka]. The publication was, therefore, corrective in both a historical and an ideological sense. All of the poets included were Black and wrote about their Blackness, and all were, relatively speaking, young. Seventy-six poets were each represented by a single poem which they themselves chose.[1] Notwithstanding, there were certain assumptions about the character of Black poetry that had gained widespread credence at the time. Among these was the conviction by many that poetry by Blacks should be written out of the Black Experience in a manner that reflected that experience. It should address itself to the concerns—the social and political and moral concerns—of the Black community. These assumptions hardened rather quickly into precepts and dogmas so that all too often ideological correctness became a substitute for poetic craftsmanship or critical acumen. Still, one of the salient theoretical assumptions implicit in the poetry, and often clearly stated by the poets themselves, was that excellence of craft and relevance of statement depended on a deep involvement in the culture and the lives of the people. This assumption, unfortunately, was not always considered by critics, who had their own notions of poetry and how best to judge it. Thus, it is fairly commonplace for critics to discuss recent Black poetry from the prevailing perspectives of the time. One such perspective is Charles Olson's theory of "projective verse," which is frequently invoked. This is understandable especially in discussions of a poet like Amiri Baraka and those poets directly influenced by him. Nevertheless, these perspectives are insufficient for much of the poetry written by poets with quite different backgrounds from Baraka's. In addition, Baraka came somewhat late to the groups which formed the kernel of the Black Arts Movement, and they were becoming aware, as he was himself, of the oral tradition which contained powerful models of its own. There were sermons, political oratory, and street raps, in addition to song lyrics and games of ritualistic dueling. Baraka in his *Autobiography* (1984; 236–37) makes the point as he recalls his move to Harlem and his association with the Umbra Workshop and particularly his attraction to the singing of Askia M. Touré, who was then known as Rolland Snellings. He was influenced by others also, most notably by Larry Neal, with whom he coedited the landmark anthology *Black Fire* in 1968.

The poetry's connections with the oral tradition are ubiquitous but still undervalued or misunderstood. For example, although Martin Luther King Jr.'s sonorous voice was the one that was most familiar in the 1960s, there were literally thousands of others that included Malcolm X, King's great contemporary, and spokespersons like Rap Brown, James Bevel, Stokely Carmichael, Wyatt Walker, James Forman, and Fannie Lou Hamer. The line—the structure—was embedded in those voices that, varied as they were in style and substance, drew upon a common heritage. One heard Daddy King's power in his son's voice, but one also heard Benjamin Elijah Mays, his mentor, and the voice of his father's ecclesiastical "rival," the Reverend William Holmes Borders, whose inflections and rhetoric resonate today in the sermons and speeches of Jesse Jackson. To assay the force of this tradition, one must recall the elder King's benediction at the Democratic National Convention in 1976—the commanding, compelling power of the moment, or the torrential rhetoric of Jackson's speeches in the 1984 presidential campaign. These voices, secular and sacred, propelled an entire generation, just as others had done throughout the history of Black people in America. Black poets have always admired this power, even when they did not agree with the message. And it is hardly an accident that the first full flowering of the free-verse line among Black poets would be in James Weldon Johnson's *God's Trombones* (1927). In his introduction to the volume, Johnson indicates his concerns with tempo, rhythm, timbre, and texture and the means by which to produce them (10–11).

The audiences for Black poetry of the sixties and seventies were already conditioned to the style and delivery that the poets exploited, and the technical problems which Johnson encountered were the same as those which faced the poets of the sixties, the adaptations of oral forms to the printed page, from, whence they would be revived into speech. Johnson had taken a further step and recorded four of his sermons in verse. Although not ineffective, they pale before real sermons by a master preacher. Still, they have received frequent forceful performance by professional actors and retain their popularity.

In the 1960s, many poets again saw a model in the preacher, but this time the preacher as musician or shaman or prophet. Larry Neal expressed most clearly this new sense of poetic and political opportunity. He was attracted to the enormous influence that James Brown wielded over an audience, for example, because his appeal in many ways was just as great as that of King or Malcolm X, so that Neal would say, "Did you ever hear a Negro poet scream like that? James Brown is the best poet we got, baby" ("Black Writers Speak Out" 83–84). While he didn't mean this in any literal way, Neal certainly implied some seriously conceived attitudes toward the function, structure, and performance of Black poetry. Not all Black poets subscribed to his views, of course, but no serious student of the poetry can afford to ignore them. Implied in Neal's position that poetry, for example, should make us stronger, should liberate the spirit, is a moral position as Karl Malkoff indicates (35). And that moral position issues forth not merely as statement, or ideology, but as technique. When we examine that technique, we uncover the confluence of the oral tradition, the verse of James Weldon Johnson, and the New Black Poetry.

Despite the confluence, however, there was something different about the new poetry. The feature which most clearly distinguishes the Black poetry of the sixties from its antecedents is its independent attitude toward language. Earlier, the poetry, when written in Standard English, tended to demonstrate the poet's linguistic mastery in terms acceptable to the general critic. That way no one, neither poet nor critic, could claim or justify a double standard for the evaluation of work by Blacks. However, this often meant, in practice, an avoidance of certain themes, subjects, and linguistic experiences derived from the Black community. These things were embarrassing to some, they did not fit. Here, clearly, the poets and writers were reacting to the negative stereotypes of their race that appeared in the minstrel shows, on the stage, in learned discourse, in fiction and poetry, and in the popular culture, which soon included radio, movies, and television. By contrast, writers like Langston Hughes, Frank Marshall Davis, and Sterling Brown were encouraged by the example of [Carl] Sandburg, [Robert] Frost, and others to explore the verbal dynamics of Black American culture itself, not some fancied version of it. These poets penetrated deeper into the language than Dunbar or James Weldon Johnson ever did, and they realized that Black spoken English was not the same thing as "Negro dialect" and indeed was capable of a full range of expressive possibilities, some of which were unattainable in Standard English. In the 1960s many of the poets not only claimed the right to legitimize the Black vernacular but sought to celebrate it by emphasizing its difference from Standard English. Although in some instances old stereotypes were refurbished in new Negro dialect and called poetry, in others the poets realized that the real subject of dispute was not vocabulary, not lexicon or diction, nor even grammar, but a view of the world and a realization of the role of language in its shaping and embodiment. It was a "struggle to define the struggle," as the saying went. In "Black Art," a popular poem from his Black Nationalist period, Amiri Baraka wrote:

> Let the world be a Black Poem
> And Let All Black People Speak This Poem
> Silently
> or LOUD (*Black Magic* 117)

There were technical correlatives to the ideology and the idealism. It was one thing to point to Aretha Franklin or to James Brown as models, it was another to capture their high-voltage energy or their sculptured microchromatics on a page. It was exhilarating to speak of "the essential energy that is Blackness, the lyricism of this consciousness," as Clarence Major did in the introduction to *The New Black Poetry* (18). It was more difficult to translate this awareness into poetry.

Nonetheless, the more dedicated of the poets pursued the cultural challenges. (Among these poets, of course, was Major himself, who has largely abandoned poetry for fiction.) For these poets the central problems appear to be: How to suggest the highly charged inventive quality of Black American vernacular on the printed page—how to indicate its dynamic range, its mixture of elegance and wit, its tonal contrasts with Standard English, its plasticity. How to appropriate the revolutionary potential uncovered by the music, both verbal and instrumental, and how to do this in linguistic terms. How to absorb and transform the diverse cultural experience bombarding all Americans without losing touch with Black traditions. How to make a poem "swing," in A. B. Spellman's words. These problems imply the traditional preoccupation of Black poets with Black speech and Black music. Since I have discussed these concerns elsewhere at some length, I need not repeat myself, except to say that one could subsume them in the concept of the jazz poem which is itself rooted in the fact of jazz music's origins in blues, hymns, and other song forms. It is amplified by the vocal inflections of instrumental music and the instrumental vocalizations of jazz singers. It is therefore useful at this point to specify some of the features of the music and the poetry inspired by it.

Joachim[-Ernst] Berendt, author of the highly acclaimed study *The Jazz Book*, defines jazz as an art music which originated in the United States and out of the "confrontation of the Negro with European music." Its basic elements are:

1. A special relationship to time, defined as "swing."
2. A spontaneity and vitality of musical production in which improvisation plays a role.
3. A sonority and manner of phrasing which mirror the individuality of the performing jazz musician. (174)

The three basic elements of jazz—swing, improvisation, and jazz sound/phrasing—interact with one another in changing relationships which result in and from the evolution of the music. While these elements can be suggested by the poet, it is not the poet's object to write music but to create a verbal analogue of the music. A good working definition of the jazz poems is given by Onwuchekwa Jemie: "Unlike classic blues, the jazz poem has no fixed form: it is a species of free verse which attempts to approximate some of the qualities of jazz" (57). He continues:

The jazz poem derives from oral performance and music. Its relaxed attitude reflects the informal atmosphere in which the music thrives, and its open verse form is reminiscent of the improvisational latitude of the music. Its language—swift-paced, informal talk—aids the impression of spontaneity. The language is most often colloquial, sometimes the hip talk of the musicians, almost always the language of the common people, rarely the language of the academies. (58)

Just as the original jazz musicians drew upon the blues, and older musical forms, the poets drew upon diverse aspects of the oral tradition, depending on their knowledge of it. There they found in the narratives, in the imagery, in the language itself the verbal equivalents of jazz sound and jazz phrasing. Some if it came from the language of the jazz life, or slang, some of it came from songs, and some came from racial attitudes toward language that antedated both jazz and its parent, the blues. Once the poets probed the language and the culture in that fashion they were rewarded. Some of their specific accomplishments I have outlined elsewhere (33–45). However, it should be useful here to point to some of the technical solutions that poets arrived at in adapting the oral tradition—the sermons, street raps, political oratory, and the like—to their political and aesthetic needs, which included professional publication. Two examples come to mind—both seeming to involve the editing of transcribed speech. The first is H. Rap Brown's autobiographical account *Die! Nigger! Die!* (1969), which was first tape-recorded and then transcribed. The second is Askia Touré's essay "Keep on Pushin': Rhythm & Blues as a Weapon" (1965), which is actually a rhapsodic prose poem, its flamboyant dynamics captured through dramatic typography, especially in the use of uppercase passages and dashes, in a manner reminiscent of Thomas Carlyle, Kenneth Fearing, or Michael McClure. In Brown's book, there is not only an account of political development but the concomitant acquisition of verbal virtuosity. In several places the narrative erupts into a kind of poetry quite similar to much that was in circulation. But Rap Brown was neither writer nor poet, but a talker, one who "raps"—and that is how he got his name.

Julius Lester, who taped Brown's account and helped to edit it, has an eye for "found" poetry, and in his *Search for the New Land* (1969) the epigraphs consist of typeset news items arranged to mimic free verse. Aside from their narrative function however, these items demonstrate the contention that lineation forces us to distinguish between poetry and prose by signaling the stance or attitude which we should bring to bear on the text. Using the same device historian Vincent Harding took passages from the prose of W. E. B. Du Bois and arranged them as the poetry which they approach so clearly, to the consternation of more conservative historians.

Since the roots of the Black vernacular are largely anchored in folk speech, one would expect considerable attention to that speech by the poets. Although no one explored this phenomenon to the extent that Langston Hughes or some of the novelists did, it was assumed to be important, and the old-time speech of grandmothers and grandfathers was dutifully quoted and transcribed. Still, the old speech was abandoned for the most part in favor of the racy urban vernacular that reflected the contemporary reality. But as formal poetry it was still valuable and accessible even across cultural lines as Jeff Titon, blues scholar, demonstrates in his transcription and notation of two narratives of the legendary bluesman Son House, that he recorded in 1969 and 1971. What is noteworthy here is the conception of the narratives as poetry and Titon's explanation of his objectives and his method. It is an excellent blend of scholarship and art (House and Titon 2–8).

What we are speaking of, to be sure, is the employment of typography to suggest the character and the dynamics of Black speech as it evolves into poetry. The entire process is not without irony as we have seen, and borders on paradox. Still we are not speaking of dialect poetry and its attendant limitations, but of the attempt of poets and scholars to achieve the special, often subtle, goal that James Weldon Johnson spoke of years ago, "a form that is freer and larger than dialect, but which will still hold the racial flavor ... which will also be capable of voicing the deepest and highest emotions and aspirations and allow of the widest range of subjects and the widest scope of treatment" (8–9).

Two poets who simulate Black speech by using altered spelling like a kind of printer's screen are Carolyn Rodgers and Ntozake Shange. With both, the degree of "screening" varies according to the dictates of the poem, and the verisimilitude depends on a subtle and precise knowledge of speech patterns. At any rate, the effort seems less directed at aural realism than at suggesting a tonal screen that identifies not only the personae but the poet. In a poem like Shange's "on becomin successful" any pejorative talk of dialect is ridiculous since the speaker is obviously middle class (Shange, *Nappy Edges* 102). In another poem, "de poems gotta come outta my crotch?," she uses the typography of Ishmael Reed, David Henderson, and Sarah W. Fabio. A comparison of the two different "screens" will disclose subtle differences created to a considerable extent by the typography.

With Carolyn Rodgers there is another typographical screen at work, one influenced by Haki Madhubuti. Although she uses it inconsistently at times, she is often highly effective, as a poem such as "The Last MF" demonstrates (346–47). Much more important is the lyricism which she, like Shange, finds in speech as sound and as typographical artifact.

This brings us to an aspect of Black musical and oral style known as "worrying the line." While it subsumes the verbal analogue of jazz sound or sonority, it is closer to the analogue of jazz phrasing. If the verbal analogue of sonority is derived from vocabulary, phonology, and the like, then the analogue of phrasing derives from syntax, grammar, and accent. In the case of Carolyn Rodgers, we may consider "Poem for Some Black Women" (47–48). In "Bosom Buddies and Lonely Hearts," Daryl C. Dance states, "The typical Black female in contemporary literature by Black women is characterized mainly by her loneliness" (18), and she cites the poem by Carolyn Rodgers. What pertains to the present study, however, is not so much the theme as the means by which it is presented. The poem begins, "I am lonely," and the narrative voice ranges over the sensitive areas of the soul in a virtuosic analysis punctuated by the tolling of the word "lonely." The language is crucial, for the women "are talented, dedicated, well read / BLACK, COMMITTED," but they suffer in silence. They "Know too much," they are too understanding. They buy too many things. They need too many things. And the poem continues:

> We need ourselves sick, we need, we need
> We lonely we grow tired of tears we grow tired of fear

What is important here is the grammar. We recall that the women are educated, sophisticated, complex, and modern. Yet here in the last despairing stanza the poet elicits a note of pathos that reveals worlds about the condition not only of Black women but of millions of people, male and female, in the modern world. These two lines consist of six simple clauses which on first glance appear to be parallel. Examination shows, however, that the pattern is broken up at the beginning of the second line, where the speaker shifts to a Black vernacular construction, "we lonely," with the so-called zero copula retained from West African language patterns (Dillard 49, 52). The effect of this grammatical "lapse" (which is really an orchestration of the lines) is to add poignancy to the situation by stripping away all vestiges of masquerade, even the ones of Standard English. The realization is intensified by Black in-house references of "bitchy" and "Sapphire," negative extensions into the vernacular, and the stammering repetition of "not too dumb not too not too." And finally, as Dance observes, the poet reinforces the thematic intensity "by setting that last word *lonely* on a single line by itself and placing a period before and after it" (Dance 19).

Worrying the line is essentially a kind of analytical play on words, on parts of words, on qualities of words. It is as firmly entrenched in current vernacular as it is in folk speech. Originally, it referred to the personal practice of altering the pitch of notes in a given passage, or to other kinds of ornamentation often associated with melismatic singing in the Black tradition. In the verbal parallel a word or phrase is broken up and the fragments sometimes distorted to allow for affective or didactic comment (Henderson 41). The late Furry Lewis, for example, has a blues in which he says, "Don't you forneverget," and the word is stretched in order to include the intensifier. In another blues song the line is worried through the use of apheresis and punning on the word fragment:

> Talkin' 'bout Birmin'ham
> That ain't no "ham" a' tall
> You should see the "ham" in my—
> Ah, you know what I mean

What he means is, "You should see the 'ham' in my over(h)alls," a sexual boast.

In Black Southern vernacular or the 1940s and 1950s the word fragment "'fliction," truncated from "affliction," was current among young males as a positive intensifier which had its own special meanings, mostly associated with elegant, aggressive macho play, whether a basketball shot, a card game, or a sexual encounter. If you really did it right, you put the "'fliction" to it.

In Rich Amerson's song "Black Woman" a similar truncation is employed both for intensification and rhythm. He sings:

> Say I feel superstitious Mamma
> 'Bout my hoggin bread, Lord help my hungry time
> I feel superstitious, Baby, 'bout my hogging bread!
> Ah-hmmm, Baby, I feel superstitious,
> I say, 'stitious, Black Woman! (Henderson 108–9)

This pattern of analysis and intensification has been effectively employed by some of the recent poets. Two examples from diverse urban poets, Amiri Baraka and June Jordan, are pertinent. In a poem titled "Malcolm Remembered (Feb. '77)," Baraka writes: "Malcolm / Callin you back thru / Years / 12 years / Murder / ago / 12 years Cia / ago / 12 years / Elijah / ago" (287). The fragmentation sets up a powerful rhythmic pattern of accusation as the two elements of time and murder play against each other, with a particularization in the beat moving from "Murder" to "Cia" to "Elijah."

Some of the best examples of the technique occur in the poetry of June Jordan. Her poem "Gettin Down to Get Over" opens with a virtuoso roll call of the Black women's name, with the positive elements ambiguously intertwined with the negative. The call begins with the loving and familiar "Momma momma momma," runs the changes on man/woman relations, on love and friendship, and then invokes *nommo*, the Bantu for the creative power of the Word. Momma and *nommo* are, in effect, equated. From then on, the poem discovers the creative force inherent in the combination. In the passage that follows, the poet plays on the names of two or perhaps three women artists—Nina Simone, the singer and pianist; Nikki Giovanni, the poet; and perhaps Nona Hendricks, the singer:

> hey!
> nina nikki nonni nommo nommo
> momma Black
> Momma (27)

The play of alliteration, consonance, and assonance helps the poet to domesticate this exotic African word which had been so quickly absorbed into the literary lexicon of the 1960s and 1970s.

A volume of sociological analysis is compressed in this rapid-fire enumeration of images of Black women generated by the white male power structure: "Black Woman / Black / Female Head of Household / Black Matriarchal

Matriarchy / Black Statistical / Lowlife Lowlevel Lowdown / Lowdown and up / to be Low-down / Black Statistical / Low Factor / Factotem / Factitious Fictitious / Figment Figuring in Lowdown Lyin / Annual Reports" (28). The furious alliteration, especially that of the "fs," is the element that "worries the line," as the repetition of the word "Black" drives the rhythm.

Jordan renders exploitation by the Black male with equal precision and even greater elaboration: "What does Mothafuckin mean? / WHO'S THE MOTHAFUCKA / FUCKED MY MOMMA / messes yours over / and right now / be trippin on my starveblack / female soul / a macktruck / mothafuck / the first primordial / the paradig/dogmatic / dogmatistic mothafucka who / is he? / hey! / momma momma" (29). As Berendt has indicated, the three basic jazz elements operate together, although one may be emphasized at the expense of the others. With that interaction in mind, we may notice how the wordplay, especially the fragmentation, may affect or determine the rhythm of the passage. We may also see how improvisation may originate from rhythm and sound. In the passage above, there is a continuation of jazz sound through the wordplay, beginning in the deliberate tautology of the subhuman "first primordial." Then, with "paradig/dogmatic," the poet scores a visual and auditory success as the formal word "paradigmatic" is exploded into a shadow version of "parody" and the hip "dig" is repeated with irony and sarcasm. The slant clarifies the relationship as the new word "digmatic" screeches from the page like a saxophone sound that eludes notation. The invention carries over to "dogmatistic," a newly created intensive modeled on the earlier sounds of "statistical," "factitious," and "fictitious," in the free association of Black speech patterns. The whole passage, we note in passing, is based on the call-and-response format.

The call-and-response pattern is one of the strongest and oldest structural features of Black music and speech, including oratory and conversation. It is found in all forms of the music and in much of the poetry which seeks a Black identification. Accordingly, we find it in religious music—in gospel and the spirituals—in popular music, and in the myriad varieties of blues and jazz. Poets who self-consciously explore these forms have thus sought to incorporate this mechanism into their work. As one traces a line from the sermons transcribed by E. C. L. Adams and Zora Neale Hurston through the poems of James Weldon Johnson and W. E. B. Du Bois, through Ralph Ellison, through the sixties, one discovers the various devices that the writers employ. First, note that two of these writers, Hurston and Johnson, omit direct references to the congregation, so that their response is simply assumed. Both, however, are concerned with the dynamics of the event, the intake of breath as a rhythmic marker, for example. In the poems of E. C. L. Adams, a physician and amateur folklorist, we find a highly sophisticated rendering of both call and response. In his second collection, *Nigger to Nigger*, he records a fragment of a sermon entitled "The Harps of God" (218–20). Technically germane to the discussion is its typography. The preacher's voice, carrying the sermon, is set in regular type and is periodically interrupted by voices responding from the congregation, set in smaller type and identified by italics. The irregular grouping of the preacher's lines suggests delivery rate, and the space separating the responses from the sermon suggests pauses in the delivery where the preacher allows for the response. In addition, the smaller type of the response suggests a lower volume of sound.

Call-and-response is not always so obvious, however, either in the music or the poetry. In his "Memphis Blues," published in 1932, for example, Sterling Brown incorporates the call-and-response pattern into a dynamic stanza based on the blues. By building jazz solos out of riffs answered by melodic improvisation, Charlie Christian, states Berendt, had a considerable impact on the creation of modern jazz. "In the improvisations of Charlie Christian, the riffs are the 'calls,' the subsequent free-swinging lines the 'responses'" (163). In effect, then, "the improvising soloist holds a conversation with himself." A practice similar to this occurs in June Jordan's poems. In section 2 of "Getting Down to Get Over" the lines are subdivided by the repeated command "Consider the Queen." It is repeated seven times, the last time closing the section. Each statement is a kind of riff which is lyrically developed. A particularly effective passage begins:

> She works when she works
> in the laundry *in jail*
> in the school house *in jail*
> in the office *in jail* (33)

And the pattern becomes a kind of cross-riffing as the "in jail" rhythm responds to the beginning of successive lines. The tempo increases as the refrain "in jail" is dropped and the fast-paced free rhyming follows the thematic arrival of the weekend.

Let us look briefly at some examples from the poetry of Larry Neal. First, there is the call-and-response pattern used in the "modern" manner indicated above. In "Don't Say Goodbye to the Porkpie Hat," Neal's poem in homage to Lester Young, Charles Mingus, John Coltrane, and other jazz greats, there is a long, lofting, high-energy solo that concludes with a kind of epiphany:

[lines 142–53 from "Don't Say Goodbye to the Porkpie Hat"]
SPIRIT!!!
SWHEEEEEEEEEEEEEEEETTT!!!

take it again
this time from the top (*Hoodoo Hollerin'* 24)

Here the pattern is reduced to its essence, both as theme and as form. Thematically speaking, the call-and-response dramatizes the interaction of sound (music), which one digs, and spirit, which one affirms. In the resolution they are one. In the epiphany they affirm the triumph of life over death, spirit over material stupidity. Man cannot create a forever, Neal's friend J. Stewart used to say, but man can create forever. So, the music is played again, this time from the beginning, from the top.

The element of improvisation becomes apparent as one reads the entire poem, but one may get a better idea of its extent by noting that the poem appears in two main versions, and in the second, from which the quote is taken, the poet changes whole sections, and creates two "takes," so to speak, of the composition. One change here involves the borrowing of a riff from another poem, "Black Boogaloo," which he compresses and intensifies in "Don't Say Goodbye to the Porkpie Hat." It goes,

Dig. Dig Black. be. be. be. be. be.
Be. be. be. be. be. (*Black Boogaloo* 43)

In the final version, the rhythmic drive of the dialectic creates the ultimate solo flight.

This riffing, this use of repeated rhythmic phrases, of "short, explosive lines," in Haki Madhubuti's (Don Lee's) words brings us to a brief consideration of the notion of "swing." In its original sense, it referred to the fluid, floating pulsation against a "fixed," steady beat laid down by the rhythm section. It has since been applied to more subtle effects deriving from the overlapping of meters, the superimposition of melodies, and the tension between melodic and rhythmic elements (Berendt 163–73). For our purposes, the original definition is a good place from which to begin. Some of the other effects will become apparent in the illustrations which follow. In Sterling Brown's poem "Puttin on Dog" we find this line:

Look at old Scrappy putting on dog
Puttin on dog, puttin on dog (*The Collected Poems* 227)

The swing-producing element comes from a prolongation and "bluing" of the words "putting" and "on" and the omission, in the vernacular, of a word which would have appeared in Standard English. Thus, the lines are actually written and read against these:

> Look at old Scrappy putting on (the) dog
> Putting on (the) dog, putting on (the) dog

In the free verse poem "The Nice Colored Man," Ted Joans sets up several contrasting rhythms which are based on the word "n[*****]." The first is the regular beat, the second, a riff. Preceding each regular beat, there is a "melodic" element created by the qualifying adjective, phrase, or adverb. Important to this discussion is the fact that little actually depends on line length as such but on the transfer of oral rhythm to the page. The grouping of repeated elements shifts and changes to produce one of the best satirical poems to come out of the period (Henderson 223–25).

In his afterword to Haki Madhubuti's *Earthquakes and Sunrise Missions*, Darwin Turner discusses the poet's use of repetition and the way overlapping words develop into separate and distinct messages (184–86). For the present study there is more to be discovered than this stereophonic effect. Let us examine the passage in question from "A Poem to Complement Other Poems":

> change n[*****] change
> know the realenemy
> change: is u is or is u aint. change. now now
>   change. for the better
> [lines 5–21 from "A Poem to Complement Other Poems"] (184–86)

In the passage the two motifs "change" and "know the realenemy" are held together and developed by the rhythmic chanting (which is apparent even when one reads the poem for the first time) of the word "change" which is repeated thirty-four times in twenty-one lines. Note the use of interlock, as described by Alan Lomax, in which the second line/motif is introduced before the first is completed. They eventually cohere into distinct statements at the end of the composition. In the first line, two out of the three words are "change," the other is "n[*****]" the heaviest word in the Black Experience. Thus the "message" is clearly and forcefully stated from the outset. The entire passage is saturated with the word "change," and even without the rapid-fire style of the poet's delivery, the word virtually inundates the page. In the last two long lines of the poem there are twelve words, and nine of them are the word "change."

Performance, to be sure, was one way to approach some of the problems we have discussed. Still the mere fact of performance was no panacea. Performance, for example, was no guarantee that the poem would "swing." And it is particularly illuminating to hear some of the early recordings of Black poetry of the sixties. If one listens to Walter Lowenfels's *New Jazz Poets*, for example, one will discover very little difference in delivery between the white "Beat" poets and poets like David Henderson (who was an original member of the Umbra Workshop), Ishmael Reed, and others. The difference appears not in their delivery but in their imagery.

But live performance became highly popular as the poets soon learned the craft that Larry Neal and Askia Touré pointed to in James Brown; they developed what was, in effect, a Black performance style. Neal himself became one of the best readers of his generation, along with Baraka, Askia Touré, June Jordan, Jayne Cortez, Nikki Giovanni, Sonia Sanchez, Eugene Redmond, Haki Madhubuti, Quincey Troupe, and others.

The performance factor, however, led to confusion as poets worked for punch lines and calculated appeals to ideological imperatives, including racial prejudice. Still one must admit the widespread appeal and importance of the poetry readings, not only to academic audiences consisting largely of undergraduate students, but also to community gatherings and consciousness-heightening sessions. Among the distinctive successes one must name Nikki Giovanni's record albums, especially the first, *Truth Is On Its Way*, which was recorded with the New York Community Gospel Choir. And there were records and tapes by other poets with music integrated into the performance. Among these were works by Baraka, Madhubuti, Fabio, [Stanley] Crouch, Sanchez, Cortez, and others. Some who made no commercial recordings nevertheless participated in hundreds of readings. Under certain conditions the musical elements tipped the balance into song, as in the phenomenon of Gil Scott-Heron, who is a novelist, poet, musician, [and] activist. He recited and sang his own poetry to the music of his own rock group, and with satirical songs like "In the Bottle," he came close to the role of the poet as entertainer that was envisioned by Larry Neal. The rap style of performance since that time has been reclaimed by Grandmaster Flash and the Furious Five with a rap like "The Message" (Sugar Hill Records, 1982). Still one can view performances like these as updated versions of The Last Poets ("The Revolution Will Not Be Televised"). And as one would expect, the enormous popularity of the rap style among young people (white and Black) was quickly noted by the business community so that today one hears TV raps on the delights of McDonald's food or some other product. And flat sounding "anti" raps are beamed by army recruiters at potential soldiers, just as a generation ago the street rhymes of Black draftees were absorbed into the cadences of hip drill sergeants, where they have grown and flourished.

In performance, stylistic features which seem muted on the page or merely suggested by the type are given greater prominence. Among those features are call-and-response patterns (especially those that may involve several voices), riff patterns, percussive rhythmic effects, and orchestrated voicings. The most obvious feature that appears is sound as sound, sound used for its own sake, not as verbal component, nor as tone, but as building material.

As we have seen, one of the problems of jazz poetry lies in suggesting tonal quality and texture. This led Langston Hughes to adopt a bebop vocabulary for his "Montage of a Dream Deferred" and for the long montage entitled *Ask Your Mama*. In those poems the written language echoes the voices of the musicians which, in turn, mimic their instruments. Instructive here is Dizzy Gillespie at the Newport Jazz Festival as he instructed the audience how to "sing along" by placing the right kind of sharp accent on the first syllable of peanuts in "Salt Peanuts! Salt Peanuts!" They found it difficult because it was not the accent that he wanted so much as the right "attack." Especially problematic to the poets of the sixties were the "atonal" sounds produced by the new musicians like Pharoah Sanders and John Coltrane. They understood how the sounds made them feel, but translating them into a poem was something else. Of course, they could describe the sounds, and they did. Many of the most interesting poems consisted of this kind of description. For instance, Neal writes:

> hear them screeching love in
>   rolling sheets of sound . . .
> crisp and moaning voices
>   leaping in the horns of destruction (Henderson 292)

Madhubuti (Don L. Lee) writes of Coltrane that he came "into the sixties . . . blowing / a-melodics / screeching / screaming, blasting" (Henderson 336). As the poem progresses, we find more direct representations of the Coltrane sound and comment on the means that the poet/performer must employ to achieve it. As he wrote these stage directions, as it were, Madhubuti—like Hughes and Frank Marshall Davis before him, and like contemporaries Sarah Webster Fabio and Sonia Sanchez—was at once admitting the inadequacy of notation and seeking an open form that had to be completed either in the reader's imagination, on the stage, or before a microphone. And the first formal jazz poet, Vachel Lindsay, knew this too, of course, for his stage directions to "The Congo" perform the very same functions.

Two poems of the sixties push the poetry even farther in the realm of sound, toward what has since become known as "sound poetry." These poets were Ronald Stone (later known as Yusuf Rahman) and Norman Pritchard. Both appear on the recording *New Jazz Poets*, edited by Walter Lowenfels. Stone's composition entitled "Lady Day Spring-Toned" is a tone poem in a literal sense, that is, its effects are achieved largely through varying the tone and pitch of the voice as it plays upon a series of loosely organized images. At points the sounds themselves are nearly abstract, though sensuously so.

With "Gyre's Galaxy" Pritchard explores even further the abstract tonal relations found in a single line. There is scarcely any verbal content as such, and the effect is nearly musical. Oddly enough, Pritchard's poetry, published in the seventies, veered toward the visual, the abstractly visual at that, toward a kind of essentialist or reductionist linguistics, where the aesthetic object becomes one or two capital letters composed of subtly placed smaller letters engaged in subliminal dialogue. Pritchard thus becomes a kind of concrete poet. The seeming paradox of his two extremes of representation—pure sound on one hand, and empty linguistic icon on the other—epitomizes the technical challenges inherent in a poetry rooted in an art form as shifting and protean as jazz. In a way, the poets envied the musicians who inspired them, and at one point, Neal indicated that the poet should struggle to free himself from the text. The text could be "destroyed" for all that the inspired poet should care, for he like the musician would improvise on materials drawn from memory (Jones and Neal 653). And A. B. Spellman, poet and jazz critic, felt that Rahman actually achieved, for a while, the kind of condition that Neal and others strove for. He states:

> You had to see him one Monday night at Slugs or East Third Street between Ave's C & D in concert with Sun Ra's Arkestra, as it was then called. Costumed and jeweled in a manner reminiscent of the Sudanese, preparing the room with incense, shaking chains of bells as he moved among the tables, Yusuf danced and sang his poems. The lines as written were like chord changes for verbal improvisation. Taken literally, from the page, we might think the author of these lines to be a silly second-rate Surrealist:

> A Gnostic frog-eyed owl / quilted by bone yards bitter
> Blacknight /
> SOMEWHERE OVER A COSMIC RAINBOW

But, in performance, the audience's mind straining to visualize the images from this whirling Black man who played on every sense and backed by the empathetic Sun Ra band, the effect was strong indeed.

Thus, the premises of craft for this poet depend as much on his ability to deliver his lines as it does his ability to write them. With recoilless lines like "SOUL-talking / SOUL-talking / SOUL-talking / could be Pops Armstrong a Black Mack-the-knife / strut strut struting [sic] with some bar-b-q." This last sung as Armstrong performed it, segueing into a sequence of quotes from the classics of jazz, crescendoing into a kind of bebop Sufic chant, it is clear that this poet had to be seen to be appreciated (Spellman 8–9).

The scat singing of Louis Armstrong, Ella Fitzgerald, Sarah Vaughan, Betty Carter, and other vocalists provided another resource for the poets. And they challenged the reader, especially the unhip reader, to understand not merely their intentions, but where they were "coming from." Spellman's article "Oral Challenges to the Written Word: The Poetry of Yusuf Rahman and Amus Mor" helps us to understand the links between scatting and the representation of jazz sounds on the page. Here he refers to a poem by Amus Mor, from his book *The Coming of John*: "The next poem could not have been written ten years earlier. For one thing, no one would have known that it was possible to sing the third and fourth bars of John Coltrane's 'Naima' on the page: 'it was the end of naima / that most beautiful melody / a dusty red crescent over the bell tower / and us fool enough to riff the head / De daaa daaa dee daaaa daaa daaaaa'" (Spellman 8–9). The technical challenge was also answered by Bob Kaufman, in "CROOTEY SONGO," from his *Golden Sardine*. The following is the last stanza of the three-stanza poem:

DEGET, SKLOKO, KURRITIF, PLOG, MANGI, PLOG MANGI,
CLOPO JAGO BREE, BREE, ASLOOPERED, AKINGO LABY.
ENGPOP, ENGPOP, BOP, PLOLO, PLOLO, BOP, BOP (Kaufman 54)

Kaufman's poem suggests the scatting of the jazz vocalist, and if its form, including the length of the lines, were determined by music, one would probably be justified in calling it a song, or simply a musical composition with a minimal tone range (see Kostelanetz, *The End of Intelligent Writing*, 373). But there are several elements that make us classify it as a poem. The first is the resemblance of these sounds to actual language, and the treatment of the forms as though they were language. The entire poem, for example, consists of three stanzas, the first containing four lines and the last two, three lines each, for a total of ten lines. Thus, we have an appeal to the visual practice of arranging poetry in stanzas, with an echo of the quatrain in the first stanza, and the triplet in the last two. There are other connections also, of grammar and punctuation, that emphasize the verbal. In the passage quoted, note the commas separating the series of "words." Note, too, the implied "grammatical" distinction between "PLOG, MANGI" and "PLOG MANGI." Note the implied grammatical parallel between "ASLOOPERED" and "AKINGO LABY." It is all very clever and very funny, and it never loses the humor and satire of jazz and its folk roots. It is also the work of a highly sophisticated poet whose fabulous verbal gifts have not been fully appreciated. And as we read lines like these we sense the mingling of the conventional and the creative. We are brought in contact with puns that are part nonsense and part slang, part satire, part play. The first stanza ends with word-play" "HEDACAZ, AX—,O,O," with the puns on the word "sax" and "sex." There is a similar playfulness at the beginning of the second stanza: "DEEREDITION, BOOMEDITION, SQUOM, SQUOM, SQUOM." Finally, we note that the poem conforms to the conventions of poetic perception and closure as cited by Barbara H. Smith (84–95) and that it benefits from the discussion "Song as Oral Communication," by Mark W. Booth (7–14).

Between the two extremes of poetry as abstract sound composition and poetry as the verbal analogue of jazz, with perhaps indeterminate form, we find a poetry that is elastic enough to be read well by a performer but fixed enough to guide the silent reader. Most of the poetry is of this type and it uses the typographical resources common to poetry in our time. Still its rhythms and musicality are often distinctive, and the whole attitude toward language which it embodies, on its deepest levels, is reflective of a vigorously flourishing Black oral tradition.

NOTE

1. Clarence Major's *The New Black Poetry* (1969) was intended as an anthology of exclusively Black poets, but John Sinclair, founder of the White Panther Party, is also included with the anti–Vietnam War poem "Breakthrough." As he has noted in conversation with this volume's editors, Major did not realize that Sinclair was white when he accepted his submission for the volume.

AFTERWORD

THE CRITICAL DISCOURSE OF
STEPHEN E. HENDERSON

PHILLIP M. RICHARDS

Stephen E. Henderson's literary criticism situates itself in a particular moment in Black cultural history amid the movements for civil rights, Black Power, and Black Arts. In the broadest possible sense, his work seeks a Black Aesthetic that can serve as a humanism to define and reproduce the Black literary tradition from the middle nineteenth century to future generations. He addressed the humanistic possibilities of his historical moment to his contemporaries and to future readers of the tradition.

In his vocation as a critic, Henderson's intention was largely pedagogical. This element of his criticism posed the question of how Black youth should be educated as a politically and aesthetically conscious middle class. His writing faced the issue of how the traditions of Black historians, writers, and social scientists could inform a worldview, a view of the world which is cosmopolitan but aware of the literate Black person's place in history. In this connection, Henderson was particularly concerned with the impact of what he saw as a Black cultural renaissance in the late fifties, sixties, and seventies. This period had been crucial for the recovery of much Black folk tradition, new artistic forms in music, dance, and speech. It saw, too, the articulation of these literary works into a new cultural, political, social, and religious consciousness that he called "Soul."[1]

It is important to remember that Henderson began his task as a critic by critiquing the absence of attention to Black Culture in the Historically Black Colleges and Universities (HBCUs). He admitted that Black colleagues in those sites had performed admirably in preparing Black people for entry into the American professional classes. However, he believed that they were inadequate to the challenge of educating young Black people for the moment of cultural change that they were encountering in midcentury America and afterward. He went on to critique American universities for their blindness to the enormous contributions of Black people to the shaping of American and global societies.[2]

Henderson's critical practice was situated in the schools, research institutions, and think tanks. His methods provided an early rationalization for the function of African American literature within Black educational and cultural institutes. His career evolved at Virginia Union University and Morehouse College, where he taught; the Atlanta Institute of the Black World; and Howard's Institute for the Arts and the Humanities. His career focused on the creation of these sites and the solicitation of funding for them, as well as the scholarly and curricular work that they produced.

The issues I raise above were of crucial importance for Henderson's critical method, his sense of literary history, and his conception of proper critical judgement. This critical method was catalyzed by the need for a literary-critical defense of the New Black Poetry, which had come under attack by the mainstream white poetry establishment during the fifties, sixties, and seventies. This attack required a justification for the formal structures of the poetry of figures such as Amiri Baraka, Sonia Sanchez, and June Jordan. Second, it necessitated an account of the character of the poetry: an explanation of the stance of the poet, the poem's dramatic situation, and an elucidation more generally of the New Black Poetry's underlying historical moment.[3] Describing his critical approach to a poem, Henderson presents a methodology for the analysis of a poem that integrates the concerns of his literary history, his approach to the New Black Poetry, and his understanding of the relation of the poem to the continuity of the African American poetic tradition. The first level of the poem is its theme, which may be taken from the mainstream Anglo-American tradition. The second level of the poem is structure, which is derived from Black American oral and written traditions. The third level of the poem is saturation: the poem's stance toward the realities of the Black historical moment.[4]

This methodology locates Henderson's practical criticism within the context of the Black literary tradition. It speaks to the New Critical approaches of those scholars who came immediately before Henderson, such as Sterling A. Brown and Arthur P. Davis. It speaks to the use of contemporary Black vernacular as poetic structure in the writing of Haki R. Madhubuti and Sonia Sanchez. And finally, the conception of saturation, a holistic Blackness, responds to the conceptions of Blackness in Amiri Baraka. Ultimately,

Henderson's practical criticism provides an empirical way of articulating poetic expression from the blues and work songs through the beginnings of formal Black verse in the late eighteenth and early nineteenth century to George McClellan and Paul Dunbar and finally to Langston Hughes. Even the verse of Phillis Wheatley or Jupiter Hammon can be submitted to the criteria of its use of Anglo-American theme, religious language, or the contemporary situation of free Black people in their period.[5]

For Henderson, the criterion of saturation is the crucial distinction in the cosmopolitan Blackness, which he seeks for cultivated Black people as well as for the Black literature of the present day. It is a stance of Black human authenticity that allows the person of color to face the existential demands of the given historical moment with an appropriate sense of its meaning in terms of his political, social, cultural, and, significantly, spiritual past. The spiritual past and its continuity from the beginning of the Black tradition is particularly important to Henderson. The spiritual continuity of Blackness developed in the sixties and seventies into the conceptual of "Soul." The unity of Black poetry, music, and dance expressed in "Soul" as a transcendent spiritual power allowed the Black person to confront and transcend the exigencies of his time.[6]

Henderson has clearly been a crucial influence on major critics who have followed him. His insistence on literary structure has pointed the way to later critics' focus on Black linguistic and grammatical forms as a means of analyzing poetry, creating canonical narratives, and stylistically defining a critical discourse.[7] Black literary critics have gone on to rely on the repetition, variation, and troping of literary structures to interpret Black literary texts individually and as an African American literary canon. In this respect, Henderson is an important link between two different generation of Black literary critics, particularly in his interest in close reading, critical theory, and their relation to literary history.

Moreover, the impetus for Henderson's Black-oriented criticism largely emerged from his experience with the Black college curriculum and the historical development of a dislocated Black presence in the recently integrated white universities. However, the great power of Henderson was in his reliance on a vast store of empirical knowledge of the music, sermonic speech, and discourse of Black folk. He combined this with an extensive knowledge of formal Black poetry in the twentieth century, as well as a capacious acquaintance with British and American literature. His sense of the structural base of Black poetry has come directly from his inquiries into the structures of Black poetry in the spirituals, the blues, and folk speech in Langston Hughes, Sterling Brown, and Larry Neal. Henderson's emphasis on the importance of saturation in the studies and mature lives of educated Black people came especially to the fore in his broad statements on culture.

This fact cannot be overlooked. Henderson's conception of structure and saturation gave his literary critiques access to the critic's specific knowledge of African American blues, work songs, spirituals, folk speech, and ballads. Henderson could write authoritatively of these forms as they appeared in the wide-ranging work of Hughes, Brown, Henry Dumas, and Mari Evans. This erudition gave specificity to Henderson's traditionally literary-critical essays such as "The Blues as Folk Poetry." This philological knowledge of the language, verse, and songs of the folk allowed him to make plausible distinctions between different interpretations of literary meaning in African American literature. Combined with his prowess as a close reader and critic of literary expression, Henderson exercised an enormous authority as a student of Black literature and a builder of Black cultural institutions. A close reading of this volume's essays reveals that we have not yet seen his kind again.

NOTES

1. See "Black Saturation: A View of the Humanities" herein.

2. See "Saturation Progress: Report on the Theory of Black Poetry" herein.

3. In his defense of the New Black Poetry, Henderson begins to deploy his criteria for the proper appreciation of poetry. See "The Question of Form and Judgment in Contemporary Black American Poetry: 1962–1977" herein.

4. For an account of Henderson's formal method of explication, see "Saturation" herein.

5. For applications of Henderson's critical method, see "The Heavy Blues of Sterling Brown: A Study of Craft and Tradition" herein. See also, in this volume, "Take Two—Larry Neal and the Blues God: Aspects of the Poetry."

6. See "Saturation."

7. See Henry Louis Gates Jr., *The Signifying Monkey: A Theory of African American Literary Criticism* (New York: Oxford University Press, 1988).

APPENDIX

SELECTED SYLLABI FOR HENDERSON'S HOWARD UNIVERSITY COURSES

Blues, Soul, and Black Identity   080-198-01
Fall Semester, 1972   Dr. Stephen Henderson

COURSE OUTLINE

Rationale: The basic assumption behind this seminar is that the term "Soul" embodies a highly compressed folk myth of Black Experience in America and that its currency among Black people of all walks of life (in Martin Luther King's phrase—"The Ph.D.'s and the no D's") indicate at once both its comprehensiveness and its pragmatic vitality. Soul in the course is thus equated to Blackness and this Blackness is examined especially as its paradoxes are expressed in the poetry and music of the blues. The further assumption is that the blues is the "touchstone" of the entire Black Experience in America.

Approach: The instructor assumes that the blues is essentially a non-academic subject (despite the folklorists and the traditional teachers of English); in fact, it is an anti-academic subject. Notwithstanding, if the education of Black young people is to be meaningful, if they are to know themselves, so that they may serve their people, then it must deal in some way with the aesthetic and psychological experience of the blues.

Since many Blacks have rejected blues, especially the earlier country blues, or know relatively little about them, the first job of the instructor is to provide information about the blues and to give students an opportunity for extensive listening and analysis.

Virtually unknown to most academic people, a sizeable body of scholarship and research has grown up around the blues. Extensive recordings have been made ever since the 20s and a small group of dedicated amateurs both in Europe and the United States continues the tedious task of amassing information. However, the critical interpretation of blues, with a few notable exceptions, has been largely naïve or misleading. Since the blues, in the opinion of the instructor, is the touchstone of the Black Experience in America, this situation is intolerable. Thus, the materials of the course are drawn, in part, from his own research and critical preoccupations—from interviews, theories, transcriptions, and critiques.

The seminar meets twice weekly—Monday and Friday from 1:40 P.M. to 3:00 P.M.

OUTLINE OF DISCUSSION AND RESEARCH AREAS

I. <u>Introduction</u>: Informal lecture: What is blues? Rationale behind the course. Cf. statement above. Approaches to the blues, geared to students' major fields of interest: psychological, sociological, philosophical, historical, aesthetic, ideological.

II. <u>Roots of the Blues</u>

    A. Africa Remembered: Illustration type based on theories of Courlander, Lomax, Work with critique of instructor.

        1. Djuka drums

        2. Song of Chango

        3. Song of Obatala

        4. Song of Lagba and Vemayá

        5. Song of Ortega Chango

        6. Ras Tafari, Jamaica

        7. John Canoe, Jamaica

        8. Junkanoo band, Key West, Florida

        9. Celta Cruz: Para ta Altar, Resurge al Omelanko

        10. Various examples from the U.S.A., including Georgia, Sea Island Singers, Rich Amerson, Moving Star Hill Singers, etc.

    B. Discussion based on experiences of the class, of some African musical features and survivals in these Afro-American sources.

    C. Africa Remembered, U.S.A.

        1. Field cries and field hollers singing style, African voice timbres, etc.

        2. Development of framework for discussion of LeRoi Jones' *Blues People*.

            Illustrations for C.1. drawn from various field recordings in prisons, etc., the "dozens," folk sermons, nick-names.

III. <u>Black Sacred and Secular Music, U.S.A:</u> Some theories of origin, some implications for the Black Aesthetic

    A. Secular

        1. Work songs, illustrated with recordings from Angola, Parchman, etc.

        2. Children's songs, recorded by Courlander and Lomax

        3. Calypso and verbal improvisation

    B. Sacred

        1. Spirituals: Theories of origin, characteristics, themes

        2. Hymns

        3. Gospel: Origin and derivation (theories) and influence on "Soul Music" style

    C. Tangencies and Congruencies of Sacred and Secular

        1. Parodies of sacred song (e.g., "I heard the voice of a pork chop say, 'Come unto me and rest'")

        2. Textual borrowings form sacred to secular and vice versa

        3. Attitudes of singers toward blues/sacred songs

4. Attitudes of church people toward blues

5. Similarities in formal and expressive devices of style and their relationship to "Soul" singing—synthesis of gospel, jazz, blues—Illustrations: Aretha Franklin (in church, 15 years old)

IV. The Blues Continuum

A. Report: *Blues People*, LeRoi Jones

B. Critique: "The Blues as a Genre," Harry Oster

C. Survey of blues style: Illustrations and critique of Charles Heil's scheme. Illustrations of geographical and other variations

D. Great representative blues artists and their importance

V. A close examination of blues texts: Central importance of the texts (documented by blues singers)

A. The blues as poetry: The language continuum, relationship to vernacular, dozens, proverbs, folksayings, toasts, critique of academic and amateur approaches to blues poetry

B. Blues as embodiment of Black Experience: Class discussions of research topics—bibliography, discography, rationale, organization

VI. Areas for Individual Research

A. Blues in literature: Hughes, S. Brown, McKay, Ellison and Baldwin; Wright; the New Black Poets, and others

B. Blues as sociology: Typical themes (to be refined)

1. Self-concept and battle of the sexes

2. Doin It and Dues

3. Attitudes toward family: mother, father, etc.

4. Implicit concept of the Black community

5. Social awareness

6. "Rejection" of the blues by the Black bourgeoisie

7. Social protest

8. Survival techniques

C. Psychology

1. Self-hatred vs. self-celebration

2. Self-hatred and self-celebration

3. Blues and the "dozens"

4. Soul as "Black Unconscious": Exploration of mythic patterns and their present day relevance

5. White "blues revival" and the hippie movement

D. Blues Form: Originals (Cf. sec. II & II above)

E. Individual performers

F. Philosophy/Aesthetics of the blues

VII. Soul and "negritude"

A. Discussion and lectures based on scholarship and the mass media

B. Critical examination of selected interviews on "Soul"

C. Critiques and criticism of negritude/Soul: Fanon, Karenga, Rustin, *et al.*

VIII. The Black Aesthetic

A. Empirical dimensions: Historical, sociological, philosophical

B. Ideological dimensions: Critique

IX. The Black Aesthetic and Black Identity

ADDENDA:

1. Reading list (tentative and selective) and discography

2. Copies of xeroxed articles to date

BLUES, SOUL, AND BLACK IDENTITY BIBLIOGRAPHY

Harold Courlander, *Negro Folk Music.* U.S.A.

John W. Work, *American Negro Songs.* New York: Bonanza Books, 1940.

Frederick Ramsey, *Been Here and Gone.* New Brunswick: Rutgers University Press, 1960.

Charles Keil, *The Urban Blues.* Chicago: University of Chicago Press, 1966. (paper $2.45)

LeRoi Jones, *Blues People.* New York: William Morrow & Co. (Apollo Edition), 1963. (paper $1.65)

———, *Black Music.* New York: William Morrow & Co., 1968.

Samuel B. Charles, *The Country Bus.* New York: Holt, Rinehart & Winston, 1959.

———, *The Bluesman.* New York: Oak Publications, 1967.

Paul Oliver, *The Meaning of the Blues.* New York: Collier Books, 1963. (95¢)

Langston Hughes, *The Weary Blues.* New York: Knopf, 1926.

Ralph Ellison, *Shadow and Act.* New York: New American Library Signet, 1966. (95¢)

Sterling Brown, "The Blues as Folk Poetry." *The Book of Negro Folklore.* L. Hughes and A. Bontemps (eds.). New York: March 1968.

Stephen E. Henderson, "Blues for the Young Blackman." *Negro Digest.* August 1967.

S. Charters, *The Poetry of the Blues.* New York: Oak Publications, 1963.

Rod Brunar, "A Closer Look at the Blues." *Down Beat: Music, '67, 12th Yearbook.* pp. 50–53.

Roger Abrahams, *Deep Down in the Jungle.* Hatboro, Pa.: Folklore Associates, 1964.

Blues Discography. $50.

S. Charters, ed., *The Rural Blues: A Study of Vocal and Instrumental Resources.* REF Records, 165 West 46th St., New Your RF #202 (2 records)

———, ed., The Asch Recordings, 1939–1947, vol. 1. Asch Co. (2 records)

———, ed., *The Country Blues.* RF #1.

Singing the Blues. Caedmon Records.

The Bessie Smith Story (Golden Era Series), 4 vols. Columbia Records.

Country Blues Classics. 3 vols. Blues Classics #5, 6, 7, Arhoolie Records, P.O. Box 5073, Berkeley, California.

Music for the South. vol. 10 (Been Here and Gone), ed. F. Ramsey, Jr. Folkways Records #FA2659.

Living Legends: Son House, Skip James, Bukka White, Big Joe Williams. Verve Folkways, #FT-3010.

The Unexpurgated Folk Songs of Men. Ed. Mack McCormick.

Leadbelly: The Library of Congress Recordings. 3 vols. Electra-301.

Rev. Gary Davis, *Say No to the Devil.* Bluesville 1049, Bluesville Records, 203 South Washington Avenue, Bergenfield, New Jersey.

Department of Afro-American
   Studies
Howard University
Instructor: Dr. Stephen E.
   Henderson
Office: 317, Founders Library

Phone: 636-7242/3
Comparative Black Literature
080-195-03 & 04
Spring 1990
Office hours: 4–6p.m. M & F &
By Appointment

SYLLABUS

Required Texts (*Ordered through the University Bookstore)
Richard Barksdale & Kenneth Kinnamon, *Black Writers of America: A Comprehensive Anthology*
Norman Shapiro, *Negritude: Black Poetry from Africa and the Caribbean*
Chinua Achebe, *Things Fall Apart*

Course Description
   Using lectures, tapes and oral reports, this course will survey the literature of African-American, Caribbean and African writers, with emphasis on the African-American. After examining eighteenth and nineteenth century Afro-American writing, we will explore contacts between writers of African descent in all three areas of the twentieth century—the Harlem Renaissance, the Negritude Movement, and the major post-World War II writers. The political, historical, and social relationships between art and society will be an underlying assumption in the work of the course.

Course Objectives

1. To generally inform students about the broad historical purposes of Black literature.
2. To generally inform students about the colonial context—traditional or internal—in which Black literature has developed.
3. To generally inform students about 18th and 19th century African-American literature, from the development of slave narratives and the appropriation of American revolutionary rhetoric and Christian principles in slave and "free" Black writing to the protest and mediation of segregated society.
4. To generally inform students about the contact—physical and ideational—among 20th century writers.
5. To generally inform students about the Harlem Renaissance as a political, artistic and cultural force in American society.
6. To generally inform students about the major post-World War II Black writers of America, Africa and the Caribbean.

Libraries—Three useful libraries are located on campus with extensive Black-oriented holdings:

The Afro-American Studies Department's Resource Center (Room 300, Founders Library)

The Moorland-Spingarn Research Center (Room 109, Founders Library)

The Undergraduate Library (new annex of Founders Library)

Course Outline

[One of the pages is missing from Henderson's syllabus file.]

4/2–4/4	Negritude Writers: Tirolien, 64–73; Brierre, 94–103; Depestre, 106–21 (Shapiro text)
4/6	Dadie, 158–61; Diop, 142–53 (Shapiro text)
4/9–4/11	African and Caribbean Narrative—TBA
4/16	"The Present Generation" (K/B text), 653–67
4/18	Hayden Brooks, Dodson (K/B text), 675–83; 712–22; 804–13
4/20	Randall, Allen, Evans, Randall, Allen, Evans, Knight, K/B, 804–20
4/23	Lee, Sanchez, Giovanni, others in K/B, 804–20
4/25	LeRoi Jones, K/B, 745–61
	REVIEW
4/27	Last Day of Formal Classes
4/28–4/30	Reading Period
**4/23–25	FINAL EXAMINATIONS FOR PROSPECTIVE MAY GRADUATES
	NOTE: Grading Seniors must arrange to take their final exams during this period. Arrangements must be made in advance in consultation with the instructor. (Grades for prospective graduates are due in the Registrar's Office by April 26.)
May 3 12:00–2:00pm	FINAL EXAMINATION for 12:10 MWF Black Literature class.
May 8 12:00–2:00pm	FINAL EXAMINATION for 2:10–3:00 MWF Black Literature class.

Probe: An inquiry into how I view African-American literature (in general), with special emphasis placed on the contributions of African-American women writers.

1. How do we read or teach the literature of African-American women so that it might lead towards empowerment? How do we use the literature to solve problems, teach values? Literature as equipment for living.

2. To what extent does Black lesbian literature shape or influence the work of women of color?

   Example: Audre Lorde's influence on Chrystos.

   The dialogue between Black gay men and Black lesbians.

3. Islam and African-American Literature. Black Arts Movement. Islam's growing presence within the U.S. How does the traditional Muslim woman merge with African-American traditions? Ex. *A Woman's Place* by Marita Golden.

4. Do working class African-American women make literature?

Middle class women in texts. Example *Betsy Brown* by Ntozake Shange and *Linden Hills* by Gloria Naylor. Contrast with *Mama* by Terry McMillan.

5. Comparative Black Women Literature. *Eva's Man* by Gayl Jones and "The Collector of Treasures" by Bessie Head. Literary Pan-Africanism. Trends in different cultures. Examining literary or cultural development. Does literature advance through certain stages? What are they?

6. What outside texts are needed in order to better understand the literature of African-American women writers? Ex. Text on African-American History. What work gives the best representation and description of women of color?

7. The issue of color and how it shapes relationships within literary texts.

8. Contrasting of images of film with literary images. The dialogue between contemporary film and contemporary literature. Ex. *The Color Purple* and the character Shug. See latest issue of *Cineaste* magazine.

9. Regional development/influence of geography and place. The role of literary migrations and the development of African-American literature. Ex. Jazz. Alice Walker and Jayne Cortez.

10. The African-American woman writer as visionary. Ex. Alice Walker, Octavia Butler.

11. A study and assessment of the major African-American critics.
    Examination of background and introduction to texts.

Department of Afro-American Studies   Spring 1990
Howard University   Dr. Stephen E. Henderson
Contemporary Black Poetry   080-198-01
T TH 2:10–3:30 p.m. LKH 118   OFFICE: 317, Founders Library
Office Hours—By Appointment   Phone: 636-7242/3

SYLLABUS

The purpose of this course is to introduce the student to one of the richest periods
in Afro-American literature, the Black Arts Movement of the 1960s and 1970s, through
a study of the poetry, one of its chief modes of literary expression. There will be roughly
equal emphasis placed upon the context of the work, its thematic content and its aesthetic
workings. Students will be expected to read as widely as possible and to acquaint themselves with the printed materials and tapes of the African-American Studies Resource
Center (Room 300, Founders Library) and the Moorland-Spingarn Research Center
located on the first floor of Founders Library.

The basic text for the course is *The Poetry of Black America*, Arnold Adoff (ed.), Harper
& Row Publishers. Additional texts used (but out of print) are *Understanding the New
Black Poetry*, Stephen E. Henderson (ed.), William Morrow & Co., 1973, and *Drumvoices:
A Critical History of Afro-American Poetry*, Eugene Redmond, Doubleday Publishers, 1974.
Reference copies are available in the African-American Resource Center.

In addition, students are encouraged to read complete volumes of poems by writers
whose work they wish to know better and to explore the literary and cultural journals
in which many of the poems originally appeared, such publications as *Negro Digest/
Black World*, *The Journal of Black Poetry*, *Dasein*, *Umbra*, *Ex Umbra*, *Soulbook*, *Nommo*,
Obsidian, *Hoo Doo*, *Callaloo*, and a range of student publications. Resources for the 1970s
through the present include tape recordings of the "Ascension" programs, an invaluable
series initiated by E. Ethelbert Miller, taped interviews and recordings dating back to
1971; tapes or readings, lectures and panel discussions at the Writers' Conference held at
Howard University from 1974–1983; critical articles in a variety of publications including
the *Washington Review of the Arts*, *SAGALA*, and *Black American Literature Forum*.

Students will be evaluated on the following basis: classroom participation, oral reports,
unit examinations, a final examination, and a term project. The oral reports will be assigned
and the term project will be developed in consultation with the instructor. Approximate
weights of each item in determining the final grade are as follows: classroom participation
and oral reports 25%; written reports or tests 25%; term project 25%; final examination 25%.
Instructional Units
I. Rationale for the course/background
    A. The Black Consciousness Movement—historical and cultural dimensions
    B. The Black Consciousness Movement—literary dimensions—the poetry
II. The Question of Form and Judgment in Black American Poetry
    A. Ideology: Right—*Saturday Review*; Left—Revolutionaries
    B. The Black Aesthetic debates

      1. Ideological dimension

      2. Formal dimension

      3. Historical dimension

   C. From the Black Aesthetic to Black Aesthetics

   D. Some challenges and opportunities

      1. The New Formalism

      2. The New Scholarship

III. Major Poets, Themes and Works

   A. The Forerunners—Langston Hughes, Sterling Brown

   B. The Middle Generation—Brooks, Walker, Randall

   C. The 1990s

      1. Dasein Group

      2. Umbra

      3. Ex Umbra

      4. Watts Writers Workshop

      5. OBAC

      6. Other groupings

   D. The 1980s

      1. The Washington Scene

      2. The National Scene

INDEX

ABOUT THE EDITORS

HAZEL ARNETT ERVIN is editor of ten books, including *The 25th Anniversary Edition, Ann Petry: A Bio-Bibliography*; *African American Literary Criticism, 1773 to 2000*; *The Handbook of African American Literature*; *A Community of Voices on Education and the African American Experience*; and *History and Memory of the Civil Rights Movement in Lexington, North Carolina*. The literary critic, professor of English, and academic consultant is also a Fulbright Scholar (Barbados), Wye (Aspen) Fellow, NEH Fellow, and UNCF-Mellon Fellow. She is recognized in *The World Who's Who of Women* (Cambridge, England), *Who's Who in Black Atlanta*, *Who's Who among African Americans*, and *Dictionary of American Scholars*.

PHILLIP M. RICHARDS is professor emeritus at Colgate University. He is the author of *Best Literature by and about Blacks* (2000), *Black Heart: The Moral Life of Recent American Letters* (2005), and *An Integrated Boyhood: Coming of Age in White Cleveland* (2012). He is the editor of Julian Mayfield's *The Hit and the Long Night* (1989). Richards's work has appeared in *Early American Literature*, *American Quarterly*, *Style*, *Massachusetts Review*, *American Poetry Review*, and *Callaloo*, among other journals and volumes.

E. ETHELBERT MILLER is a literary activist and author of two memoirs and several poetry collections. He hosts the WPFW morning radio show *On the Margin with E. Ethelbert Miller* and hosts and produces *The Scholars* on UDC-TV, which received a 2020 Telly Award. Miller is associate editor and a columnist for the *American Book Review*. He was given a 2020 congressional award from Congressman Jamie Raskin in recognition of his literary activism, awarded the 2022 Howard Zinn Lifetime Achievement Award by the Peace and Justice Studies Association, and named a 2023 Grammy-nominee finalist for Best Spoken Word Poetry Album. Miller's latest book is *How I Found Love behind the Catcher's Mask*, published by City Point Press.

EMILY RUTH RUTTER is author of *Invisible Ball of Dreams: Literary Representations of Baseball behind the Color Line*, *The Blues Muse: Race, Gender, and Musical Celebrity in American Poetry*, *Black Celebrity: Contemporary Representations of Postbellum Athletes and Artists*, and *White Lies and Allies in Contemporary Black Media*. She is coeditor of *Revisiting the Elegy in the Black Lives Matter Era*. Her scholarship appears in *African American Review*, *MELUS*, and *Tulsa Studies in Women's Literature*, among other journals and edited collections. Rutter is professor of English, associate dean of the Honors College, and affiliate faculty in the Department of Women's, Gender, and African American Studies at Ball State University.